CTHULHU
TALES

THE DARKNESS BEYOND

ROSS RICHIE
chief executive officer

MARK WAID
editor-in-chief

ADAM FORTIER
vice president,
publishing

CHIP MOSHER
marketing director

MATT GAGNON
managing editor

JENNY CHRISTOPHER
sales director

Cthulhu Tales: The Darkness Beyond — published by Boom! Studios. Cthulhu Tales is copyright © Boom Entertainment, Inc. Boom! Studios™ and the Boom! logo are trademarks of Boom Entertainment, Inc., registered in various countries and categories. All rights reserved. The characters and events depicted herein are fictional. Any similarity to actual persons, demons, anti-Christs, aliens, vampires, face-suckers or political figures, whether living, dead or undead, or to any actual or supernatural events is coincidental and unintentional. So don't come whining to us.

Office of publication: 6310 San Vicente Blvd, Ste 404, Los Angeles, CA 90048-5457.

A catalog record for this book is available from the Library of Congress and on our website at www.boom-studios.com on the Librarian Resource Page.

First Edition: March 2009

10 9 8 7 6 5 4 3 2 1
PRINTED IN KOREA

THE ZOO

STORY RAVEN GREGORY

ART SERGIO CARRERA

IT MUST HAVE BEEN SOMETHING YOU ATE

STORY SAM COSTELLO

ART AXEL MEDELLIN MACHAIN

FACE OF THE COMPETITION

STORY ROBERT TINNELL

ART MILTON SOBRIERO

EDITOR MARK WAID

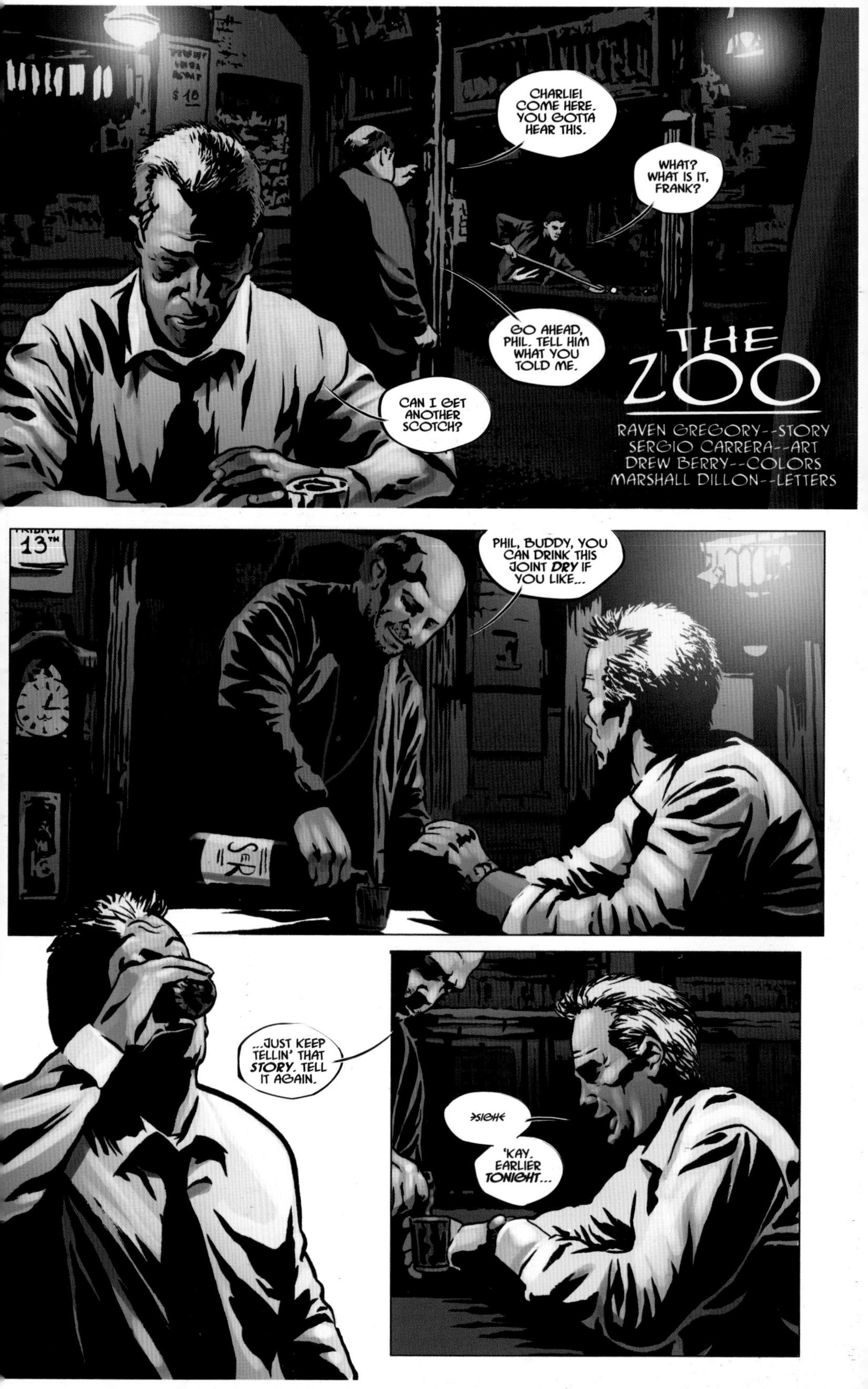
CHARLIE! COME HERE. YOU GOTTA HEAR THIS.
WHAT? WHAT IS IT, FRANK?
GO AHEAD, PHIL. TELL HIM WHAT YOU TOLD ME.
CAN I GET ANOTHER SCOTCH?
THE ZOO
RAVEN GREGORY--STORY
SERGIO CARRERA--ART
DREW BERRY--COLORS
MARSHALL DILLON--LETTERS
13TH
PHIL, BUDDY, YOU CAN DRINK THIS JOINT DRY IF YOU LIKE...
...JUST KEEP TELLIN' THAT STORY. TELL IT AGAIN.
>SIGH<
'KAY. EARLIER TONIGHT...

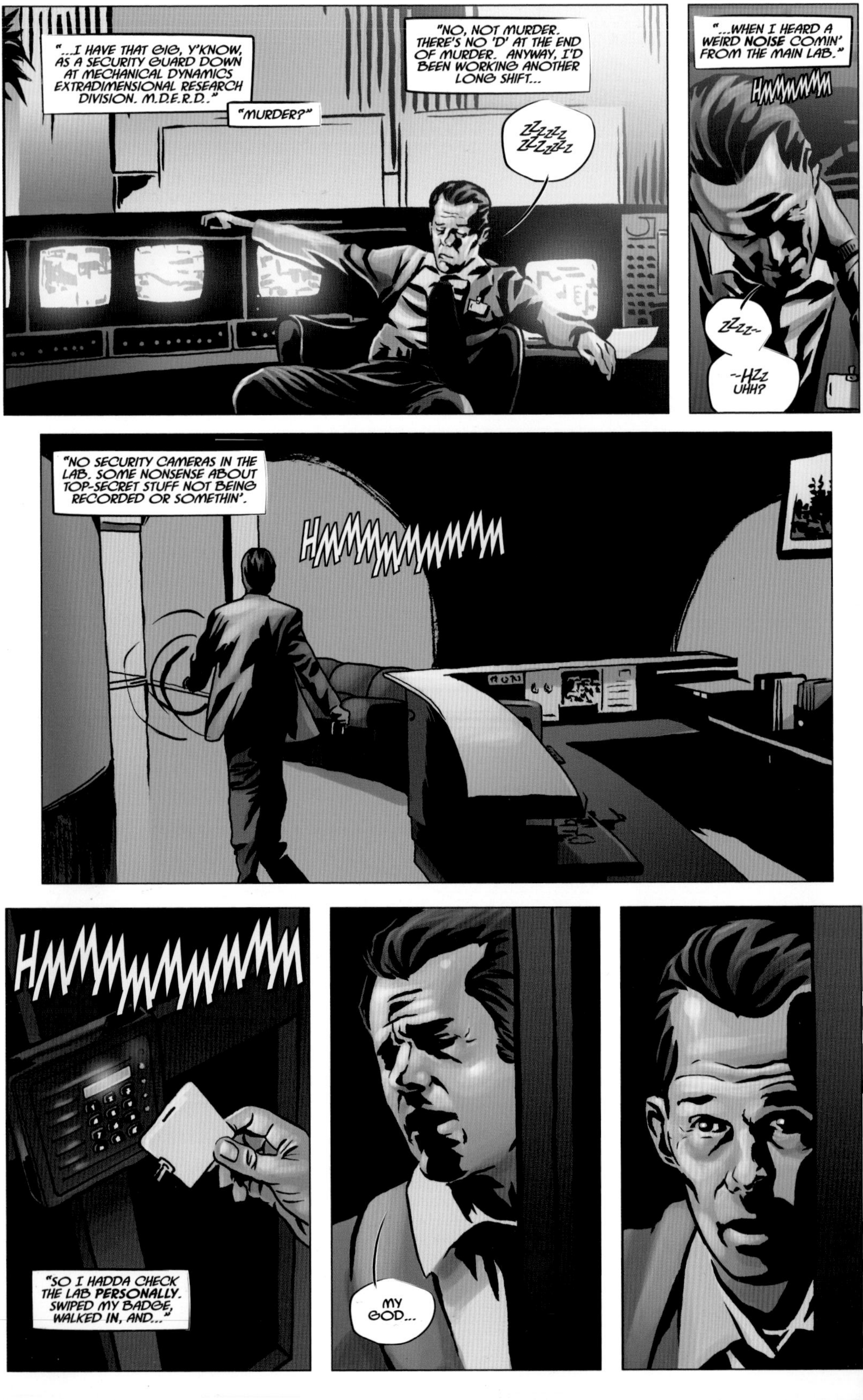
"...I HAVE THAT GIG, Y'KNOW, AS A SECURITY GUARD DOWN AT MECHANICAL DYNAMICS EXTRADIMENSIONAL RESEARCH DIVISION. M.D.E.R.D."
"MURDER?"
"NO, NOT MURDER. THERE'S NO 'D' AT THE END OF MURDER. ANYWAY, I'D BEEN WORKING ANOTHER LONG SHIFT...
ZZZZZZZ ZZZZZZZ
"...WHEN I HEARD A WEIRD NOISE COMIN' FROM THE MAIN LAB."
HMMMMMM
ZZZZ--
--HZZ UHH?
"NO SECURITY CAMERAS IN THE LAB. SOME NONSENSE ABOUT TOP-SECRET STUFF NOT BEING RECORDED OR SOMETHIN'.
HMMMMMMMMMM
HMMMMMMMMMMM
"SO I HADDA CHECK THE LAB PERSONALLY. SWIPED MY BADGE, WALKED IN, AND..."
MY GOD...

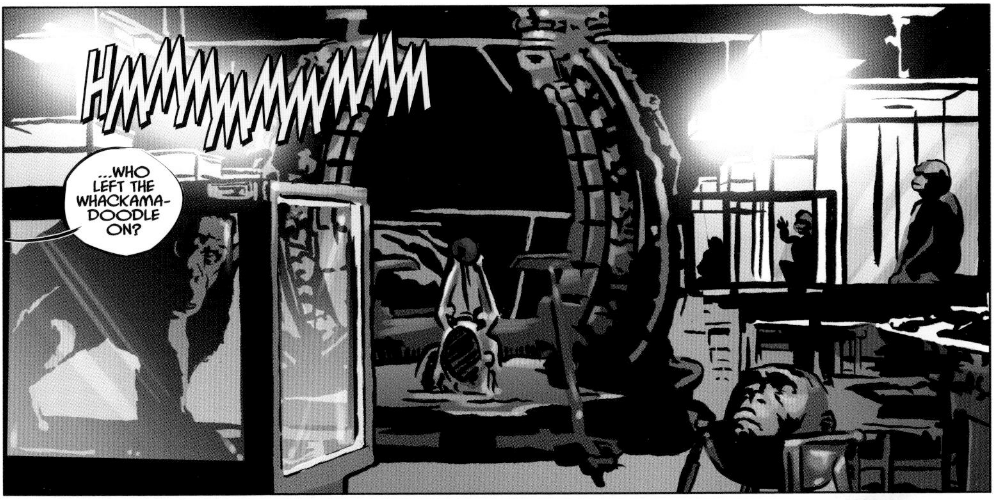
HMMMMMMMMM
...WHO LEFT THE WHACKAMA-DOODLE ON?

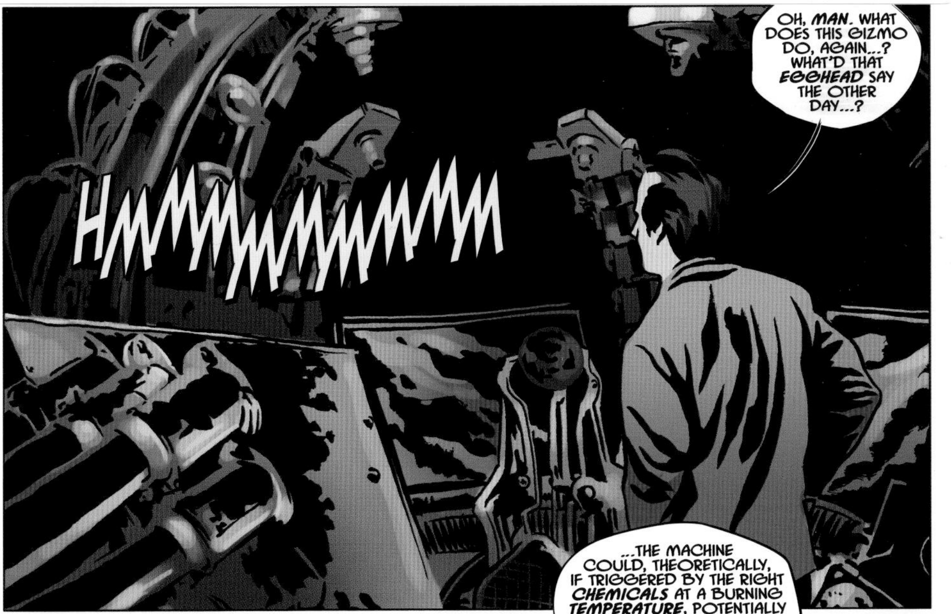
OH, MAN. WHAT DOES THIS GIZMO DO, AGAIN...? WHAT'D THAT EGGHEAD SAY THE OTHER DAY...?
HMMMMMMMMMM
...THE MACHINE COULD, THEORETICALLY, IF TRIGGERED BY THE RIGHT CHEMICALS AT A BURNING TEMPERATURE, POTENTIALLY TEAR A TEMPORARY HOLE IN THE FABRIC OF SPACE AND TIME. WHY DO YOU ASK?

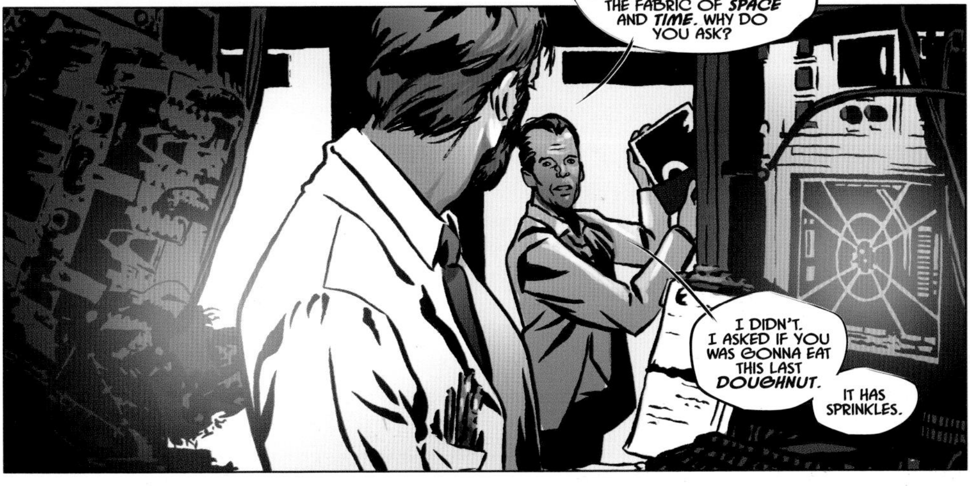
I DIDN'T. I ASKED IF YOU WAS GONNA EAT THIS LAST DOUGHNUT.
IT HAS SPRINKLES.

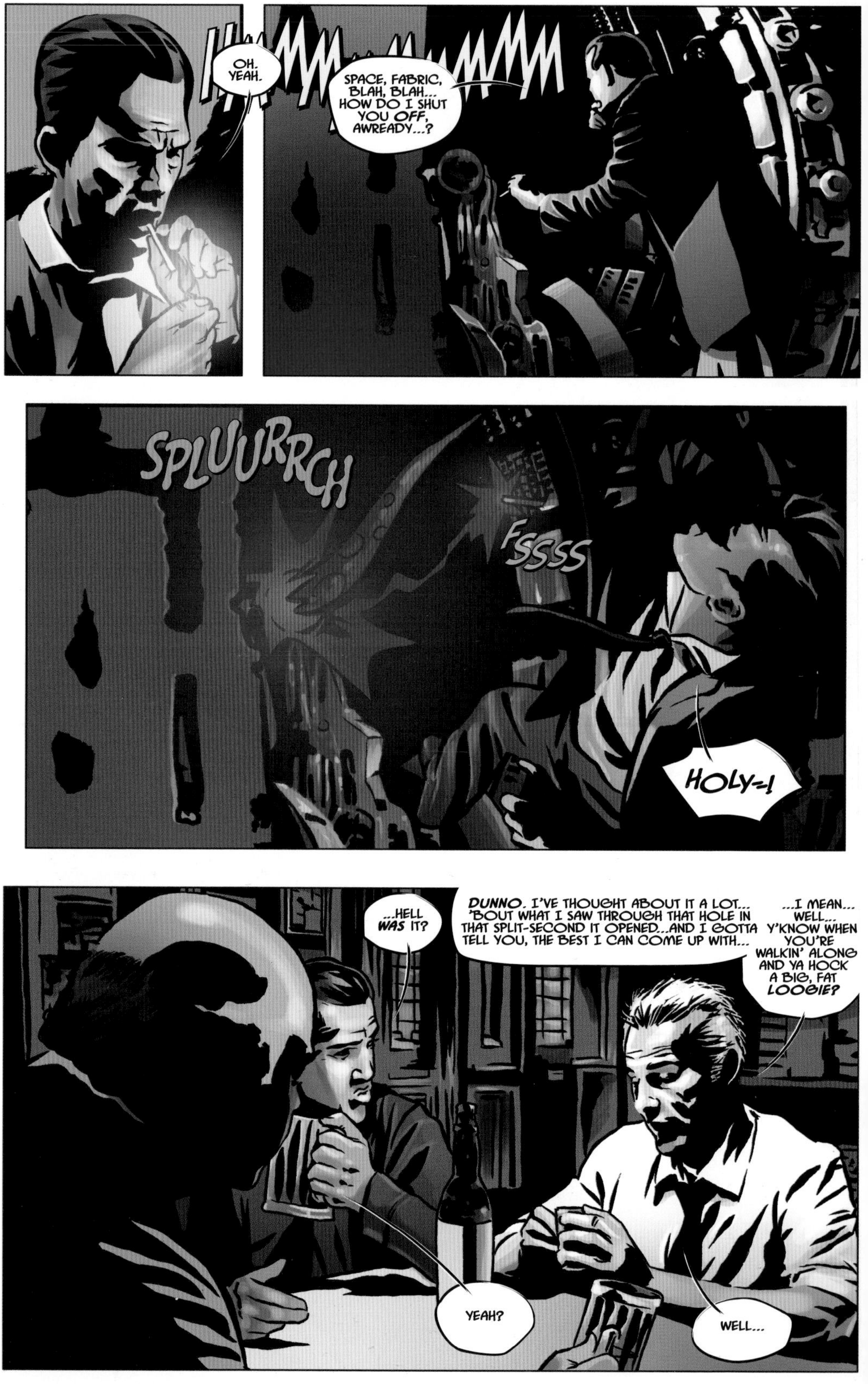
OH. YEAH.
SPACE, FABRIC, BLAH, BLAH... HOW DO I SHUT YOU OFF, AWREADY...?
SPLUURRCH
FSSSS
HOLY--!
...HELL WAS IT?
DUNNO. I'VE THOUGHT ABOUT IT A LOT... 'BOUT WHAT I SAW THROUGH THAT HOLE IN THAT SPLIT-SECOND IT OPENED...AND I GOTTA TELL YOU, THE BEST I CAN COME UP WITH...
...I MEAN... WELL... Y'KNOW WHEN YOU'RE WALKIN' ALONG AND YA HOCK A BIG, FAT LOOGIE?
YEAH?
WELL...

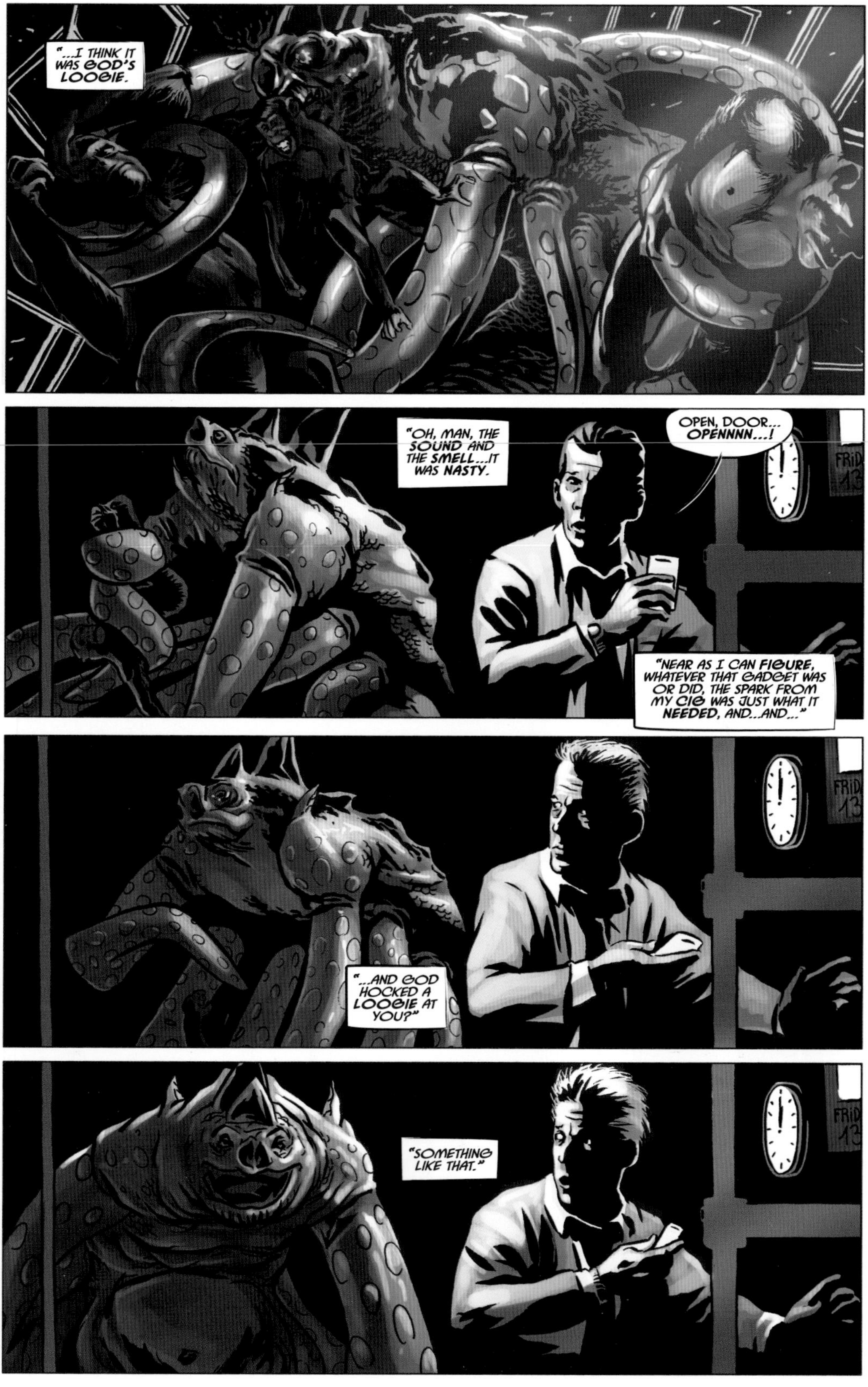
"...I THINK IT WAS GOD'S LOOGIE.
"OH, MAN, THE SOUND AND THE SMELL...IT WAS NASTY.
OPEN, DOOR... OPENNNN...!
"NEAR AS I CAN FIGURE, WHATEVER THAT GADGET WAS OR DID, THE SPARK FROM MY CIG WAS JUST WHAT IT NEEDED, AND...AND..."
"...AND GOD HOCKED A LOOGIE AT YOU?"
"SOMETHING LIKE THAT."

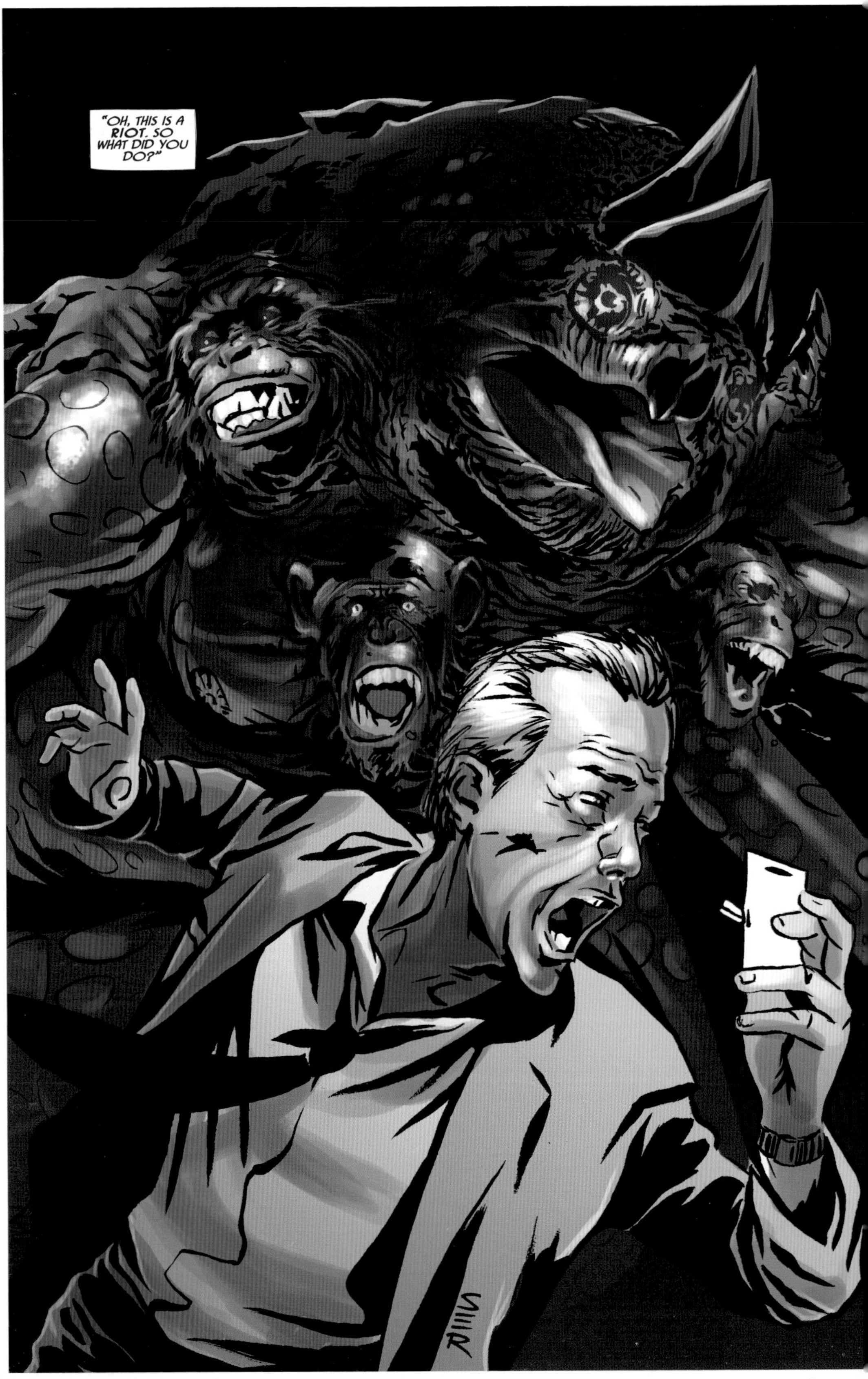
"OH, THIS IS A RIOT. SO WHAT DID YOU DO?"

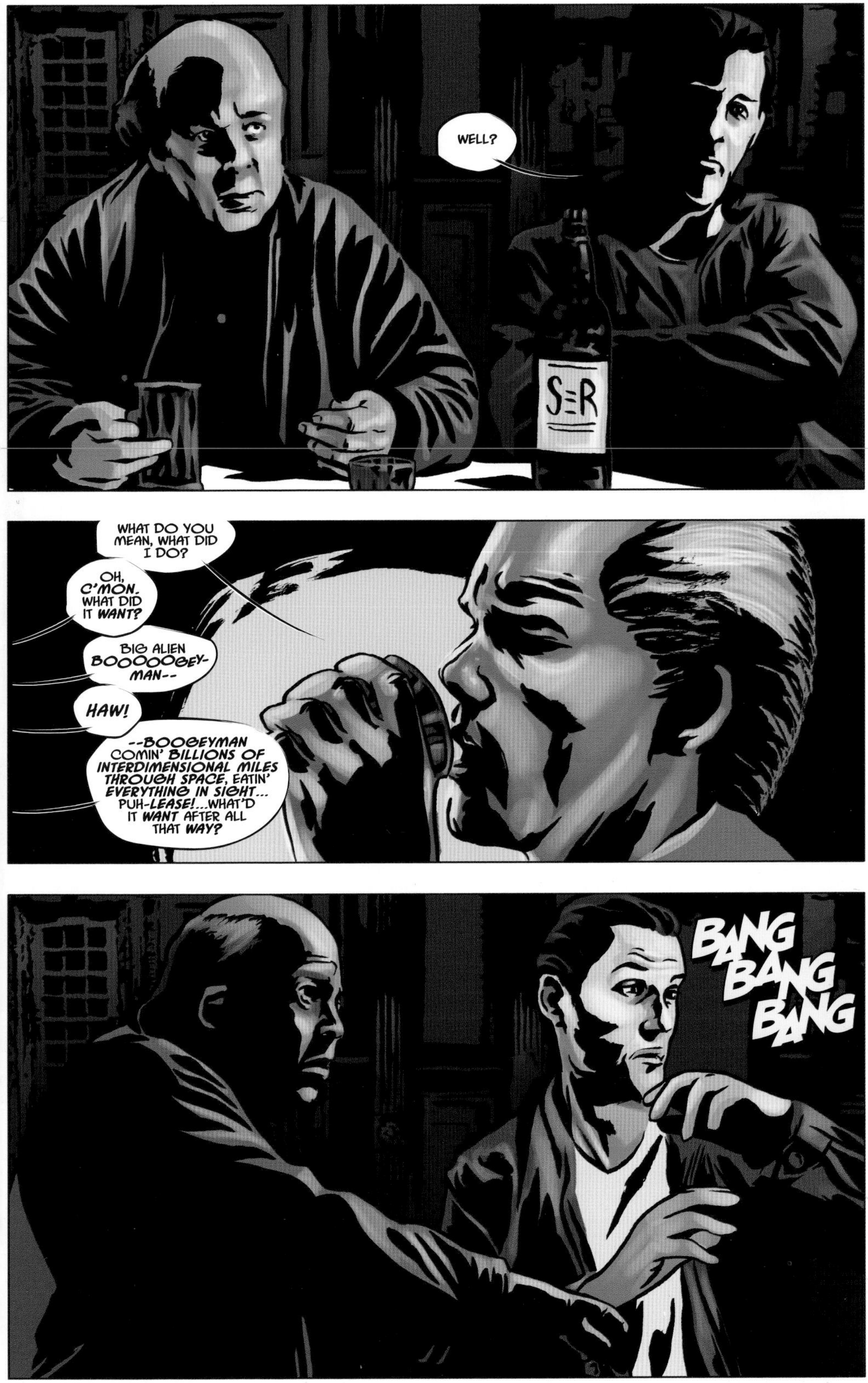
WELL?
WHAT DO YOU MEAN, WHAT DID I DO?
OH, C'MON. WHAT DID IT WANT?
BIG ALIEN BOOOOOOGEY-MAN--
HAW!
--BOOGEYMAN COMIN' BILLIONS OF INTERDIMENSIONAL MILES THROUGH SPACE, EATIN' EVERYTHING IN SIGHT... PUH-LEASE!...WHAT'D IT WANT AFTER ALL THAT WAY?
BANG
BANG
BANG

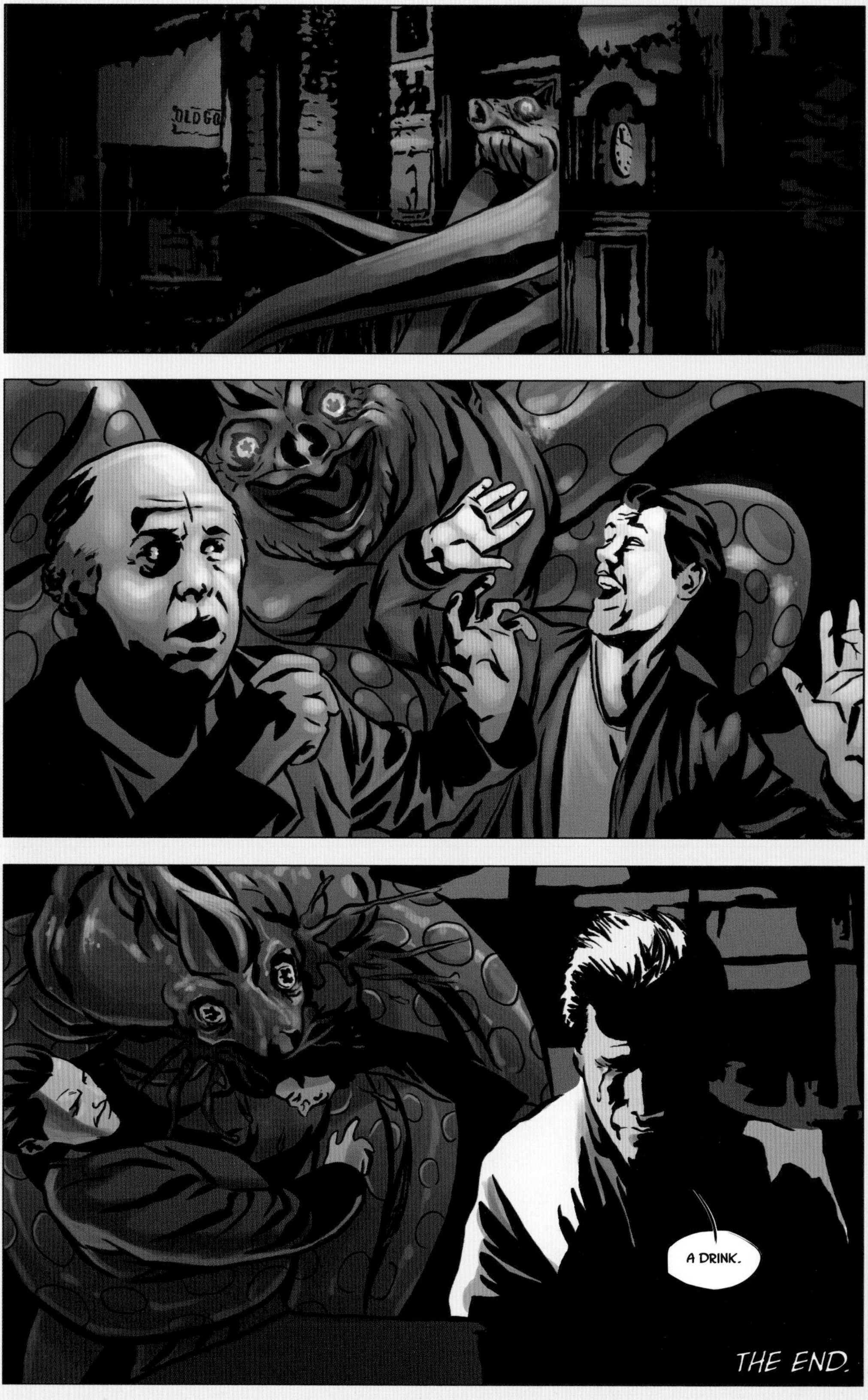
A DRINK.
THE END.

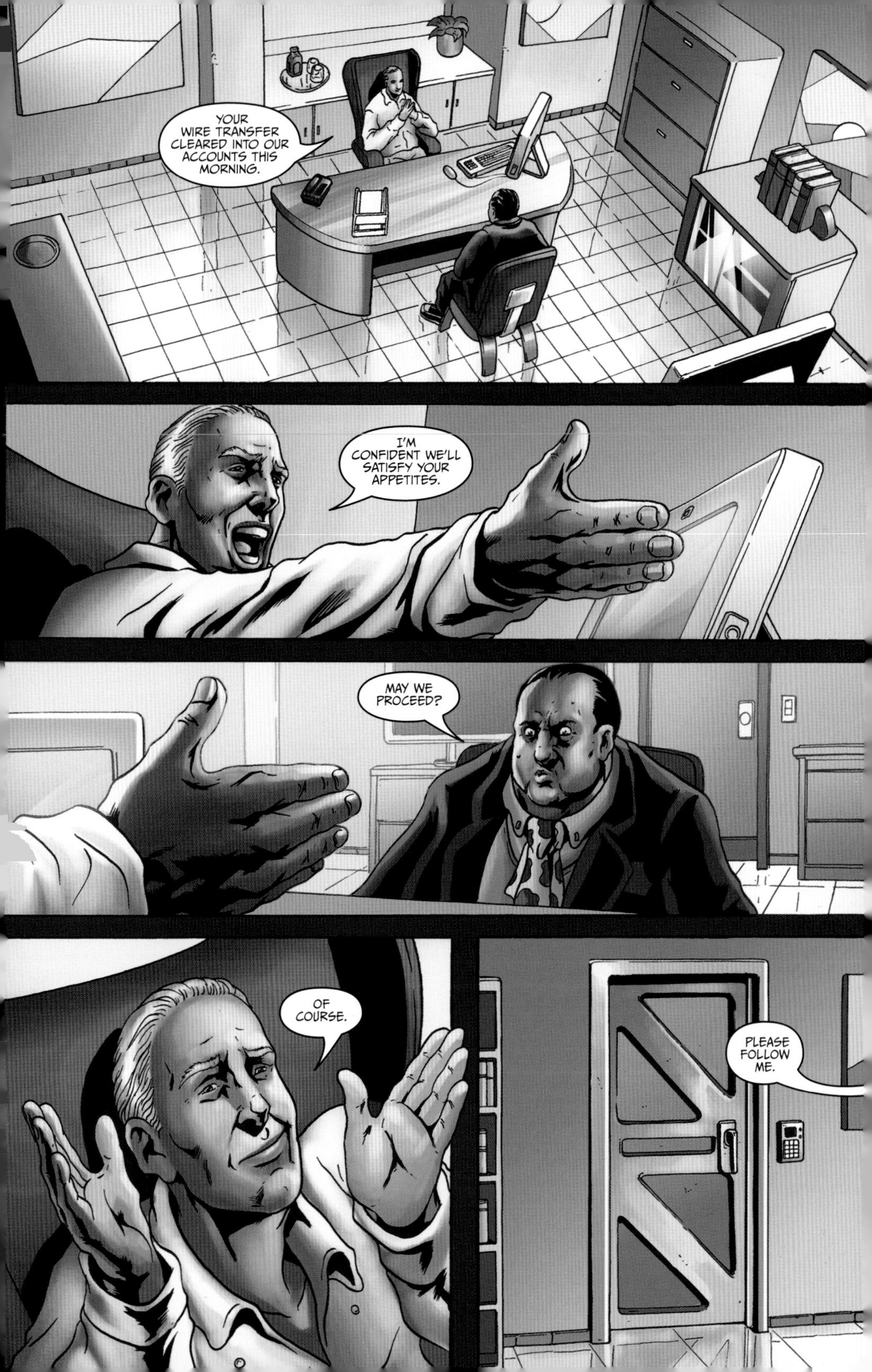
YOUR WIRE TRANSFER CLEARED INTO OUR ACCOUNTS THIS MORNING.
I'M CONFIDENT WE'LL SATISFY YOUR APPETITES.
MAY WE PROCEED?
OF COURSE.
PLEASE FOLLOW ME.

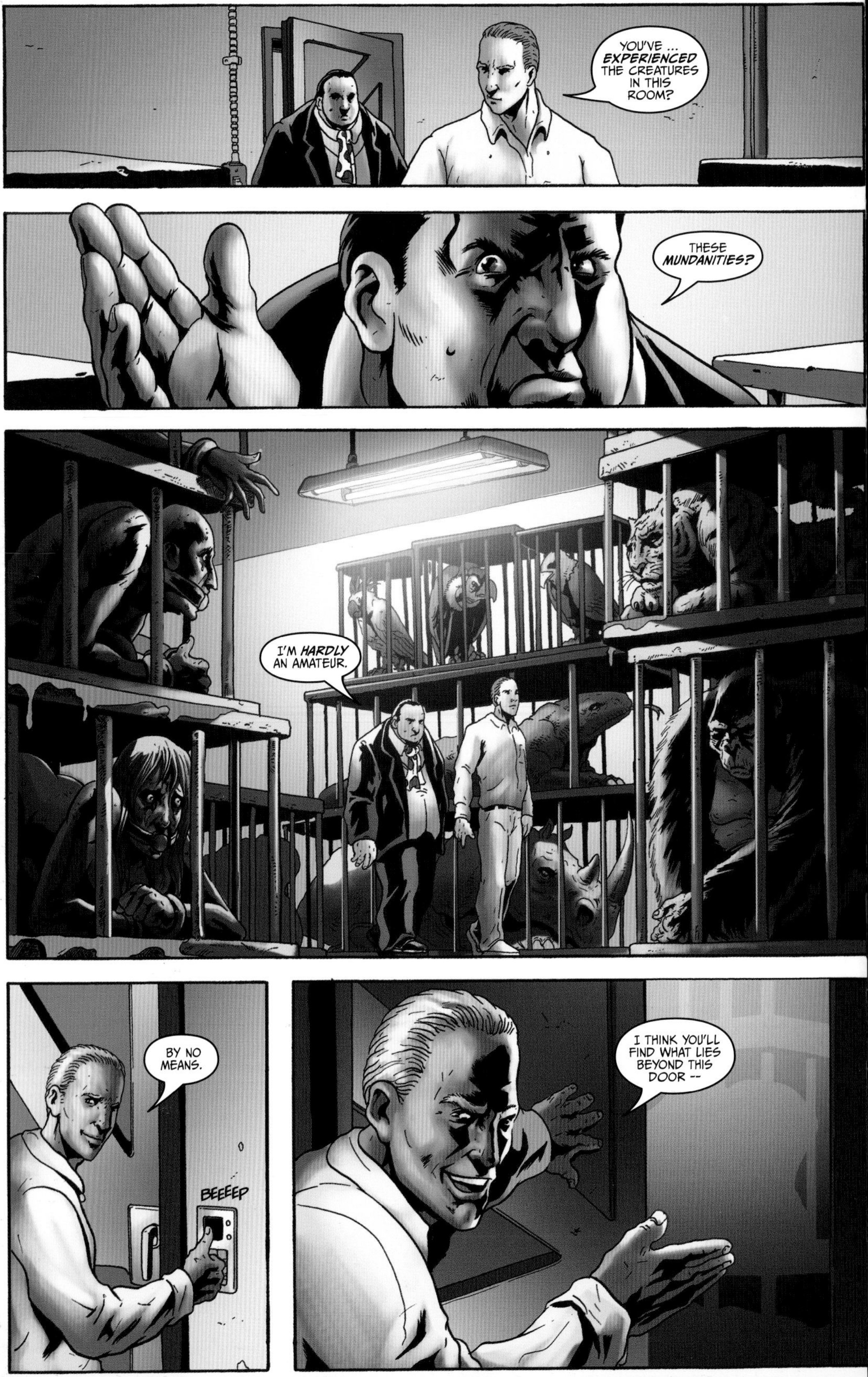

YOU'VE ... EXPERIENCED THE CREATURES IN THIS ROOM?
THESE MUNDANITIES?
I'M HARDLY AN AMATEUR.
BY NO MEANS.
BEEEEP
I THINK YOU'LL FIND WHAT LIES BEYOND THIS DOOR --

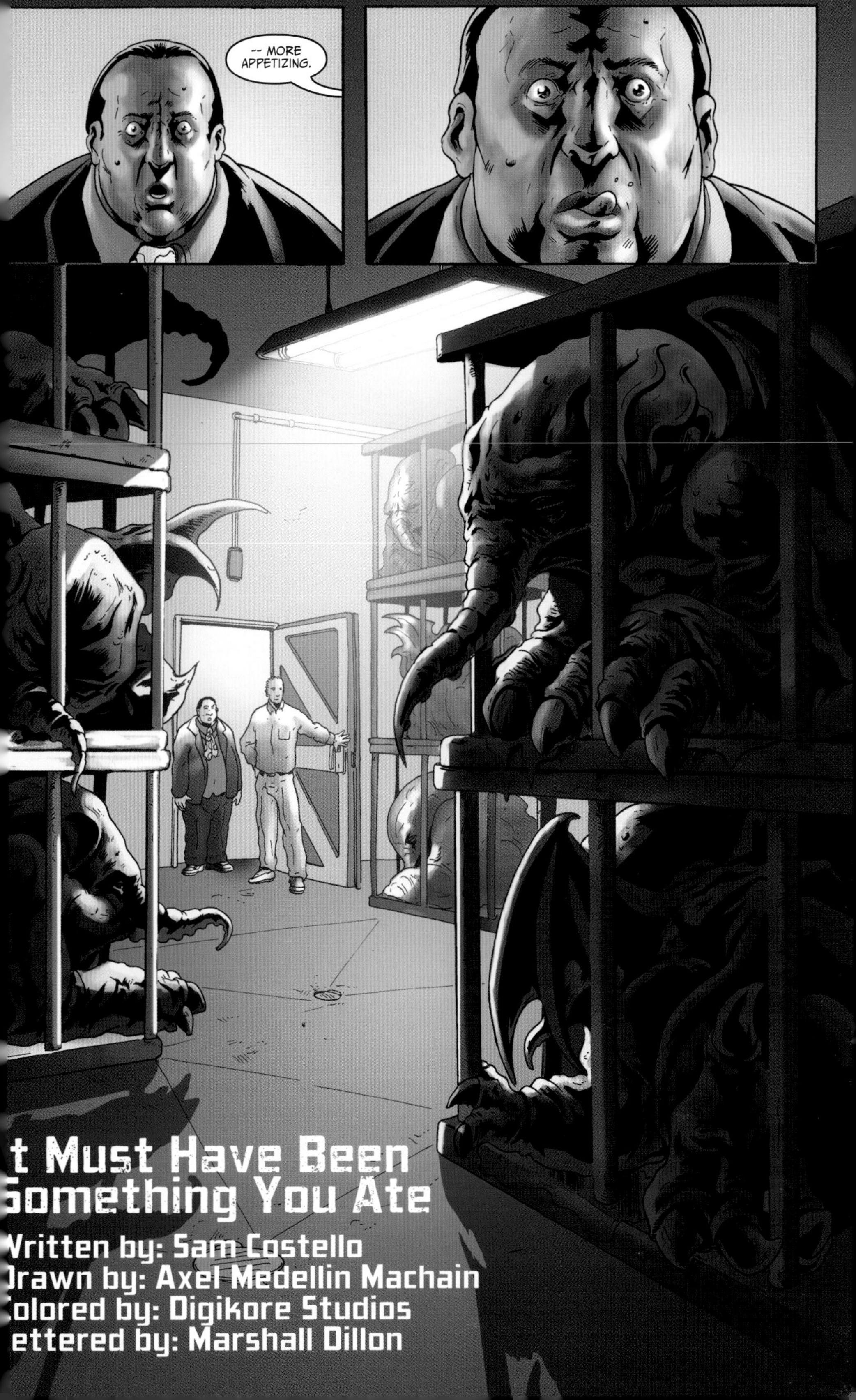
-- MORE APPETIZING.
t Must Have Been
Something You Ate
Vritten by: Sam Costello
Jrawn by: Axel Medellin Machain
olored by: Digikore Studios
ettered by: Marshall Dillon

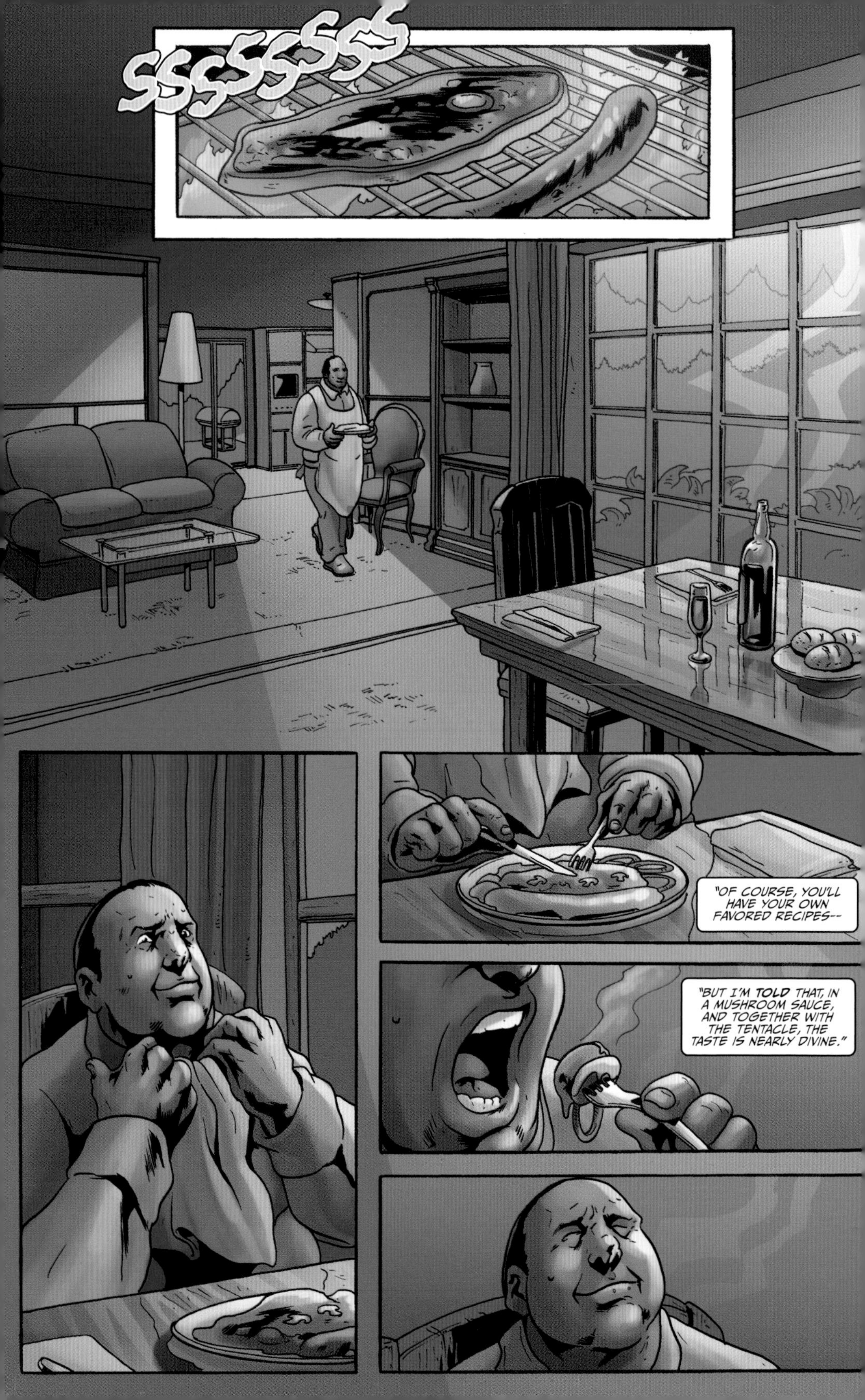
SSSSSSSS
"OF COURSE, YOU'LL HAVE YOUR OWN FAVORED RECIPES--
"BUT I'M TOLD THAT, IN A MUSHROOM SAUCE, AND TOGETHER WITH THE TENTACLE, THE TASTE IS NEARLY DIVINE."

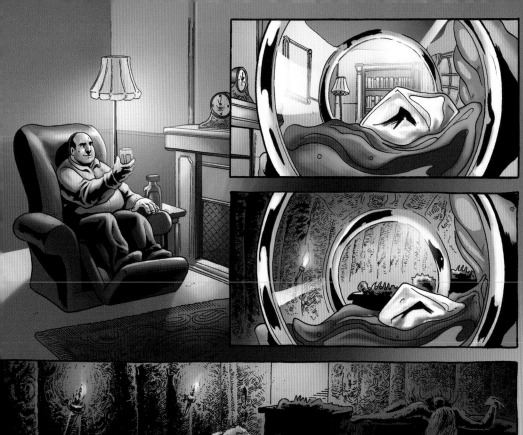

-- TO THE DELIVERY ROOM.

HARHHH!

A DREAM. JUST A DREAM.

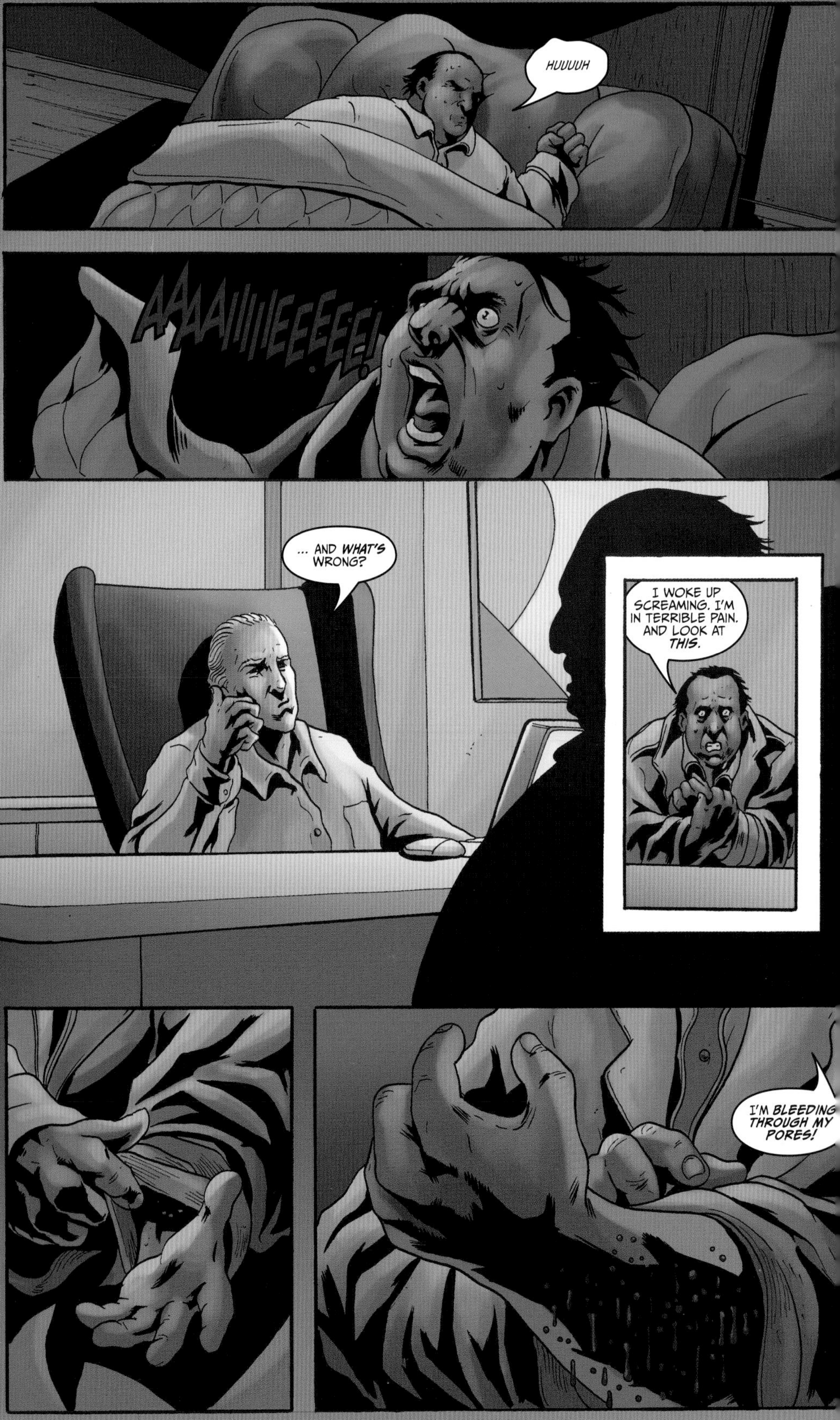
HUUUUH
AAAAIIIIIEEEEEE!
... AND WHAT'S WRONG?
I WOKE UP SCREAMING. I'M IN TERRIBLE PAIN. AND LOOK AT THIS.
I'M BLEEDING THROUGH MY PORES!

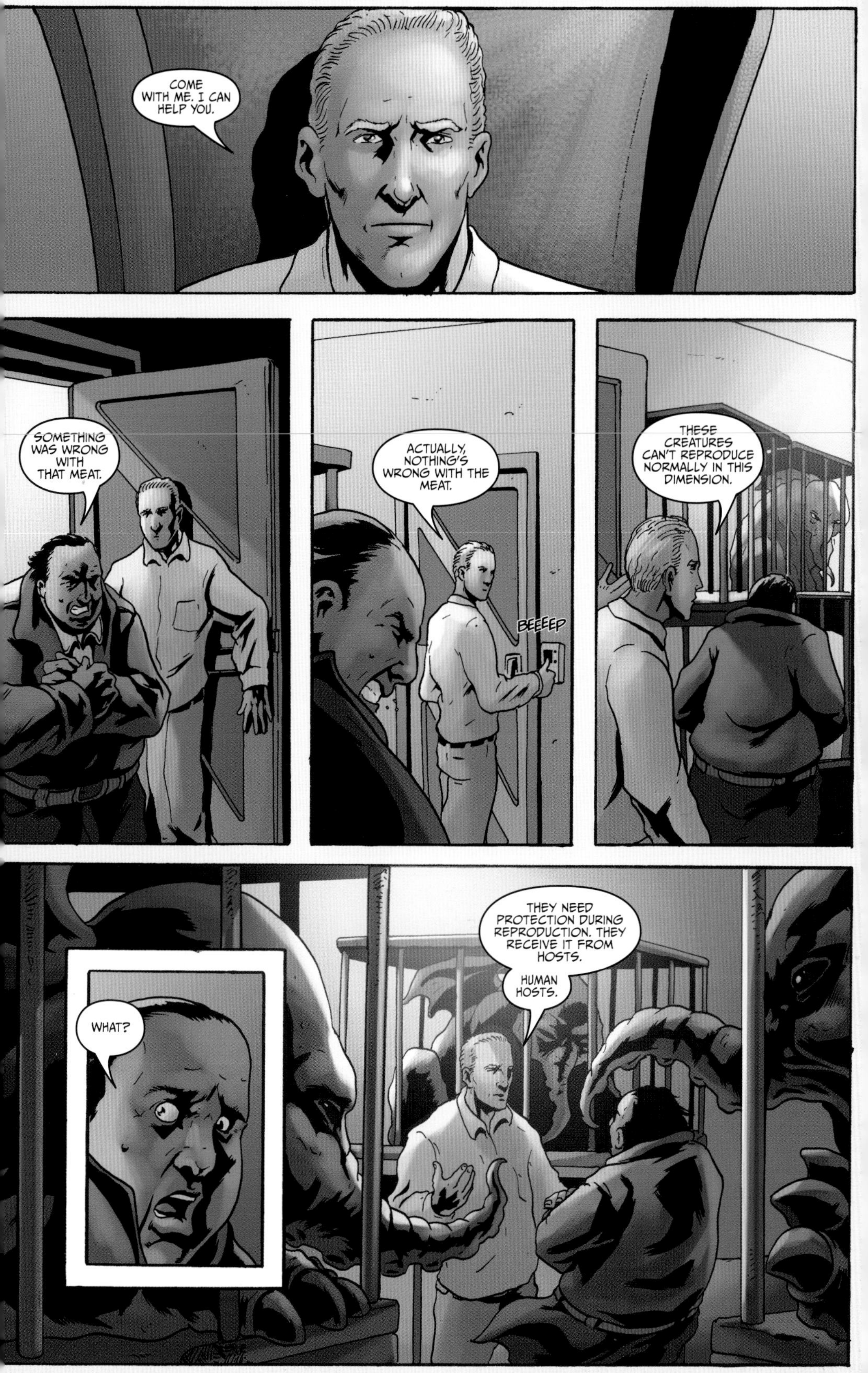
COME WITH ME. I CAN HELP YOU.
SOMETHING WAS WRONG WITH THAT MEAT.
ACTUALLY, NOTHING'S WRONG WITH THE MEAT.
BEEEEP
THESE CREATURES CAN'T REPRODUCE NORMALLY IN THIS DIMENSION.
THEY NEED PROTECTION DURING REPRODUCTION. THEY RECEIVE IT FROM HOSTS.
HUMAN HOSTS.
WHAT?

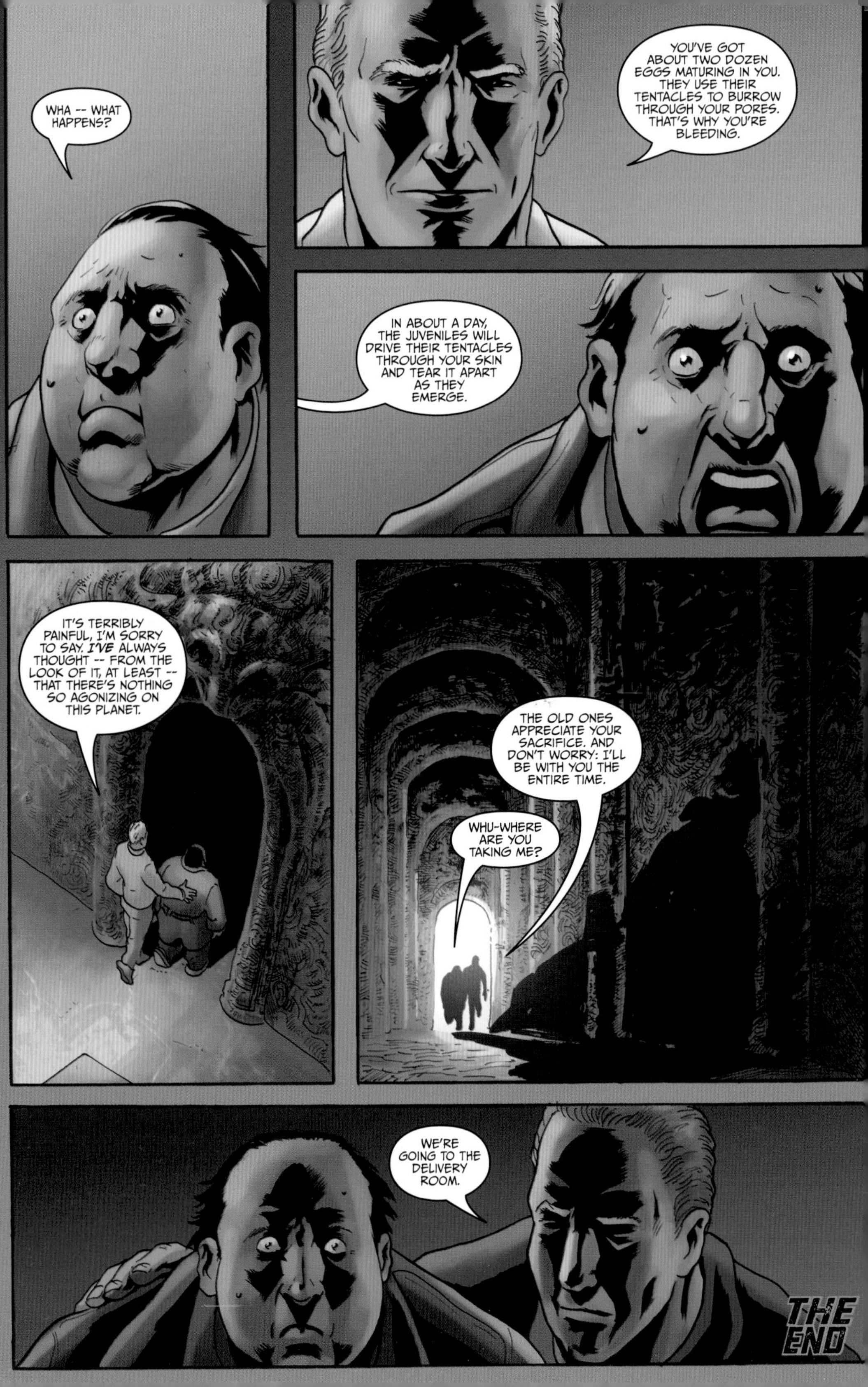
WHA -- WHAT HAPPENS?
YOU'VE GOT ABOUT TWO DOZEN EGGS MATURING IN YOU. THEY USE THEIR TENTACLES TO BURROW THROUGH YOUR PORES. THAT'S WHY YOU'RE BLEEDING.
IN ABOUT A DAY, THE JUVENILES WILL DRIVE THEIR TENTACLES THROUGH YOUR SKIN AND TEAR IT APART AS THEY EMERGE.
IT'S TERRIBLY PAINFUL, I'M SORRY TO SAY. *I'VE* ALWAYS THOUGHT -- FROM THE LOOK OF IT, AT LEAST -- THAT THERE'S NOTHING SO AGONIZING ON THIS PLANET.
THE OLD ONES APPRECIATE YOUR SACRIFICE. AND DON'T WORRY: I'LL BE WITH YOU THE ENTIRE TIME.
WHU-WHERE ARE YOU TAKING ME?
WE'RE GOING TO THE DELIVERY ROOM.
THE END

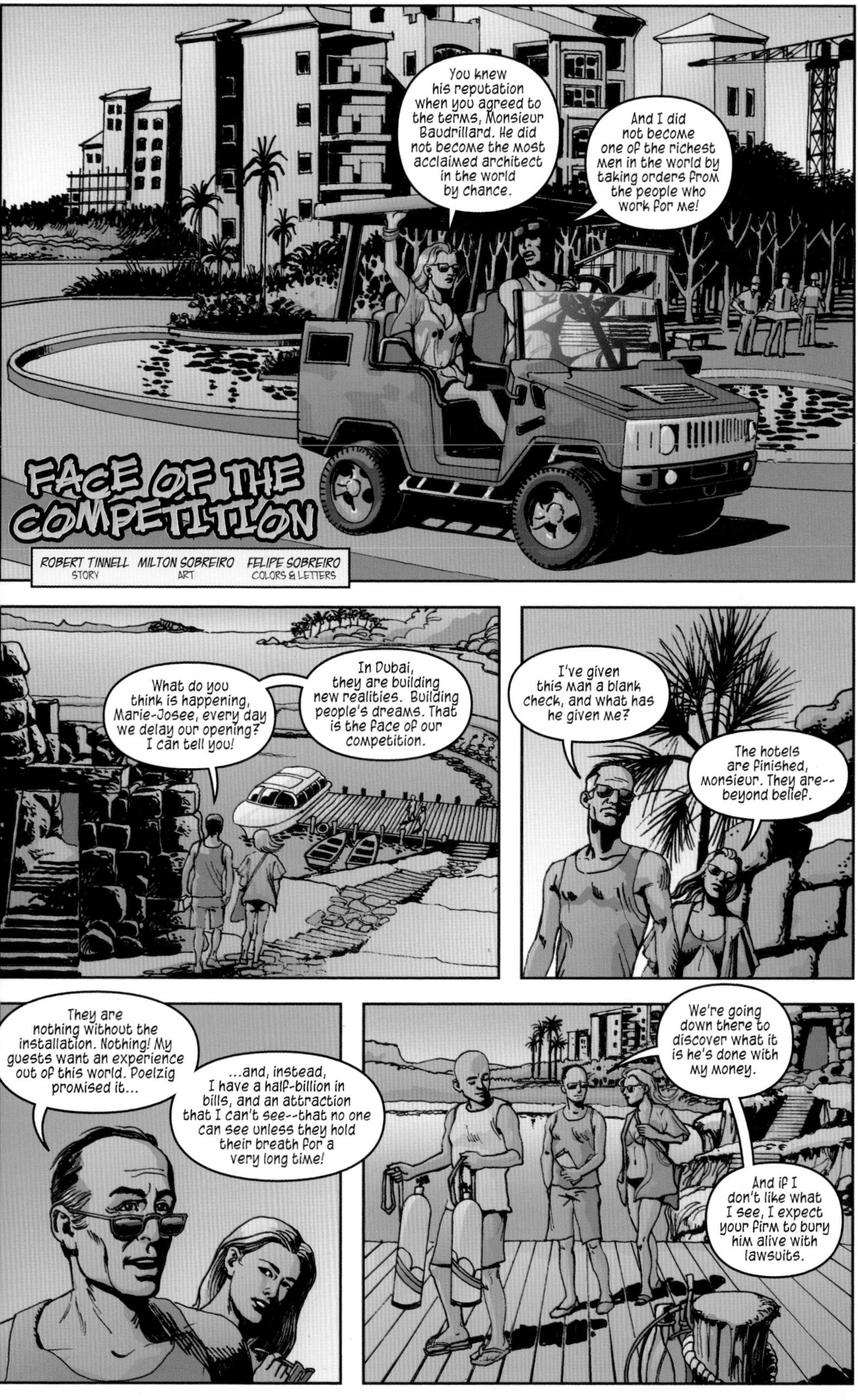
You knew his reputation when you agreed to the terms, Monsieur Baudrillard. He did not become the most acclaimed architect in the world by chance.
And I did not become one of the richest men in the world by taking orders from the people who work for me!
FACE OF THE COMPETITION
ROBERT TINNELL STORY
MILTON SOBREIRO ART
FELIPE SOBREIRO COLORS & LETTERS
What do you think is happening, Marie-Josee, every day we delay our opening? I can tell you!
In Dubai, they are building new realities. Building people's dreams. That is the face of our competition.
I've given this man a blank check, and what has he given me?
The hotels are finished, Monsieur. They are--beyond belief.
They are nothing without the installation. Nothing! My guests want an experience out of this world. Poelzig promised it...
...and, instead, I have a half-billion in bills, and an attraction that I can't see--that no one can see unless they hold their breath for a very long time!
We're going down there to discover what it is he's done with my money.
And if I don't like what I see, I expect your firm to bury him alive with lawsuits.

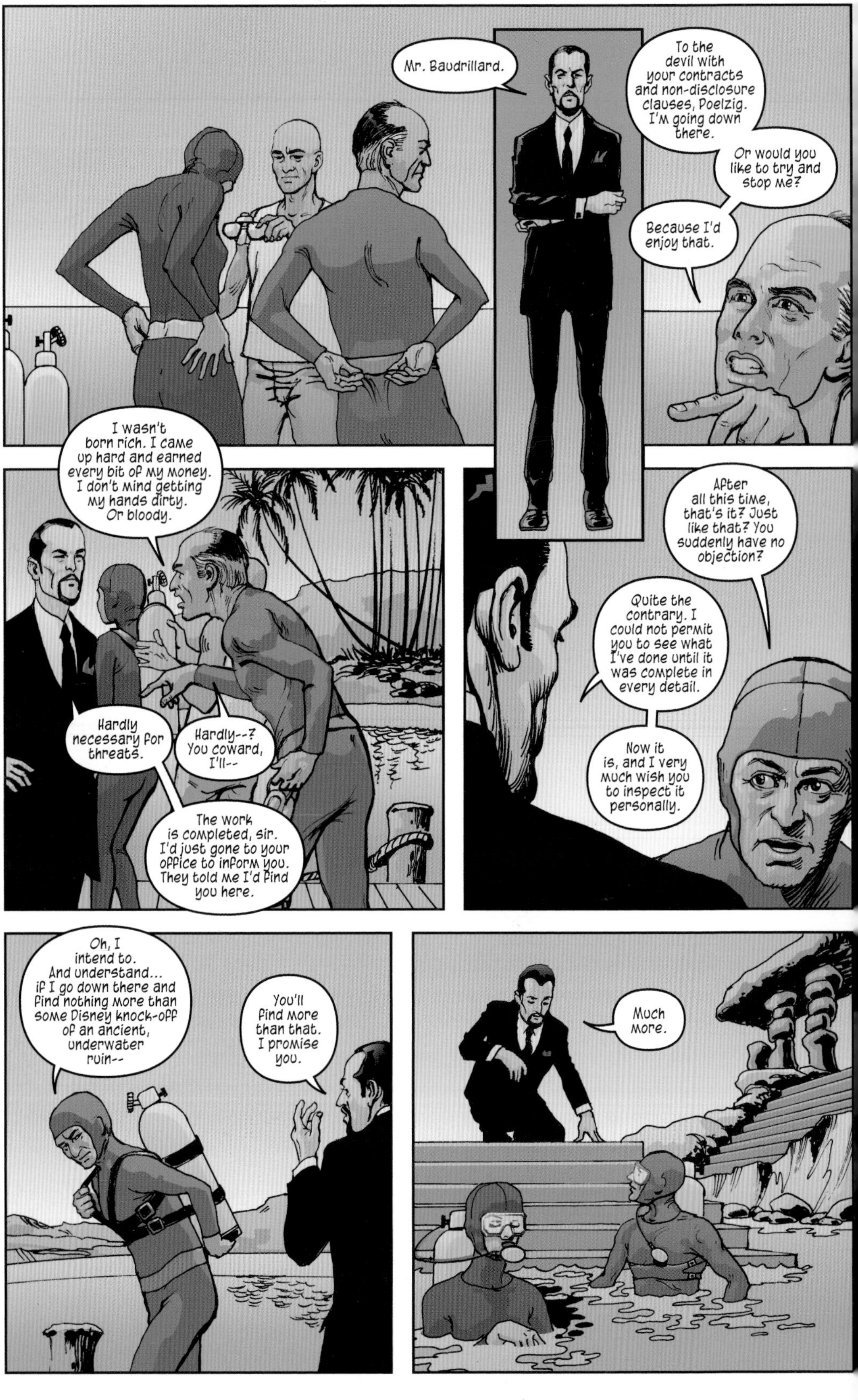
Mr. Baudrillard.
To the devil with your contracts and non-disclosure clauses, Poelzig. I'm going down there.
Or would you like to try and stop me?
Because I'd enjoy that.
I wasn't born rich. I came up hard and earned every bit of my money. I don't mind getting my hands dirty. Or bloody.
Hardly necessary for threats.
Hardly--? You coward, I'll--
The work is completed, sir. I'd just gone to your office to inform you. They told me I'd find you here.
After all this time, that's it? Just like that? You suddenly have no objection?
Quite the contrary. I could not permit you to see what I've done until it was complete in every detail.
Now it is, and I very much wish you to inspect it personally.
Oh, I intend to. And understand... if I go down there and find nothing more than some Disney knock-off of an ancient, underwater ruin--
You'll find more than that. I promise you.
Much more.

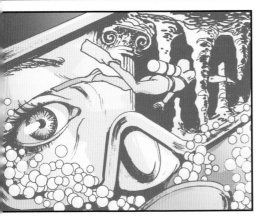

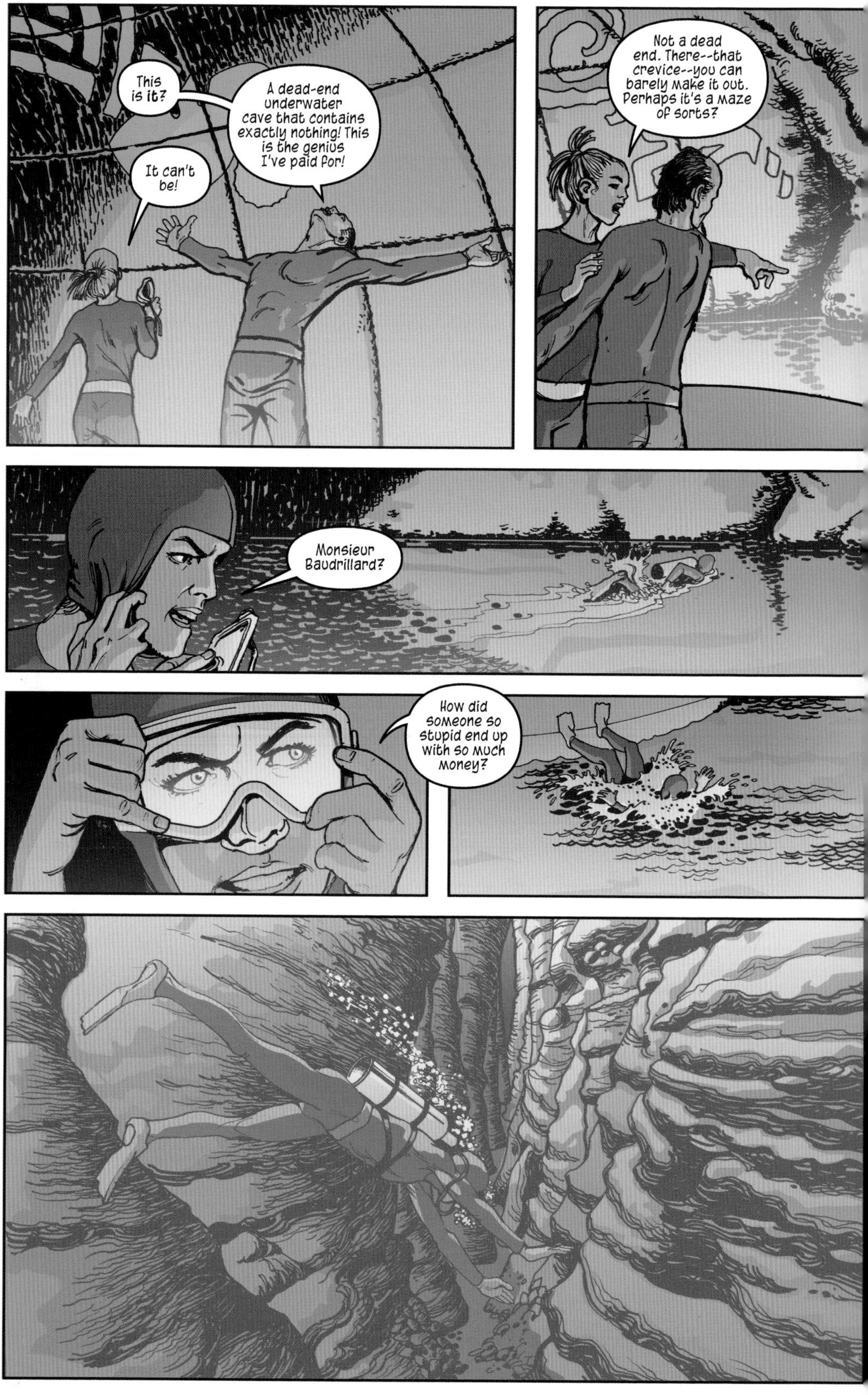
This is it?
A dead-end underwater cave that contains exactly nothing! This is the genius I've paid for!
It can't be!
Not a dead end. There--that crevice--you can barely make it out. Perhaps it's a maze of sorts?
Monsieur Baudrillard?
How did someone so stupid end up with so much money?

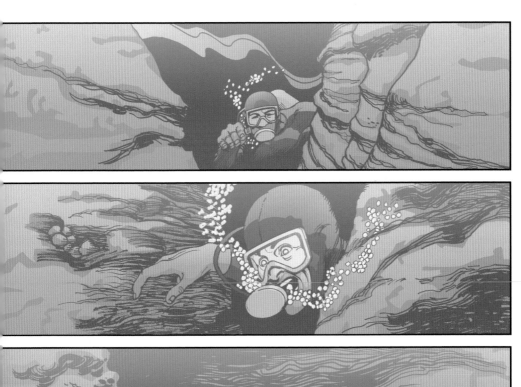

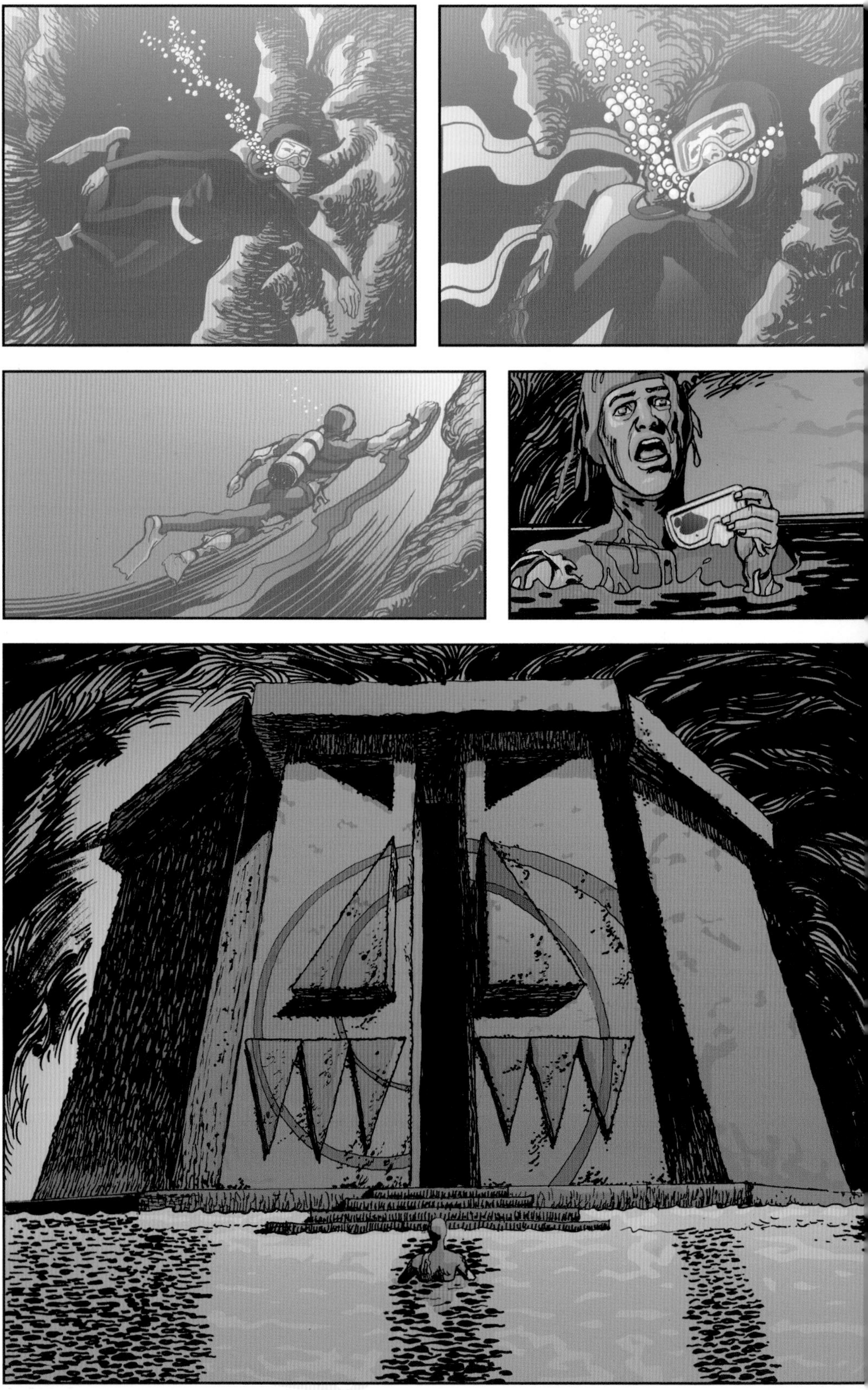

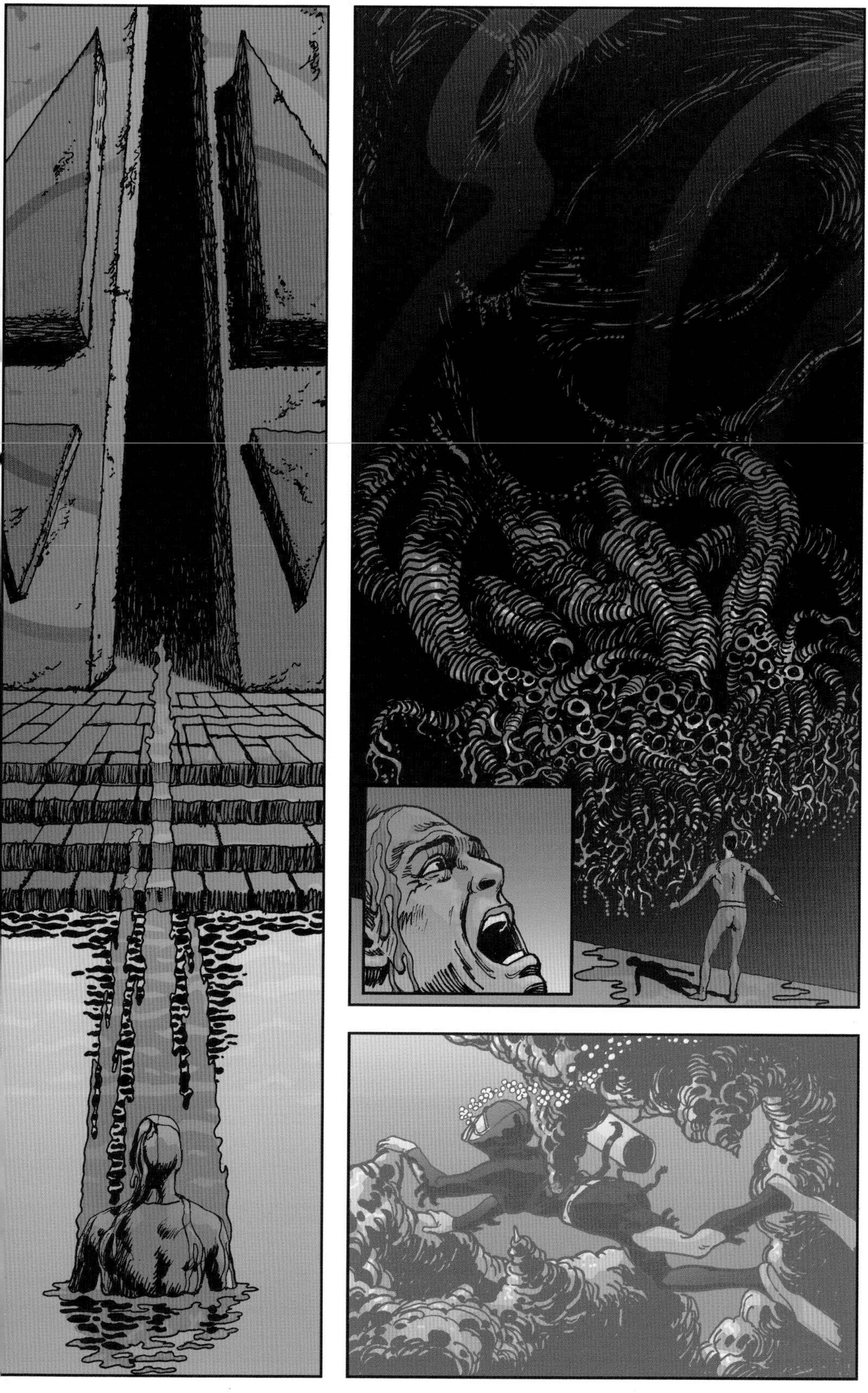

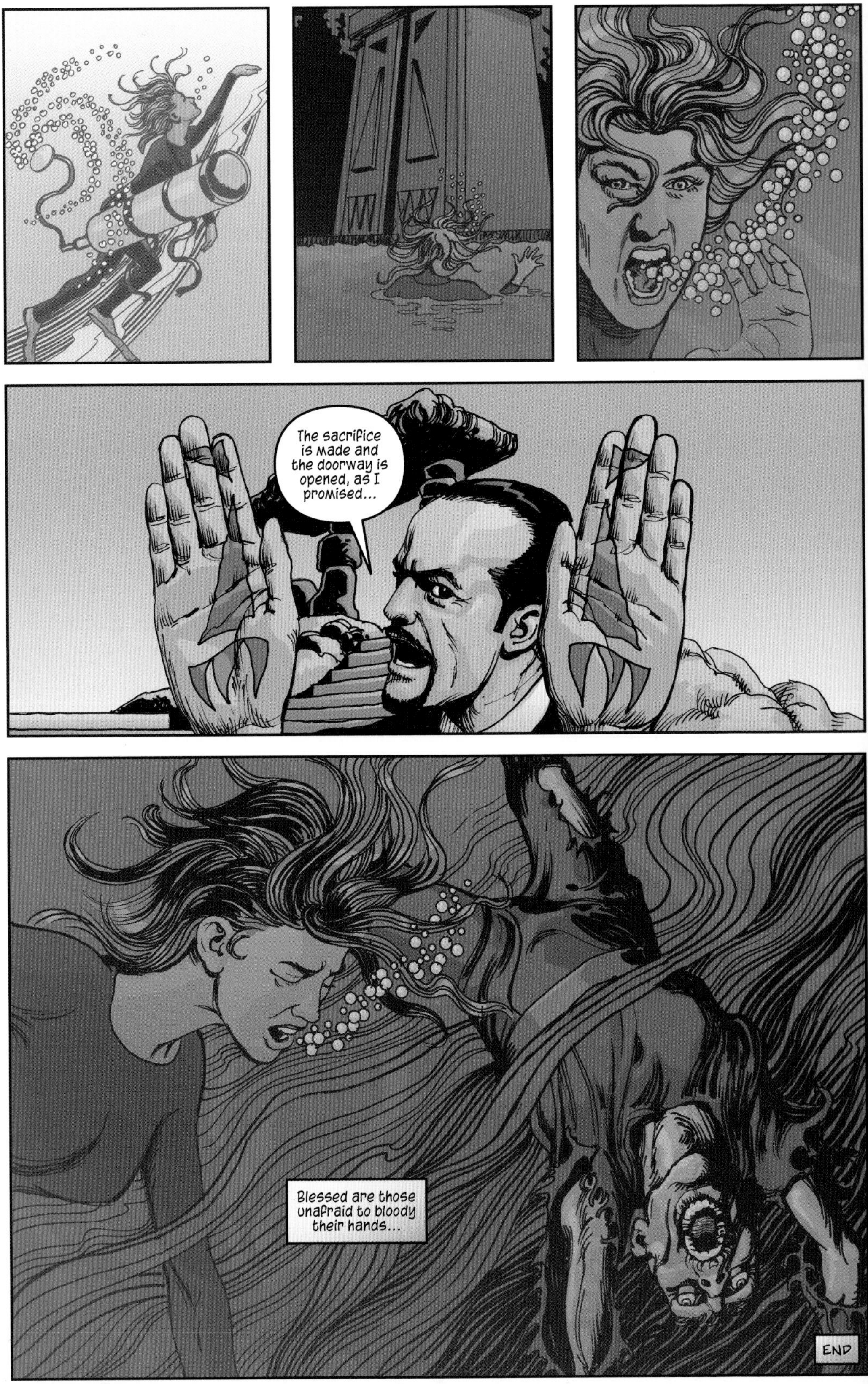
The sacrifice is made and the doorway is opened, as I promised...
Blessed are those unafraid to bloody their hands...
END

COMEBACK TOUR

STORY JEFF LESTER

ART CHEE

RITE TO LIFE

STORY MARK RAHNER

ART UNAI

WHERE AM I? [PART 1]

STORY MICHAEL ALAN NELSON

ART ARITZ

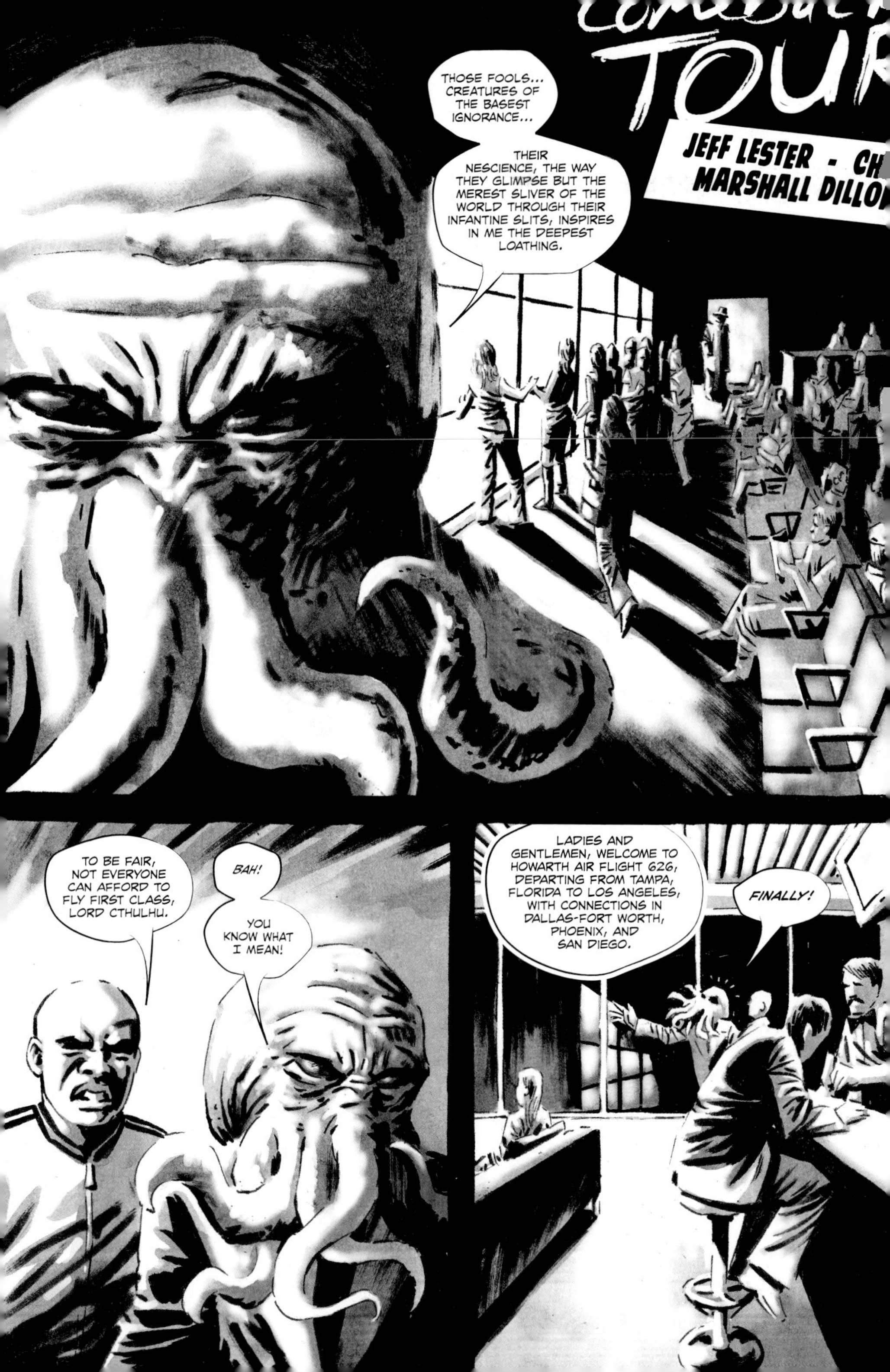

TOUR
JEFF LESTER - CH
MARSHALL DILLO
THOSE FOOLS... CREATURES OF THE BASEST IGNORANCE...
THEIR NESCIENCE, THE WAY THEY GLIMPSE BUT THE MEREST SLIVER OF THE WORLD THROUGH THEIR INFANTINE SLITS, INSPIRES IN ME THE DEEPEST LOATHING.
TO BE FAIR, NOT EVERYONE CAN AFFORD TO FLY FIRST CLASS, LORD CTHULHU.
BAH!
YOU KNOW WHAT I MEAN!
LADIES AND GENTLEMEN, WELCOME TO HOWARTH AIR FLIGHT 626, DEPARTING FROM TAMPA, FLORIDA TO LOS ANGELES, WITH CONNECTIONS IN DALLAS-FORT WORTH, PHOENIX, AND SAN DIEGO.
FINALLY!

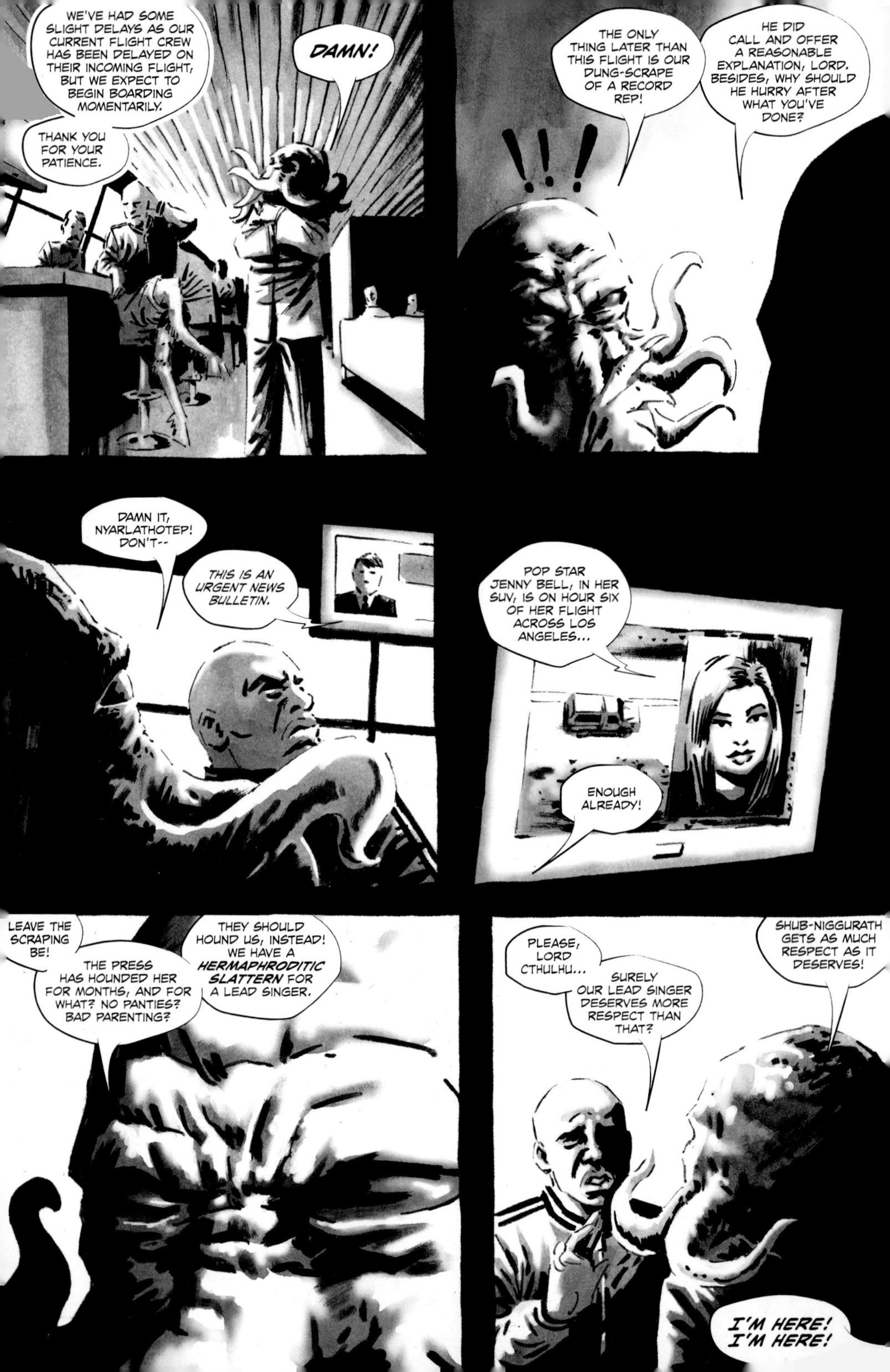
WE'VE HAD SOME SLIGHT DELAYS AS OUR CURRENT FLIGHT CREW HAS BEEN DELAYED ON THEIR INCOMING FLIGHT, BUT WE EXPECT TO BEGIN BOARDING MOMENTARILY.
THANK YOU FOR YOUR PATIENCE.
DAMN!
THE ONLY THING LATER THAN THIS FLIGHT IS OUR DUNG-SCRAPE OF A RECORD REP!
HE DID CALL AND OFFER A REASONABLE EXPLANATION, LORD. BESIDES, WHY SHOULD HE HURRY AFTER WHAT YOU'VE DONE?
!!!
DAMN IT, NYARLATHOTEP! DON'T--
THIS IS AN URGENT NEWS BULLETIN.
POP STAR JENNY BELL, IN HER SUV, IS ON HOUR SIX OF HER FLIGHT ACROSS LOS ANGELES...
ENOUGH ALREADY!
LEAVE THE SCRAPING BE!
THE PRESS HAS HOUNDED HER FOR MONTHS, AND FOR WHAT? NO PANTIES? BAD PARENTING?
THEY SHOULD HOUND US, INSTEAD! WE HAVE A HERMAPHRODITIC SLATTERN FOR A LEAD SINGER.
PLEASE, LORD CTHULHU...
SURELY OUR LEAD SINGER DESERVES MORE RESPECT THAN THAT?
SHUB-NIGGURATH GETS AS MUCH RESPECT AS IT DESERVES!
I'M HERE! I'M HERE!

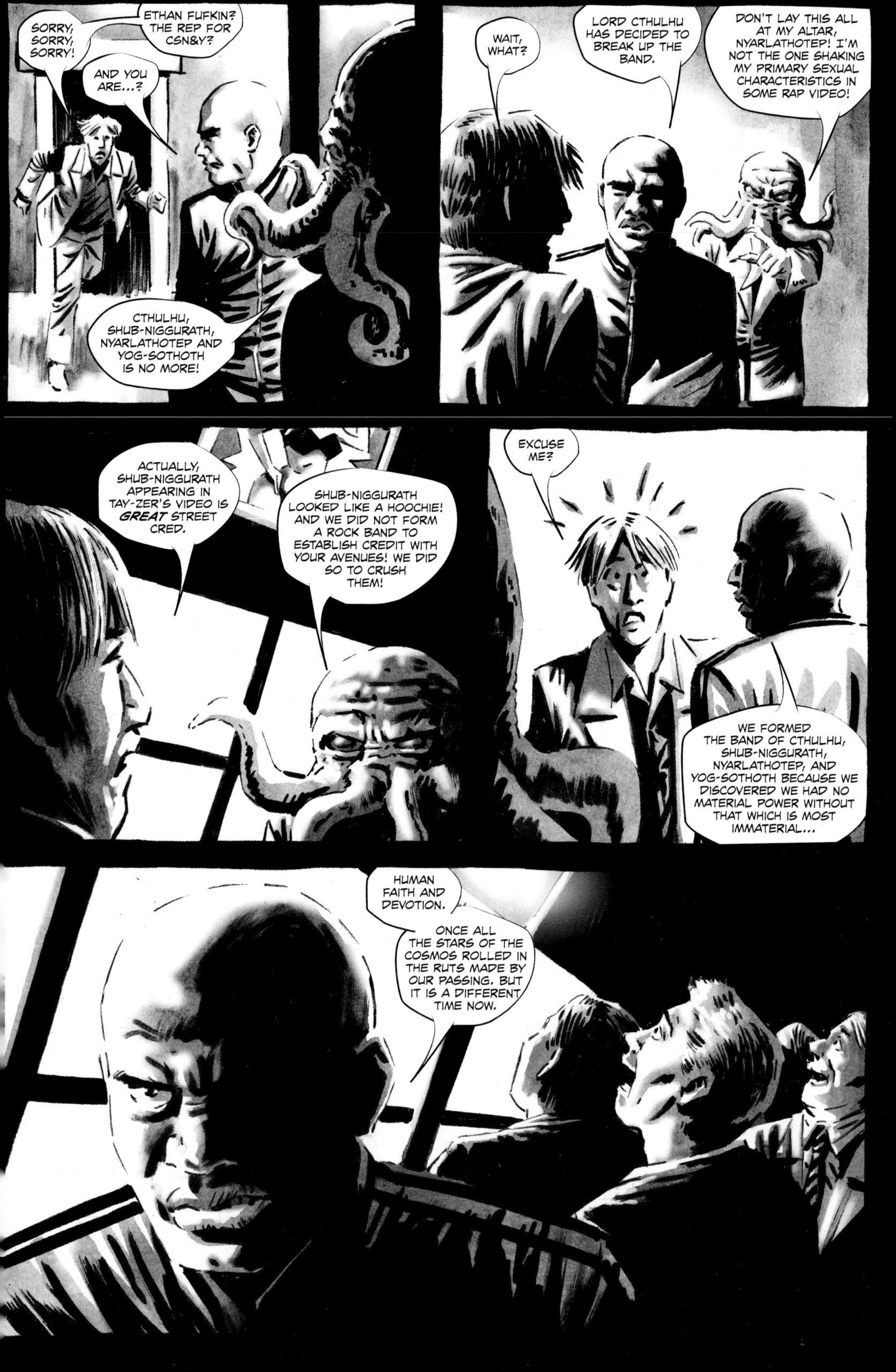
SORRY, SORRY, SORRY!
ETHAN FUFKIN? THE REP FOR CSN&Y?
AND YOU ARE...?
CTHULHU, SHUB-NIGGURATH, NYARLATHOTEP AND YOG-SOTHOTH IS NO MORE!
WAIT, WHAT?
LORD CTHULHU HAS DECIDED TO BREAK UP THE BAND.
DON'T LAY THIS ALL AT MY ALTAR, NYARLATHOTEP! I'M NOT THE ONE SHAKING MY PRIMARY SEXUAL CHARACTERISTICS IN SOME RAP VIDEO!
ACTUALLY, SHUB-NIGGURATH APPEARING IN TAY-ZER'S VIDEO IS GREAT STREET CRED.
SHUB-NIGGURATH LOOKED LIKE A HOOCHIE! AND WE DID NOT FORM A ROCK BAND TO ESTABLISH CREDIT WITH YOUR AVENUES! WE DID SO TO CRUSH THEM!
EXCUSE ME?
WE FORMED THE BAND OF CTHULHU, SHUB-NIGGURATH, NYARLATHOTEP, AND YOG-SOTHOTH BECAUSE WE DISCOVERED WE HAD NO MATERIAL POWER WITHOUT THAT WHICH IS MOST IMMATERIAL...
HUMAN FAITH AND DEVOTION.
ONCE ALL THE STARS OF THE COSMOS ROLLED IN THE RUTS MADE BY OUR PASSING. BUT IT IS A DIFFERENT TIME NOW.

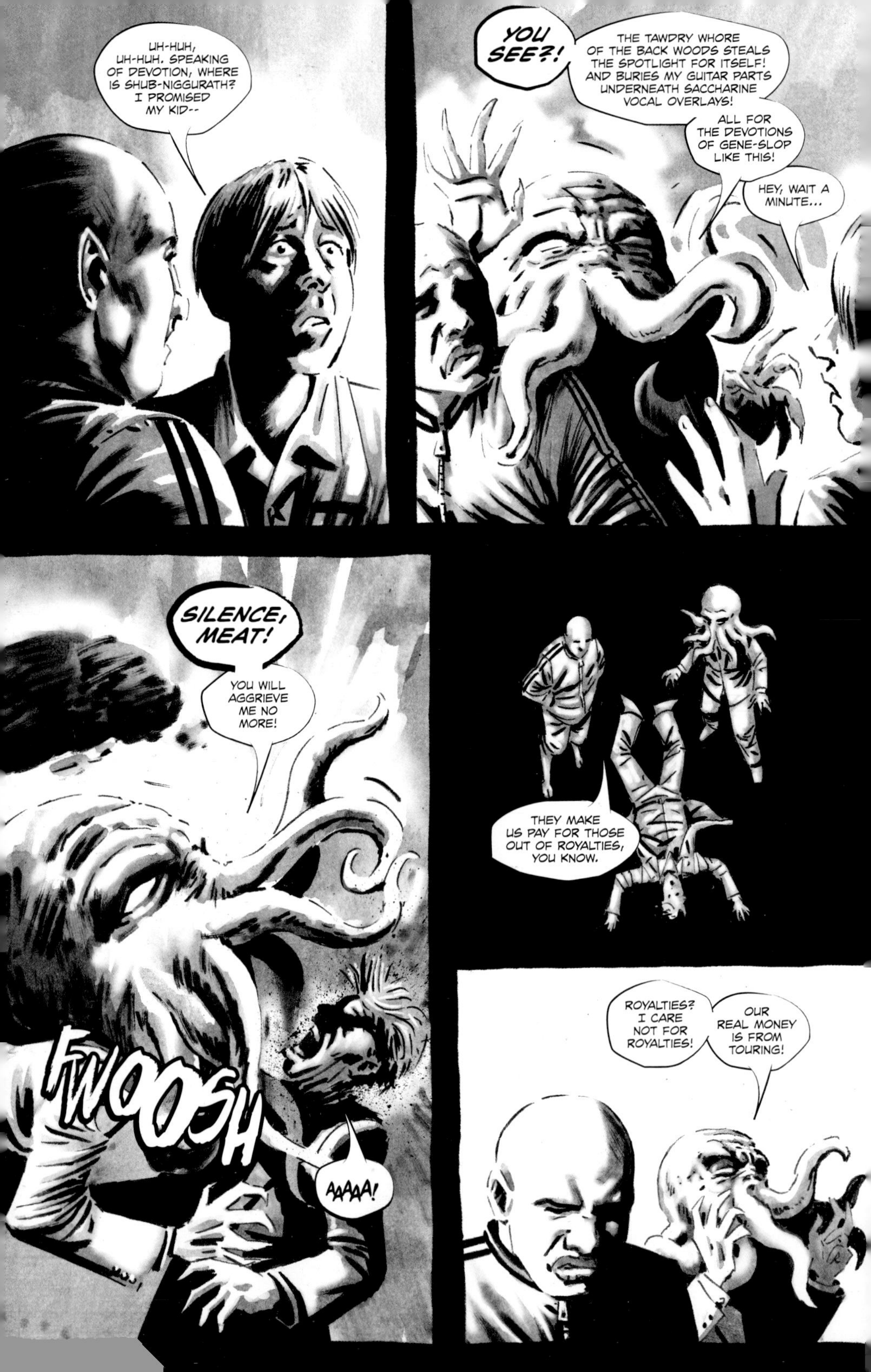
UH-HUH, UH-HUH. SPEAKING OF DEVOTION, WHERE IS SHUB-NIGGURATH? I PROMISED MY KID--
YOU SEE?!
THE TAWDRY WHORE OF THE BACK WOODS STEALS THE SPOTLIGHT FOR ITSELF! AND BURIES MY GUITAR PARTS UNDERNEATH SACCHARINE VOCAL OVERLAYS!
ALL FOR THE DEVOTIONS OF GENE-SLOP LIKE THIS!
HEY, WAIT A MINUTE...
SILENCE, MEAT!
YOU WILL AGGRIEVE ME NO MORE!
TWOOSH
AAAAA!
THEY MAKE US PAY FOR THOSE OUT OF ROYALTIES, YOU KNOW.
ROYALTIES? I CARE NOT FOR ROYALTIES!
OUR REAL MONEY IS FROM TOURING!

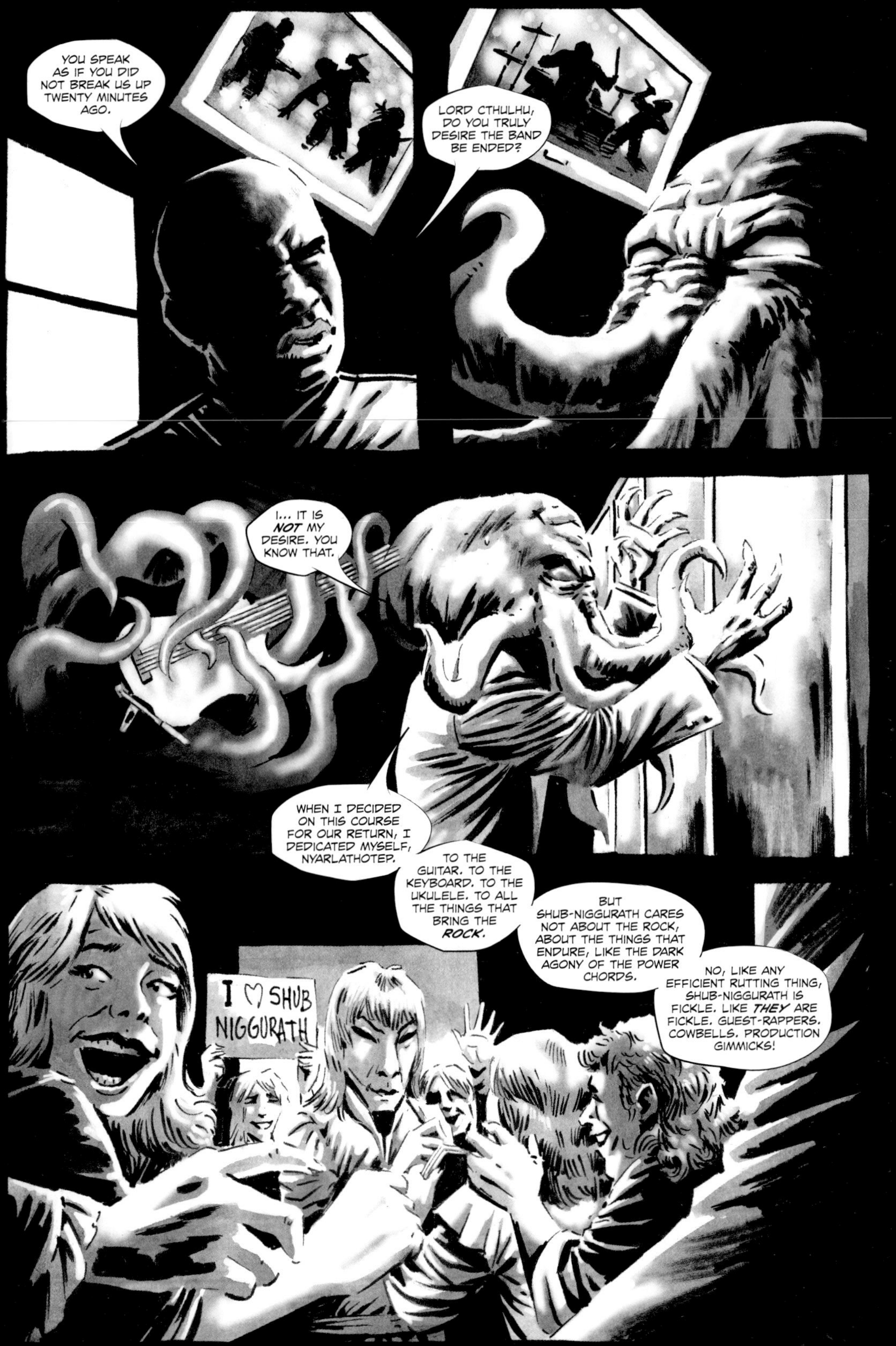
YOU SPEAK AS IF YOU DID NOT BREAK US UP TWENTY MINUTES AGO.
LORD CTHULHU, DO YOU TRULY DESIRE THE BAND BE ENDED?
I... IT IS NOT MY DESIRE. YOU KNOW THAT.
WHEN I DECIDED ON THIS COURSE FOR OUR RETURN, I DEDICATED MYSELF, NYARLATHOTEP.
TO THE GUITAR. TO THE KEYBOARD. TO THE UKULELE. TO ALL THE THINGS THAT BRING THE ROCK.
BUT SHUB-NIGGURATH CARES NOT ABOUT THE ROCK, ABOUT THE THINGS THAT ENDURE, LIKE THE DARK AGONY OF THE POWER CHORDS.
NO, LIKE ANY EFFICIENT RUTTING THING, SHUB-NIGGURATH IS FICKLE. LIKE THEY ARE FICKLE. GUEST-RAPPERS. COWBELLS. PRODUCTION GIMMICKS!
I ♡ SHUB NIGGURATH

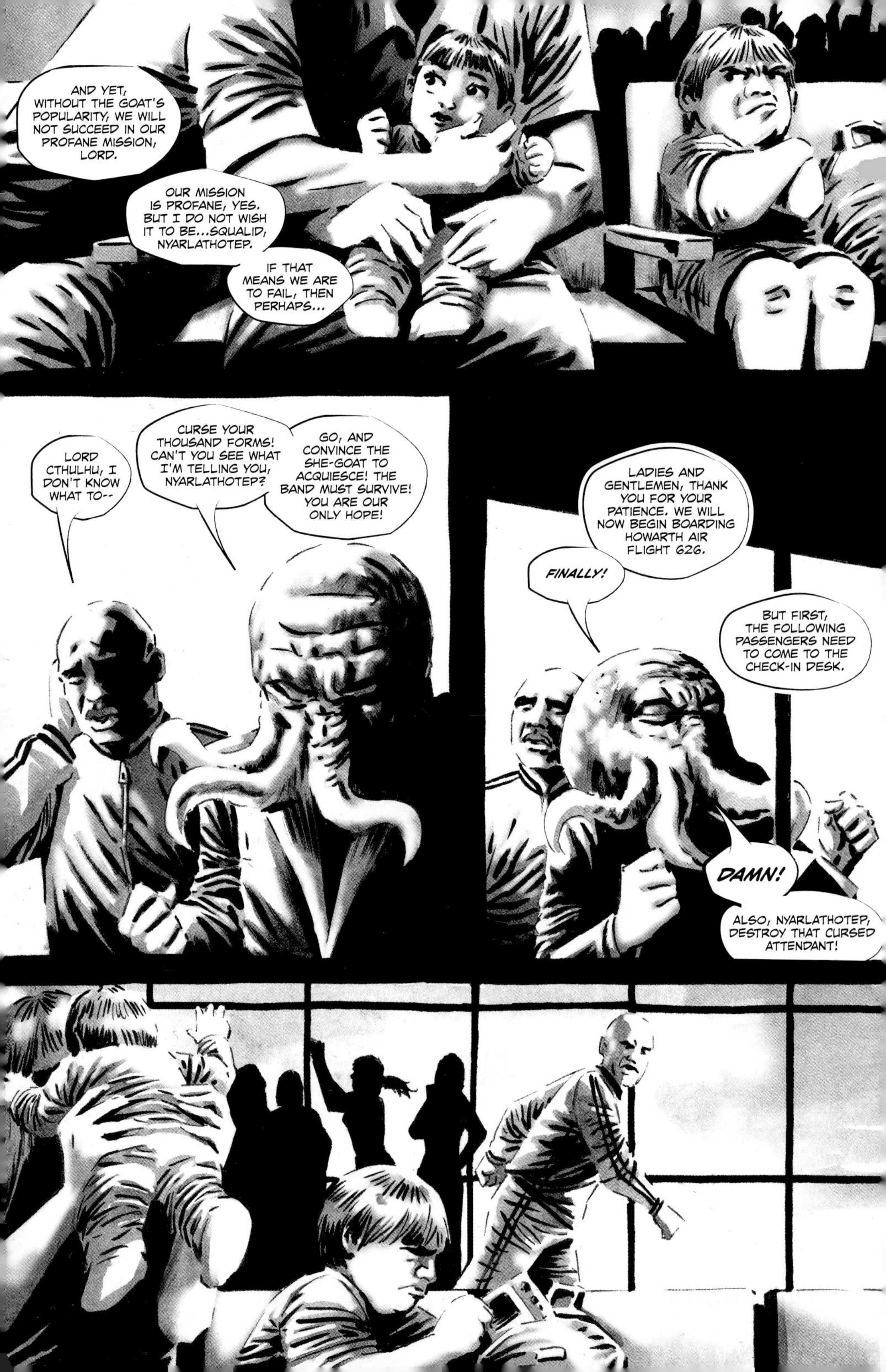
AND YET, WITHOUT THE GOAT'S POPULARITY, WE WILL NOT SUCCEED IN OUR PROFANE MISSION, LORD.
OUR MISSION IS PROFANE, YES. BUT I DO NOT WISH IT TO BE...SQUALID, NYARLATHOTEP.
IF THAT MEANS WE ARE TO FAIL, THEN PERHAPS...
LORD CTHULHU, I DON'T KNOW WHAT TO--
CURSE YOUR THOUSAND FORMS! CAN'T YOU SEE WHAT I'M TELLING YOU, NYARLATHOTEP?
GO, AND CONVINCE THE SHE-GOAT TO ACQUIESCE! THE BAND MUST SURVIVE! YOU ARE OUR ONLY HOPE!
LADIES AND GENTLEMEN, THANK YOU FOR YOUR PATIENCE. WE WILL NOW BEGIN BOARDING HOWARTH AIR FLIGHT 626.
FINALLY!
BUT FIRST, THE FOLLOWING PASSENGERS NEED TO COME TO THE CHECK-IN DESK.
DAMN!
ALSO, NYARLATHOTEP, DESTROY THAT CURSED ATTENDANT!

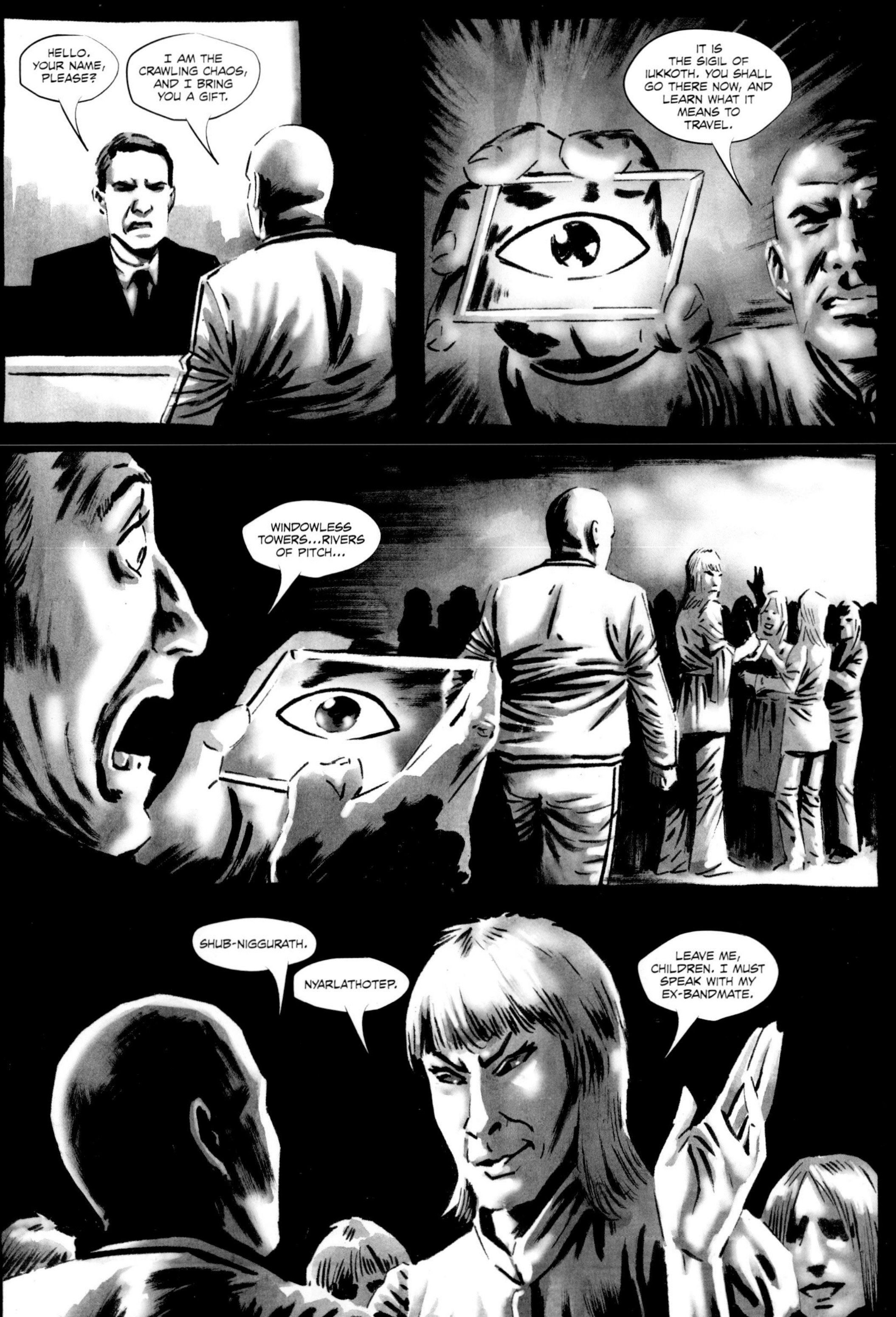
HELLO. YOUR NAME, PLEASE?
I AM THE CRAWLING CHAOS, AND I BRING YOU A GIFT.
IT IS THE SIGIL OF ILKKOTH. YOU SHALL GO THERE NOW, AND LEARN WHAT IT MEANS TO TRAVEL.
WINDOWLESS TOWERS...RIVERS OF PITCH...
SHUB-NIGGURATH.
NYARLATHOTEP.
LEAVE ME, CHILDREN. I MUST SPEAK WITH MY EX-BANDMATE.

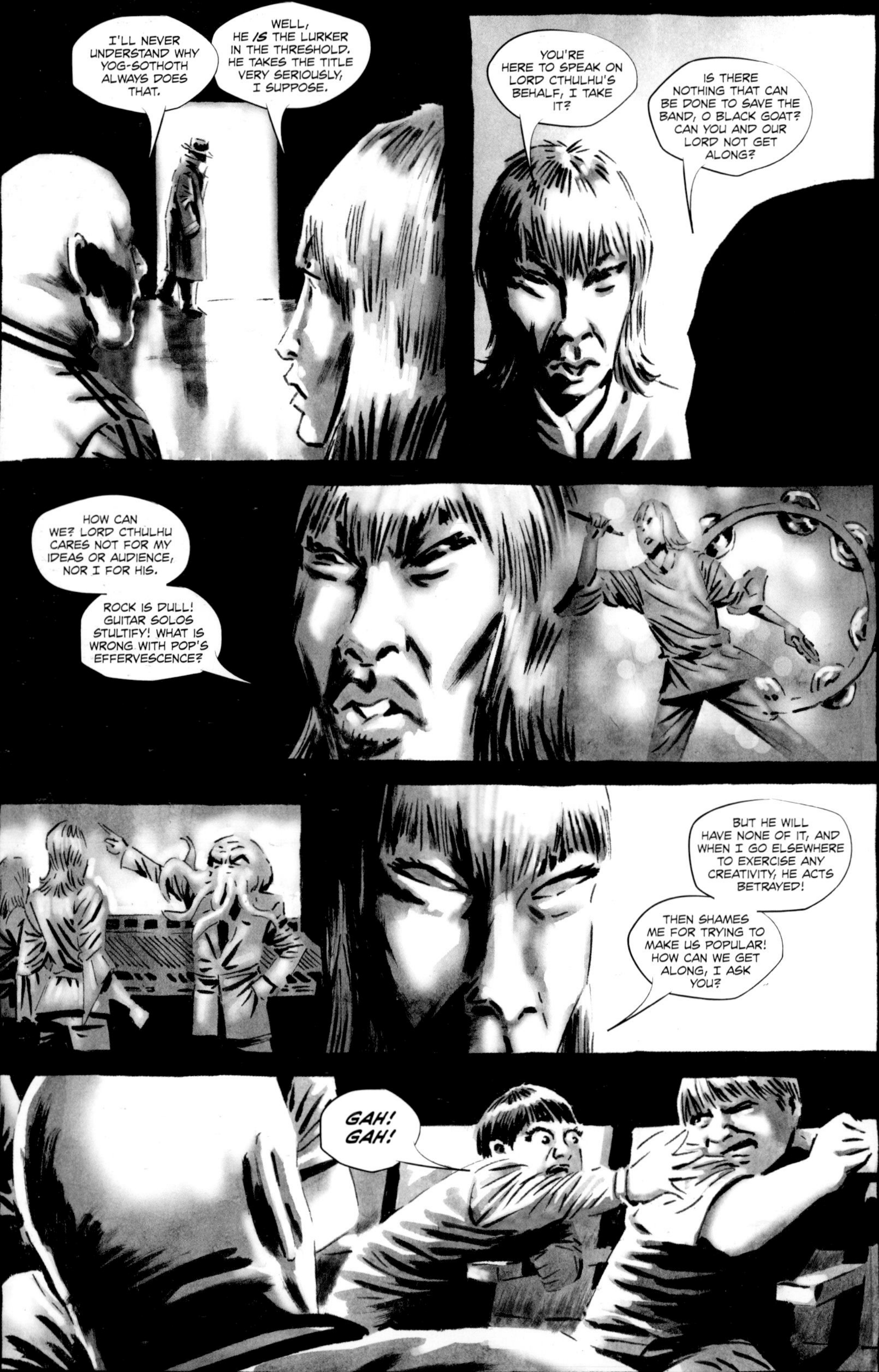
I'LL NEVER UNDERSTAND WHY YOG-SOTHOTH ALWAYS DOES THAT.
WELL, HE *IS* THE LURKER IN THE THRESHOLD. HE TAKES THE TITLE VERY SERIOUSLY, I SUPPOSE.
YOU'RE HERE TO SPEAK ON LORD CTHULHU'S BEHALF, I TAKE IT?
IS THERE NOTHING THAT CAN BE DONE TO SAVE THE BAND, O BLACK GOAT? CAN YOU AND OUR LORD NOT GET ALONG?
HOW CAN WE? LORD CTHULHU CARES NOT FOR MY IDEAS OR AUDIENCE, NOR I FOR HIS.
ROCK IS DULL! GUITAR SOLOS STULTIFY! WHAT IS WRONG WITH POP'S EFFERVESCENCE?
BUT HE WILL HAVE NONE OF IT, AND WHEN I GO ELSEWHERE TO EXERCISE ANY CREATIVITY, HE ACTS BETRAYED!
THEN SHAMES ME FOR TRYING TO MAKE US POPULAR! HOW CAN WE GET ALONG, I ASK YOU?
GAH! GAH!

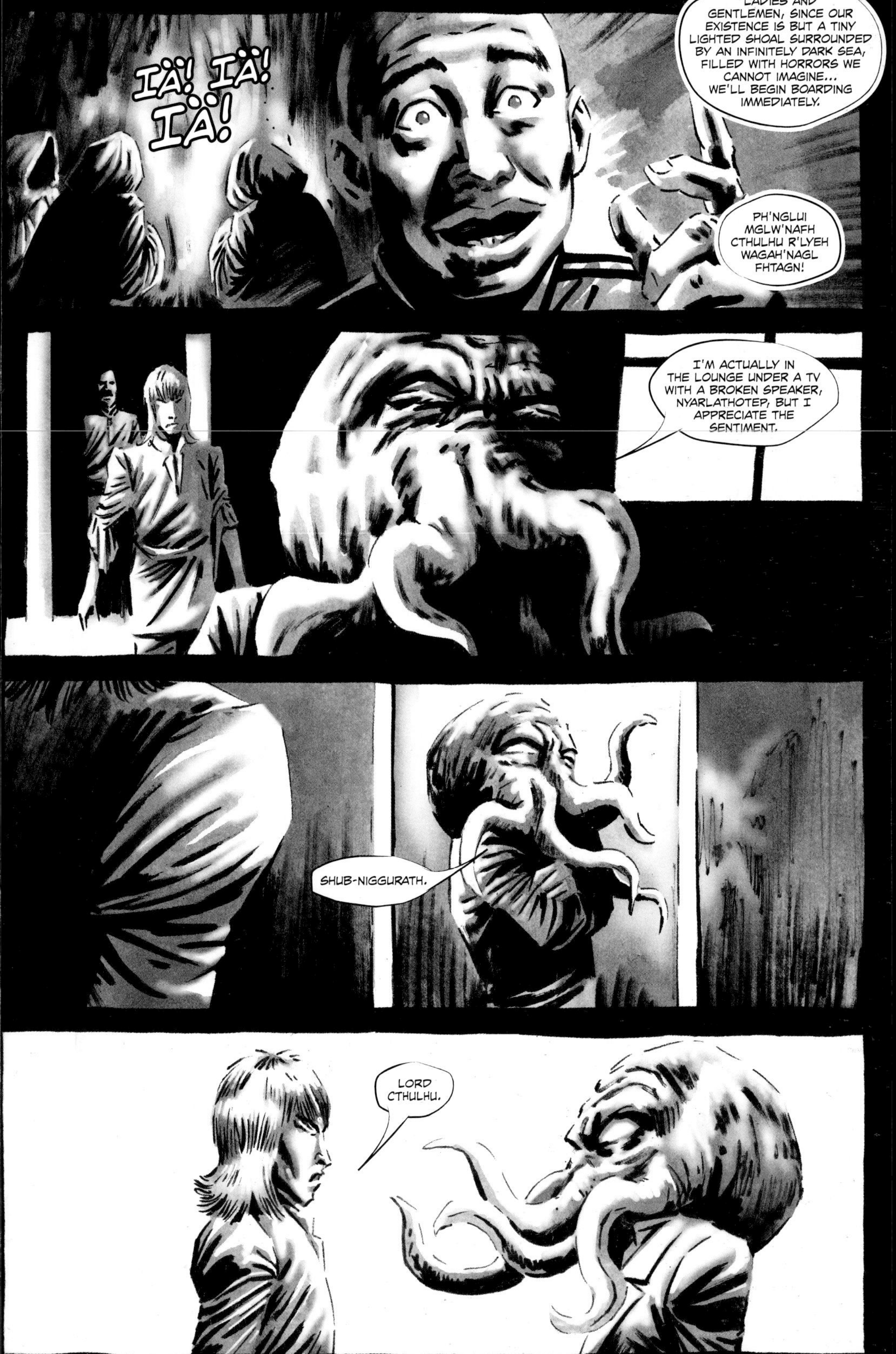
IÄ! IÄ! IÄ!
LADIES AND GENTLEMEN, SINCE OUR EXISTENCE IS BUT A TINY LIGHTED SHOAL SURROUNDED BY AN INFINITELY DARK SEA, FILLED WITH HORRORS WE CANNOT IMAGINE... WE'LL BEGIN BOARDING IMMEDIATELY.
PH'NGLUI MGLW'NAFH CTHULHU R'LYEH WAGAH'NAGL FHTAGN!
I'M ACTUALLY IN THE LOUNGE UNDER A TV WITH A BROKEN SPEAKER, NYARLATHOTEP, BUT I APPRECIATE THE SENTIMENT.
SHUB-NIGGURATH.
LORD CTHULHU.

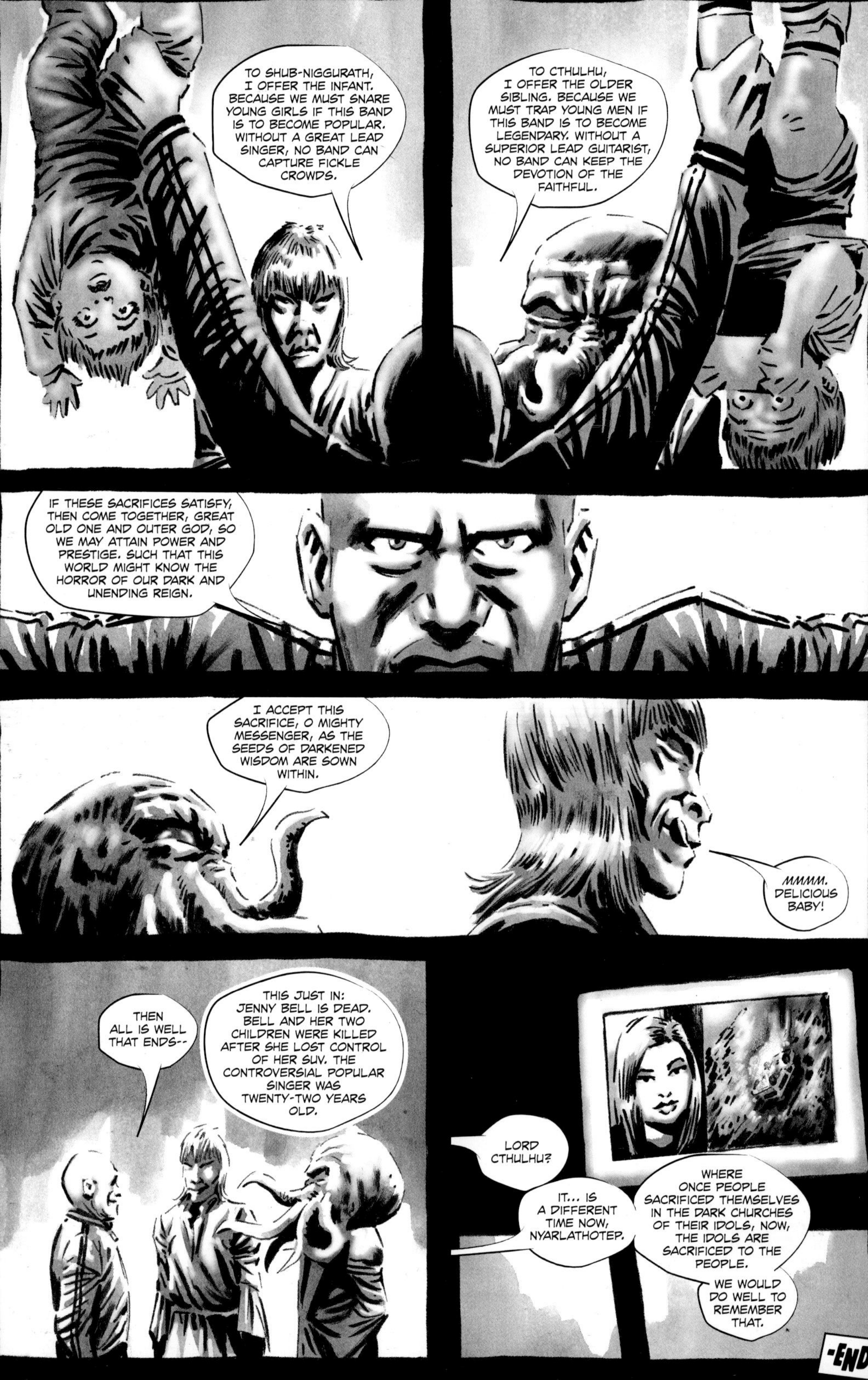
TO SHUB-NIGGURATH, I OFFER THE INFANT. BECAUSE WE MUST SNARE YOUNG GIRLS IF THIS BAND IS TO BECOME POPULAR. WITHOUT A GREAT LEAD SINGER, NO BAND CAN CAPTURE FICKLE CROWDS.
TO CTHULHU, I OFFER THE OLDER SIBLING. BECAUSE WE MUST TRAP YOUNG MEN IF THIS BAND IS TO BECOME LEGENDARY. WITHOUT A SUPERIOR LEAD GUITARIST, NO BAND CAN KEEP THE DEVOTION OF THE FAITHFUL.
IF THESE SACRIFICES SATISFY, THEN COME TOGETHER, GREAT OLD ONE AND OUTER GOD, SO WE MAY ATTAIN POWER AND PRESTIGE. SUCH THAT THIS WORLD MIGHT KNOW THE HORROR OF OUR DARK AND UNENDING REIGN.
I ACCEPT THIS SACRIFICE, O MIGHTY MESSENGER, AS THE SEEDS OF DARKENED WISDOM ARE SOWN WITHIN.
MMMM. DELICIOUS BABY!
THEN ALL IS WELL THAT ENDS--
THIS JUST IN: JENNY BELL IS DEAD. BELL AND HER TWO CHILDREN WERE KILLED AFTER SHE LOST CONTROL OF HER SUV. THE CONTROVERSIAL POPULAR SINGER WAS TWENTY-TWO YEARS OLD.
LORD CTHULHU?
IT... IS A DIFFERENT TIME NOW, NYARLATHOTEP.
WHERE ONCE PEOPLE SACRIFICED THEMSELVES IN THE DARK CHURCHES OF THEIR IDOLS, NOW, THE IDOLS ARE SACRIFICED TO THE PEOPLE.
WE WOULD DO WELL TO REMEMBER THAT.
-END

RITE TO LIFE

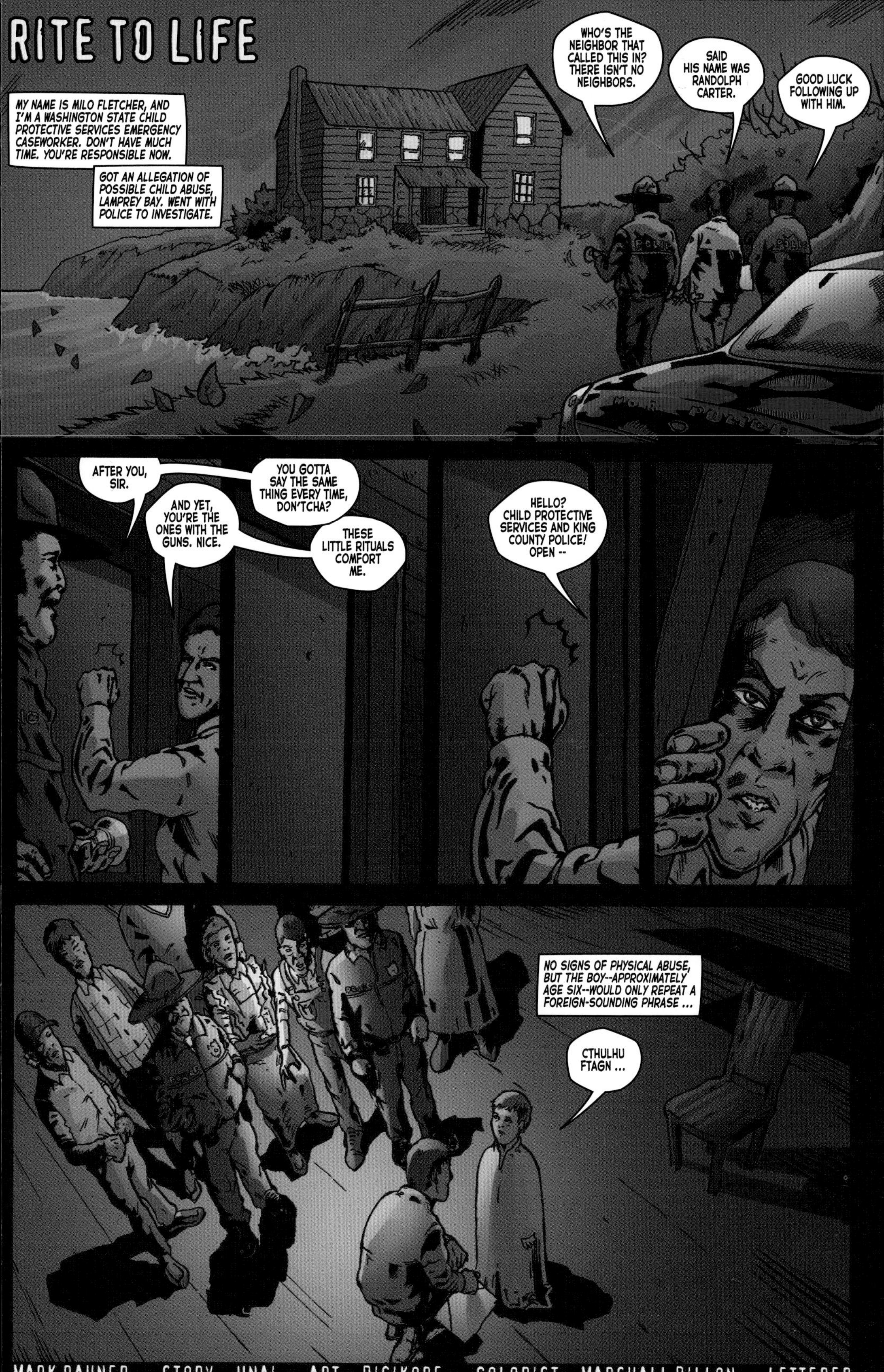

MY NAME IS MILO FLETCHER, AND I'M A WASHINGTON STATE CHILD PROTECTIVE SERVICES EMERGENCY CASEWORKER. DON'T HAVE MUCH TIME. YOU'RE RESPONSIBLE NOW.
GOT AN ALLEGATION OF POSSIBLE CHILD ABUSE, LAMPREY BAY. WENT WITH POLICE TO INVESTIGATE.
WHO'S THE NEIGHBOR THAT CALLED THIS IN? THERE ISN'T NO NEIGHBORS.
SAID HIS NAME WAS RANDOLPH CARTER.
GOOD LUCK FOLLOWING UP WITH HIM.
AFTER YOU, SIR.
YOU GOTTA SAY THE SAME THING EVERY TIME, DON'TCHA?
AND YET, YOU'RE THE ONES WITH THE GUNS. NICE.
THESE LITTLE RITUALS COMFORT ME.
HELLO? CHILD PROTECTIVE SERVICES AND KING COUNTY POLICE! OPEN --
NO SIGNS OF PHYSICAL ABUSE, BUT THE BOY--APPROXIMATELY AGE SIX--WOULD ONLY REPEAT A FOREIGN-SOUNDING PHRASE ...
CTHULHU FTAGN ...

MARK RAHNER -- STORY UNAI -- ART DIGIKORE -- COLORIST MARSHALL DILLON -- LETTERER

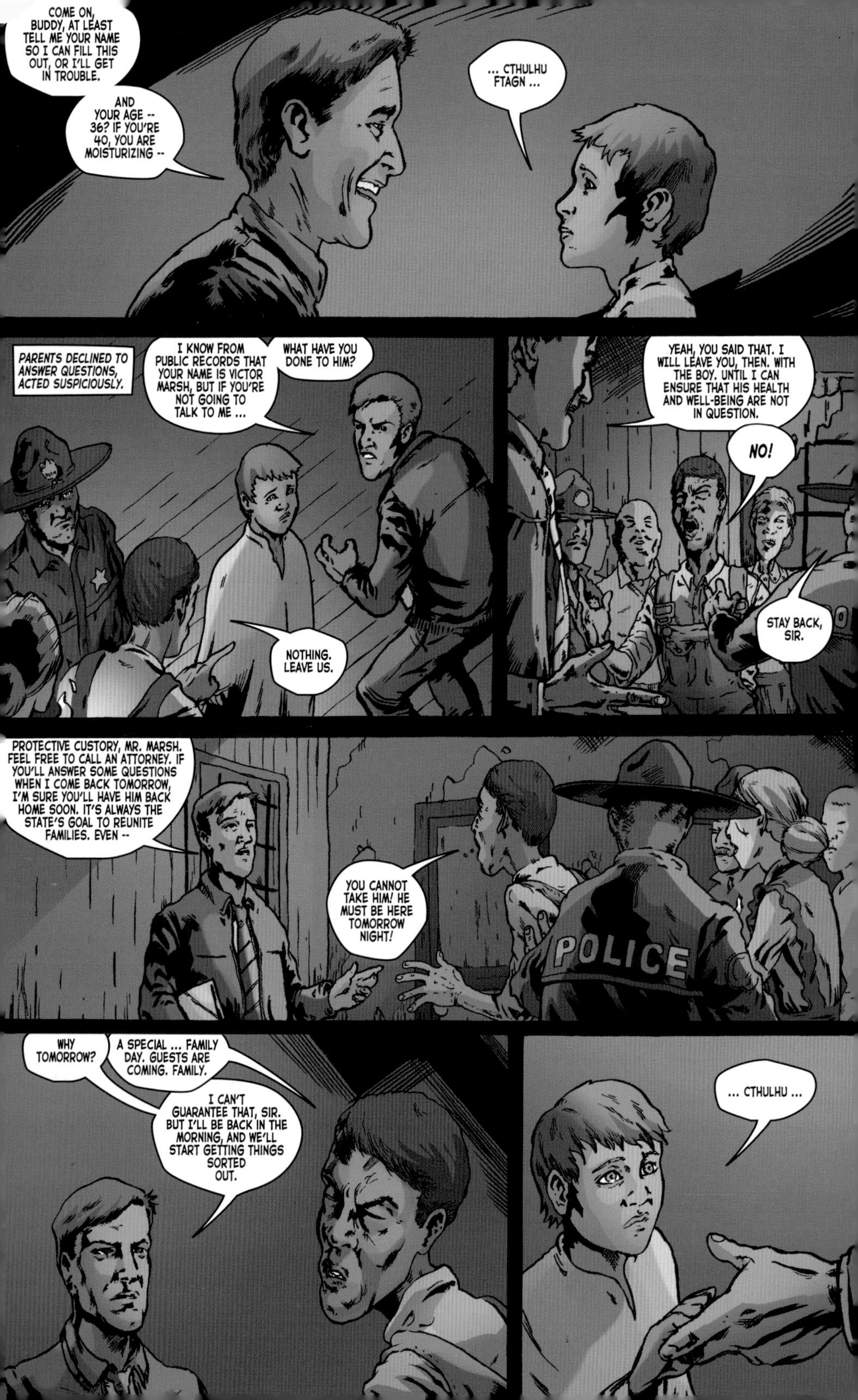
COME ON, BUDDY, AT LEAST TELL ME YOUR NAME SO I CAN FILL THIS OUT, OR I'LL GET IN TROUBLE.
AND YOUR AGE -- 36? IF YOU'RE 40, YOU ARE MOISTURIZING --
... CTHULHU FTAGN ...
PARENTS DECLINED TO ANSWER QUESTIONS, ACTED SUSPICIOUSLY.
I KNOW FROM PUBLIC RECORDS THAT YOUR NAME IS VICTOR MARSH, BUT IF YOU'RE NOT GOING TO TALK TO ME ...
WHAT HAVE YOU DONE TO HIM?
NOTHING. LEAVE US.
YEAH, YOU SAID THAT. I WILL LEAVE YOU, THEN. WITH THE BOY. UNTIL I CAN ENSURE THAT HIS HEALTH AND WELL-BEING ARE NOT IN QUESTION.
NO!
STAY BACK, SIR.
PROTECTIVE CUSTORY, MR. MARSH. FEEL FREE TO CALL AN ATTORNEY. IF YOU'LL ANSWER SOME QUESTIONS WHEN I COME BACK TOMORROW, I'M SURE YOU'LL HAVE HIM BACK HOME SOON. IT'S ALWAYS THE STATE'S GOAL TO REUNITE FAMILIES. EVEN --
YOU CANNOT TAKE HIM! HE MUST BE HERE TOMORROW NIGHT!
POLICE
WHY TOMORROW?
A SPECIAL ... FAMILY DAY. GUESTS ARE COMING. FAMILY.
I CAN'T GUARANTEE THAT, SIR. BUT I'LL BE BACK IN THE MORNING, AND WE'LL START GETTING THINGS SORTED OUT.
... CTHULHU ...

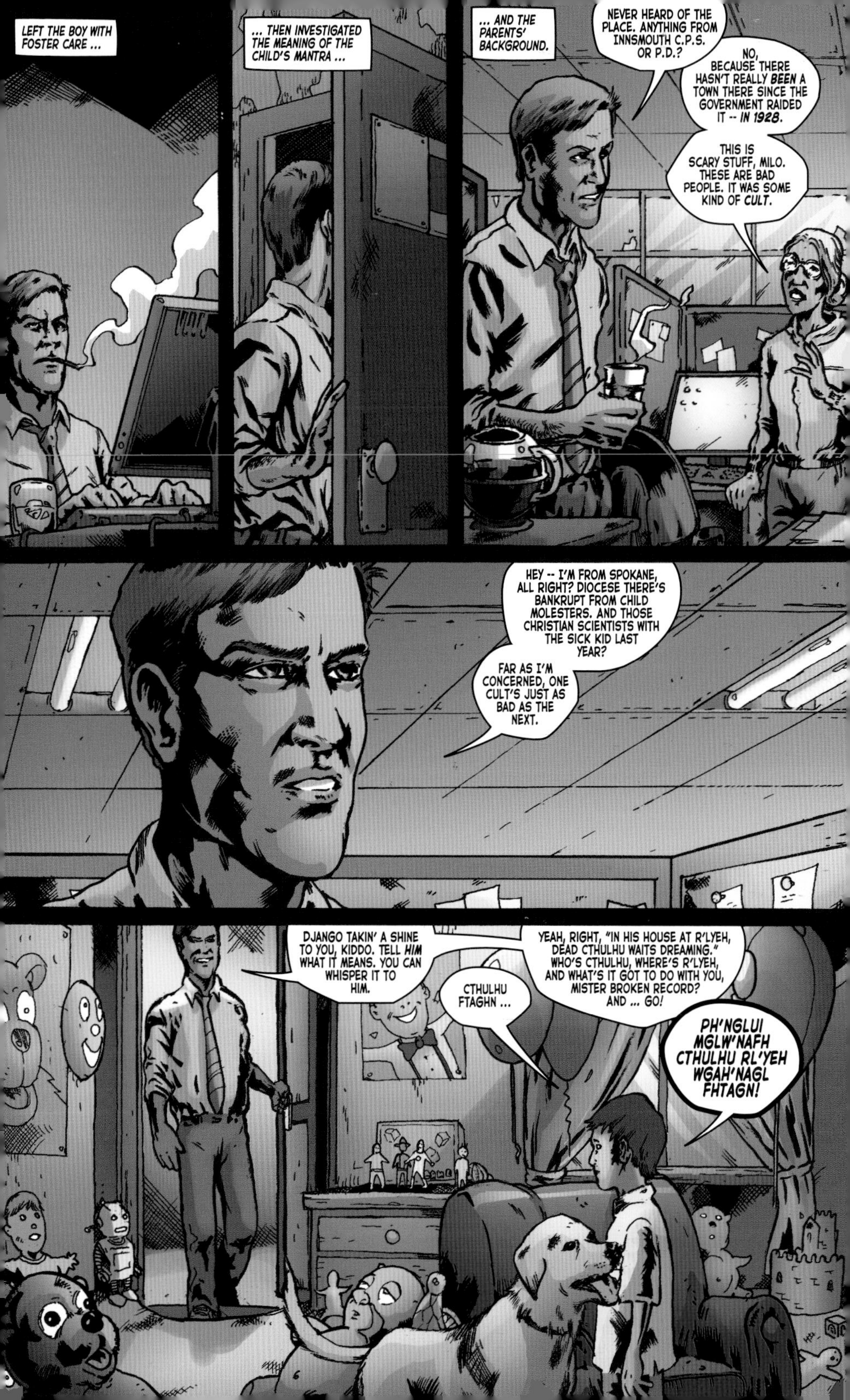
LEFT THE BOY WITH FOSTER CARE ...
... THEN INVESTIGATED THE MEANING OF THE CHILD'S MANTRA ...
... AND THE PARENTS' BACKGROUND.
NEVER HEARD OF THE PLACE. ANYTHING FROM INNSMOUTH C.P.S. OR P.D.?
NO, BECAUSE THERE HASN'T REALLY BEEN A TOWN THERE SINCE THE GOVERNMENT RAIDED IT -- IN 1928.
THIS IS SCARY STUFF, MILO. THESE ARE BAD PEOPLE. IT WAS SOME KIND OF CULT.
HEY -- I'M FROM SPOKANE, ALL RIGHT? DIOCESE THERE'S BANKRUPT FROM CHILD MOLESTERS. AND THOSE CHRISTIAN SCIENTISTS WITH THE SICK KID LAST YEAR?
FAR AS I'M CONCERNED, ONE CULT'S JUST AS BAD AS THE NEXT.
DJANGO TAKIN' A SHINE TO YOU, KIDDO. TELL HIM WHAT IT MEANS. YOU CAN WHISPER IT TO HIM.
CTHULHU FTAGHN ...
YEAH, RIGHT, "IN HIS HOUSE AT R'LYEH, DEAD CTHULHU WAITS DREAMING." WHO'S CTHULHU, WHERE'S R'LYEH, AND WHAT'S IT GOT TO DO WITH YOU, MISTER BROKEN RECORD? AND ... GO!
PH'NGLUI MGLW'NAFH CTHULHU RL'YEH WGAH'NAGL FHTAGN!

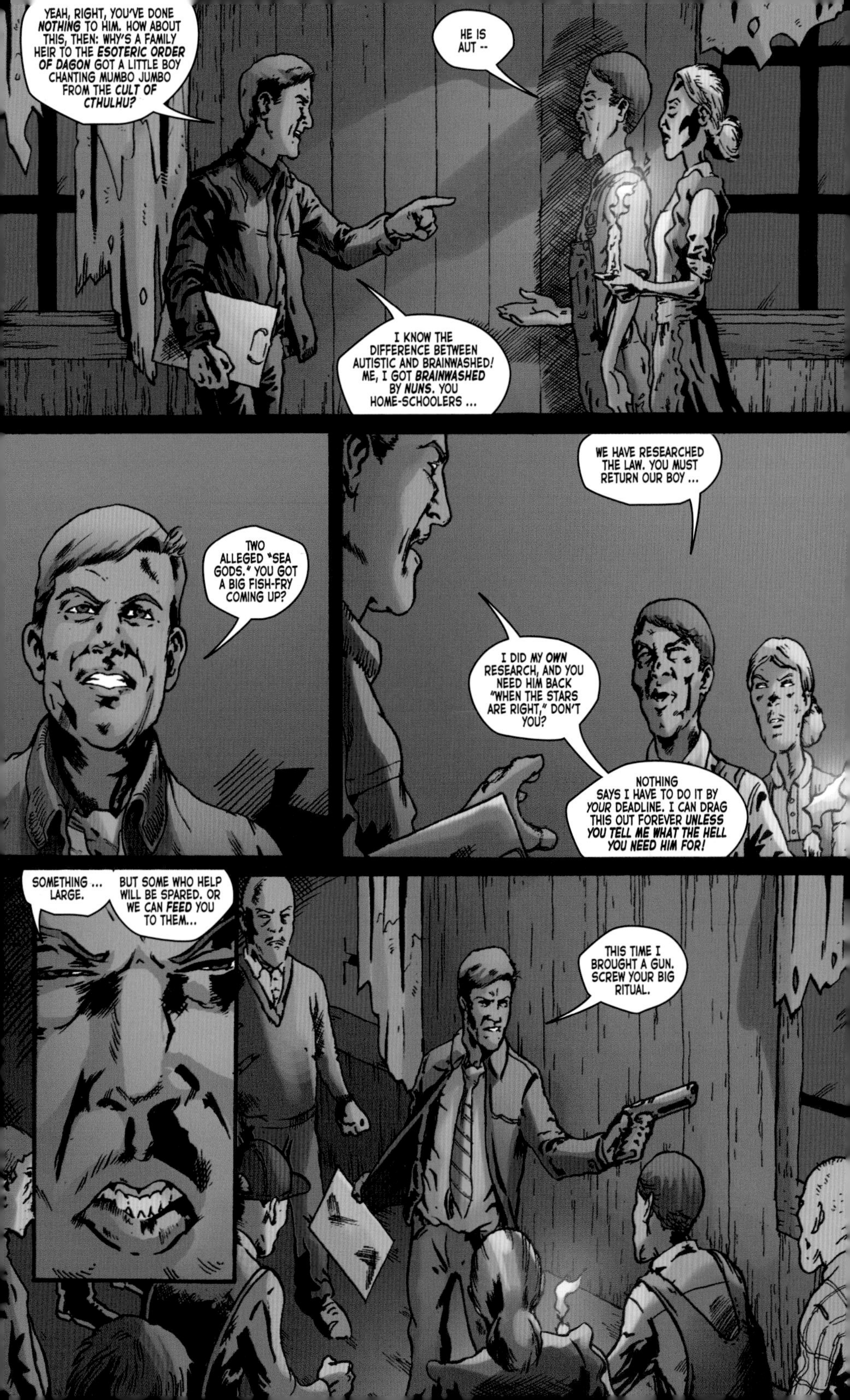
YEAH, RIGHT, YOU'VE DONE NOTHING TO HIM. HOW ABOUT THIS, THEN: WHY'S A FAMILY HEIR TO THE ESOTERIC ORDER OF DAGON GOT A LITTLE BOY CHANTING MUMBO JUMBO FROM THE CULT OF CTHULHU?
HE IS AUT --
I KNOW THE DIFFERENCE BETWEEN AUTISTIC AND BRAINWASHED! ME, I GOT BRAINWASHED BY NUNS. YOU HOME-SCHOOLERS ...
TWO ALLEGED "SEA GODS." YOU GOT A BIG FISH-FRY COMING UP?
WE HAVE RESEARCHED THE LAW. YOU MUST RETURN OUR BOY ...
I DID MY OWN RESEARCH, AND YOU NEED HIM BACK "WHEN THE STARS ARE RIGHT," DON'T YOU?
NOTHING SAYS I HAVE TO DO IT BY YOUR DEADLINE. I CAN DRAG THIS OUT FOREVER UNLESS YOU TELL ME WHAT THE HELL YOU NEED HIM FOR!
SOMETHING ... LARGE.
BUT SOME WHO HELP WILL BE SPARED. OR WE CAN FEED YOU TO THEM...
THIS TIME I BROUGHT A GUN. SCREW YOUR BIG RITUAL.

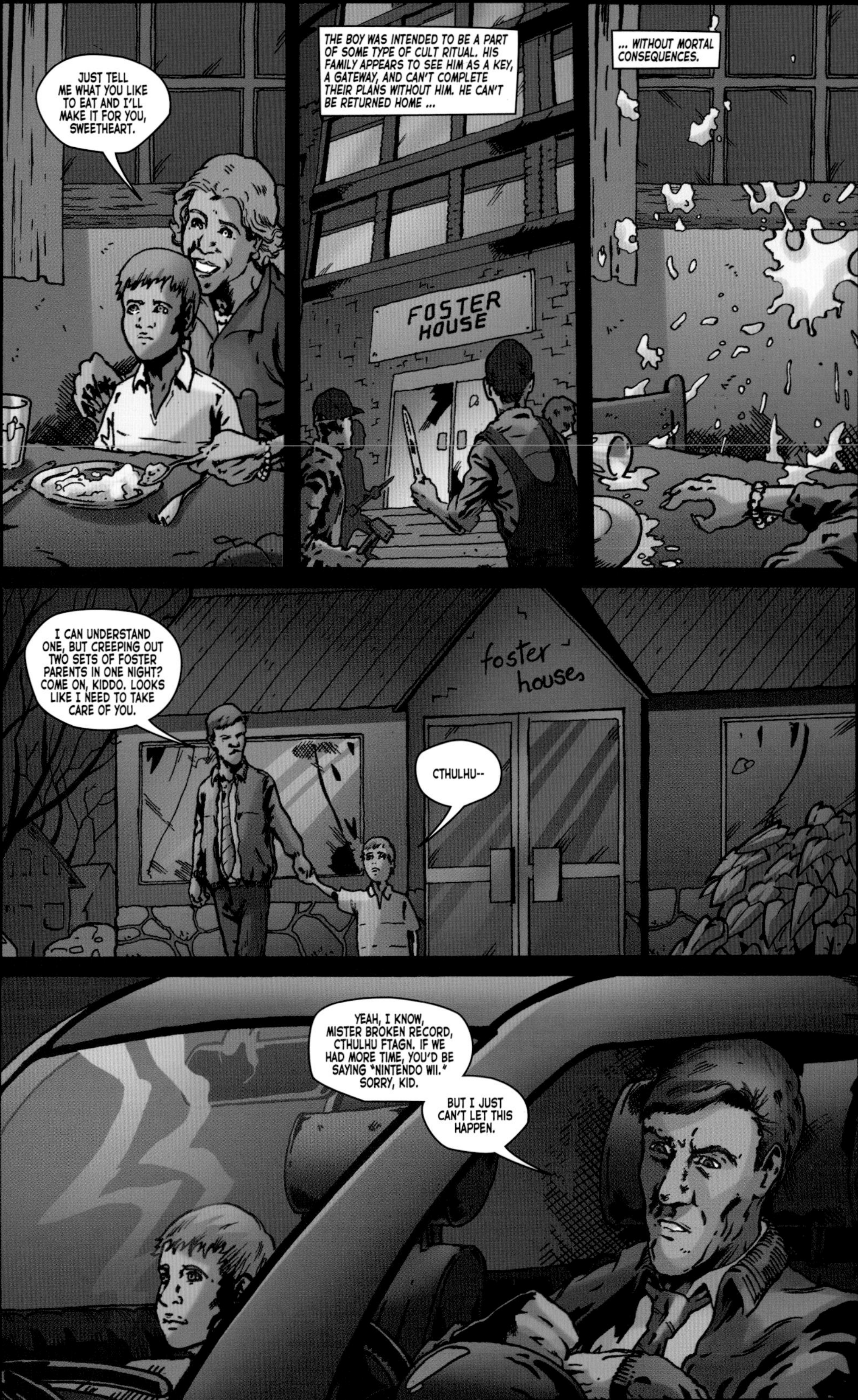
JUST TELL ME WHAT YOU LIKE TO EAT AND I'LL MAKE IT FOR YOU, SWEETHEART.
THE BOY WAS INTENDED TO BE A PART OF SOME TYPE OF CULT RITUAL. HIS FAMILY APPEARS TO SEE HIM AS A KEY, A GATEWAY, AND CAN'T COMPLETE THEIR PLANS WITHOUT HIM. HE CAN'T BE RETURNED HOME ...
FOSTER HOUSE
... WITHOUT MORTAL CONSEQUENCES.
I CAN UNDERSTAND ONE, BUT CREEPING OUT TWO SETS OF FOSTER PARENTS IN ONE NIGHT? COME ON, KIDDO. LOOKS LIKE I NEED TO TAKE CARE OF YOU.
foster houses
CTHULHU--
YEAH, I KNOW, MISTER BROKEN RECORD, CTHULHU FTAGN. IF WE HAD MORE TIME, YOU'D BE SAYING "NINTENDO WII." SORRY, KID.
BUT I JUST CAN'T LET THIS HAPPEN.

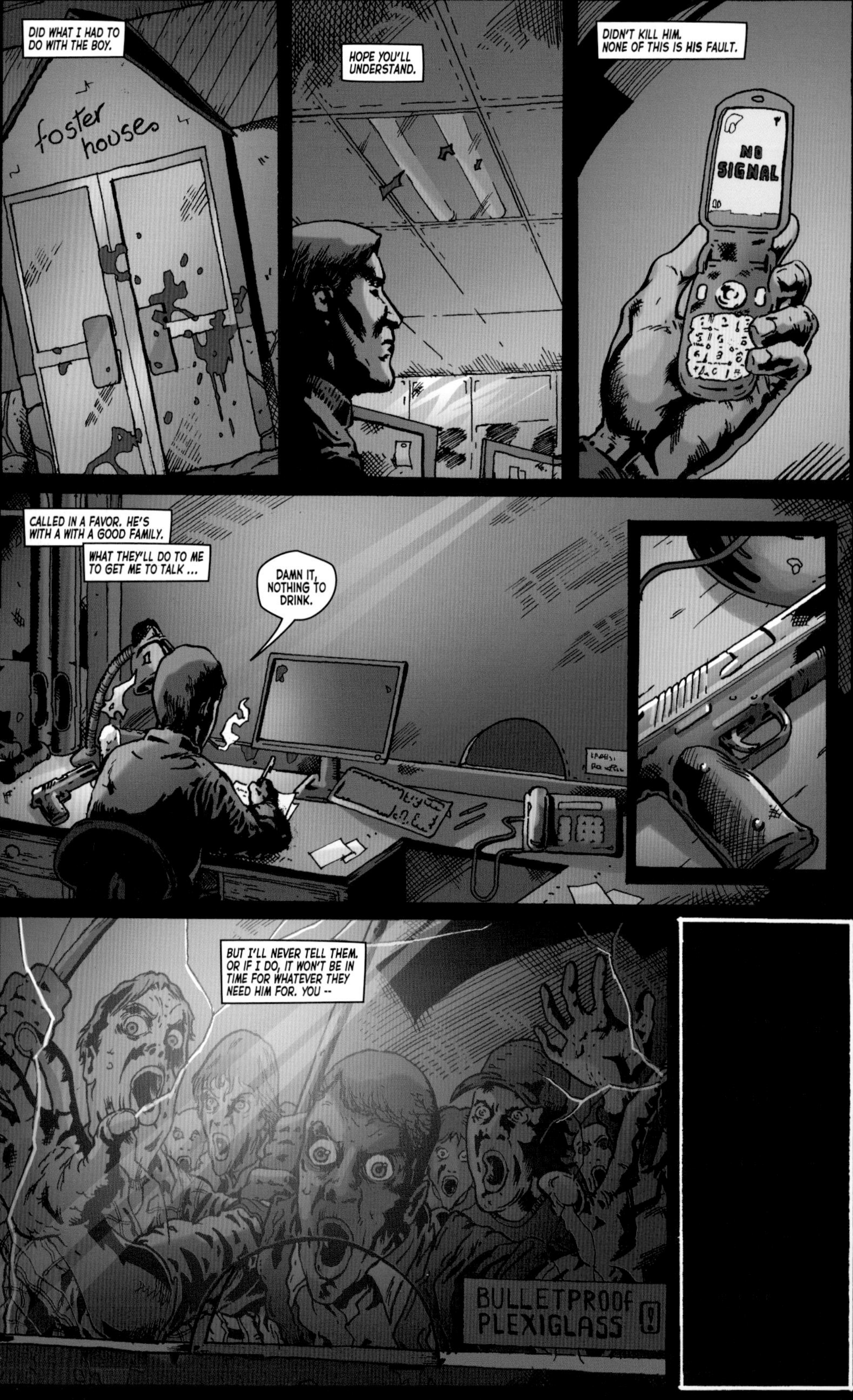
DID WHAT I HAD TO DO WITH THE BOY.
foster houses
HOPE YOU'LL UNDERSTAND.
DIDN'T KILL HIM. NONE OF THIS IS HIS FAULT.
NO SIGNAL
CALLED IN A FAVOR. HE'S WITH A WITH A GOOD FAMILY.
WHAT THEY'LL DO TO ME TO GET ME TO TALK ...
DAMN IT, NOTHING TO DRINK.
BUT I'LL NEVER TELL THEM. OR IF I DO, IT WON'T BE IN TIME FOR WHATEVER THEY NEED HIM FOR. YOU --
BULLETPROOF PLEXIGLASS

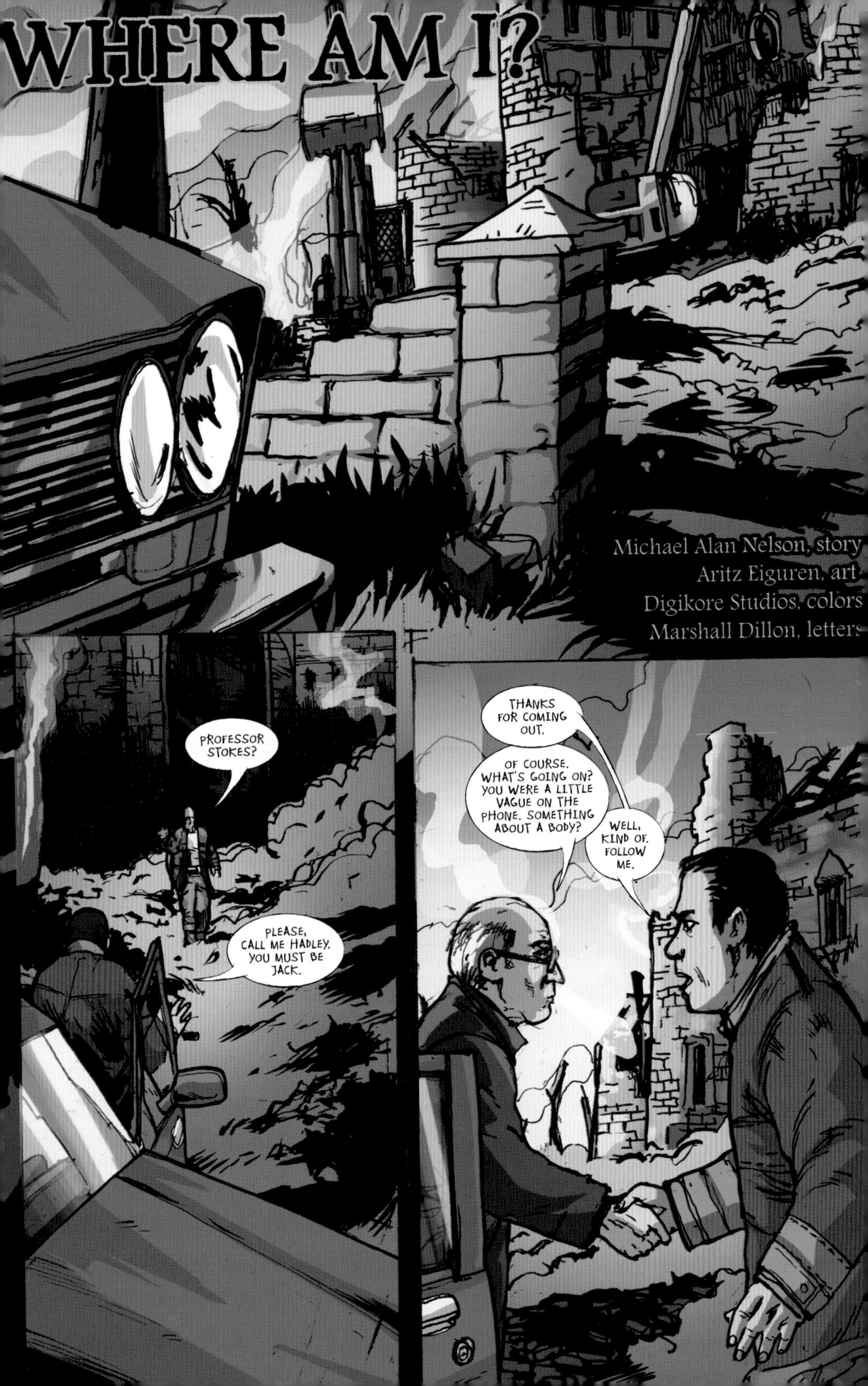
WHERE AM I?
Michael Alan Nelson, story
Aritz Eiguren, art
Digikore Studios, colors
Marshall Dillon, letters
PROFESSOR STOKES?
PLEASE, CALL ME HADLEY. YOU MUST BE JACK.
THANKS FOR COMING OUT.
OF COURSE. WHAT'S GOING ON? YOU WERE A LITTLE VAGUE ON THE PHONE. SOMETHING ABOUT A BODY?
WELL, KIND OF. FOLLOW ME.

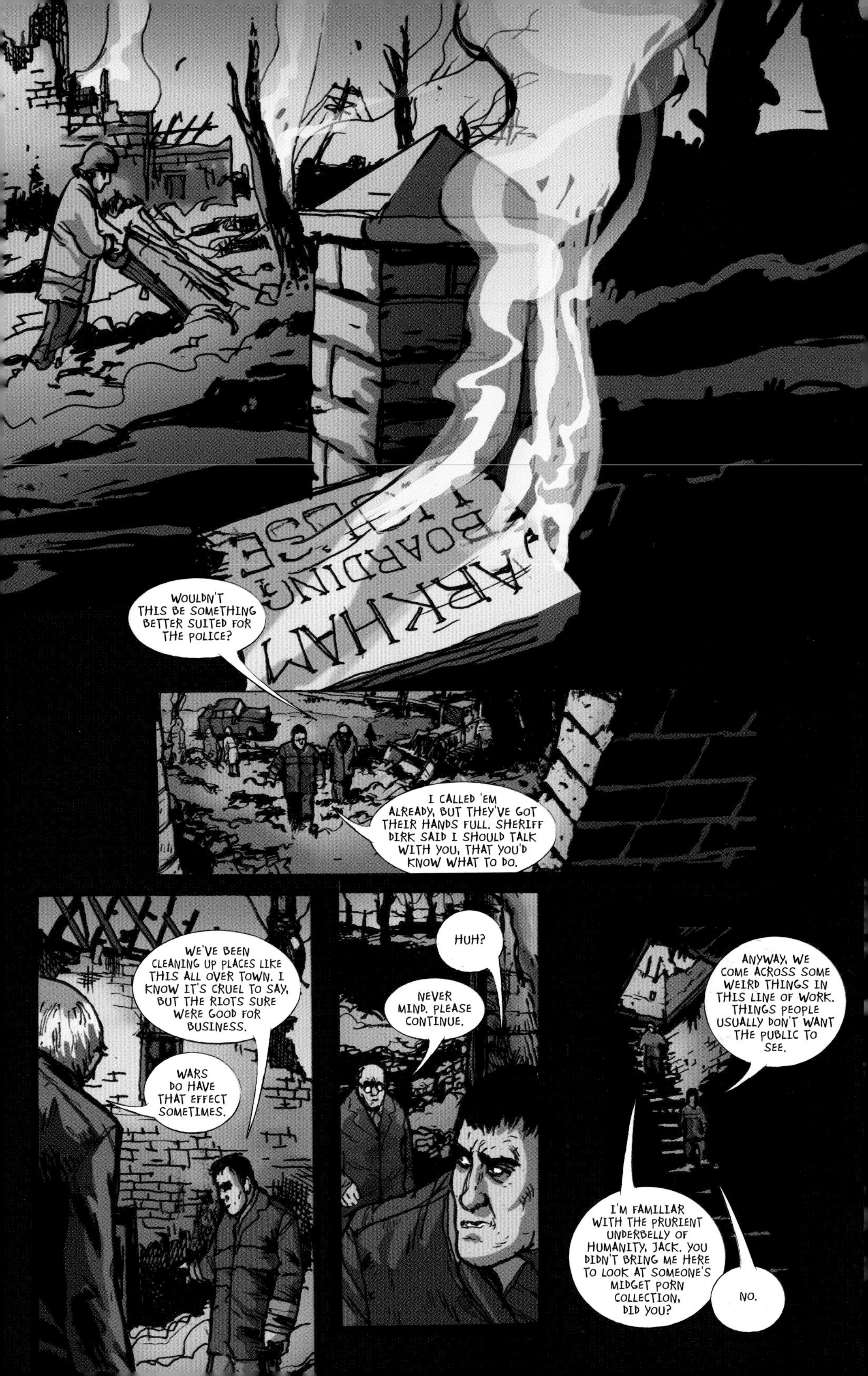
ARKHAM BOARDING HOUSE
WOULDN'T THIS BE SOMETHING BETTER SUITED FOR THE POLICE?
I CALLED 'EM ALREADY, BUT THEY'VE GOT THEIR HANDS FULL. SHERIFF DIRK SAID I SHOULD TALK WITH YOU, THAT YOU'D KNOW WHAT TO DO.
WE'VE BEEN CLEANING UP PLACES LIKE THIS ALL OVER TOWN. I KNOW IT'S CRUEL TO SAY, BUT THE RIOTS SURE WERE GOOD FOR BUSINESS.
WARS DO HAVE THAT EFFECT SOMETIMES.
HUH?
NEVER MIND. PLEASE CONTINUE.
ANYWAY, WE COME ACROSS SOME WEIRD THINGS IN THIS LINE OF WORK. THINGS PEOPLE USUALLY DON'T WANT THE PUBLIC TO SEE.
I'M FAMILIAR WITH THE PRURIENT UNDERBELLY OF HUMANITY, JACK. YOU DIDN'T BRING ME HERE TO LOOK AT SOMEONE'S MIDGET PORN COLLECTION, DID YOU?
NO.

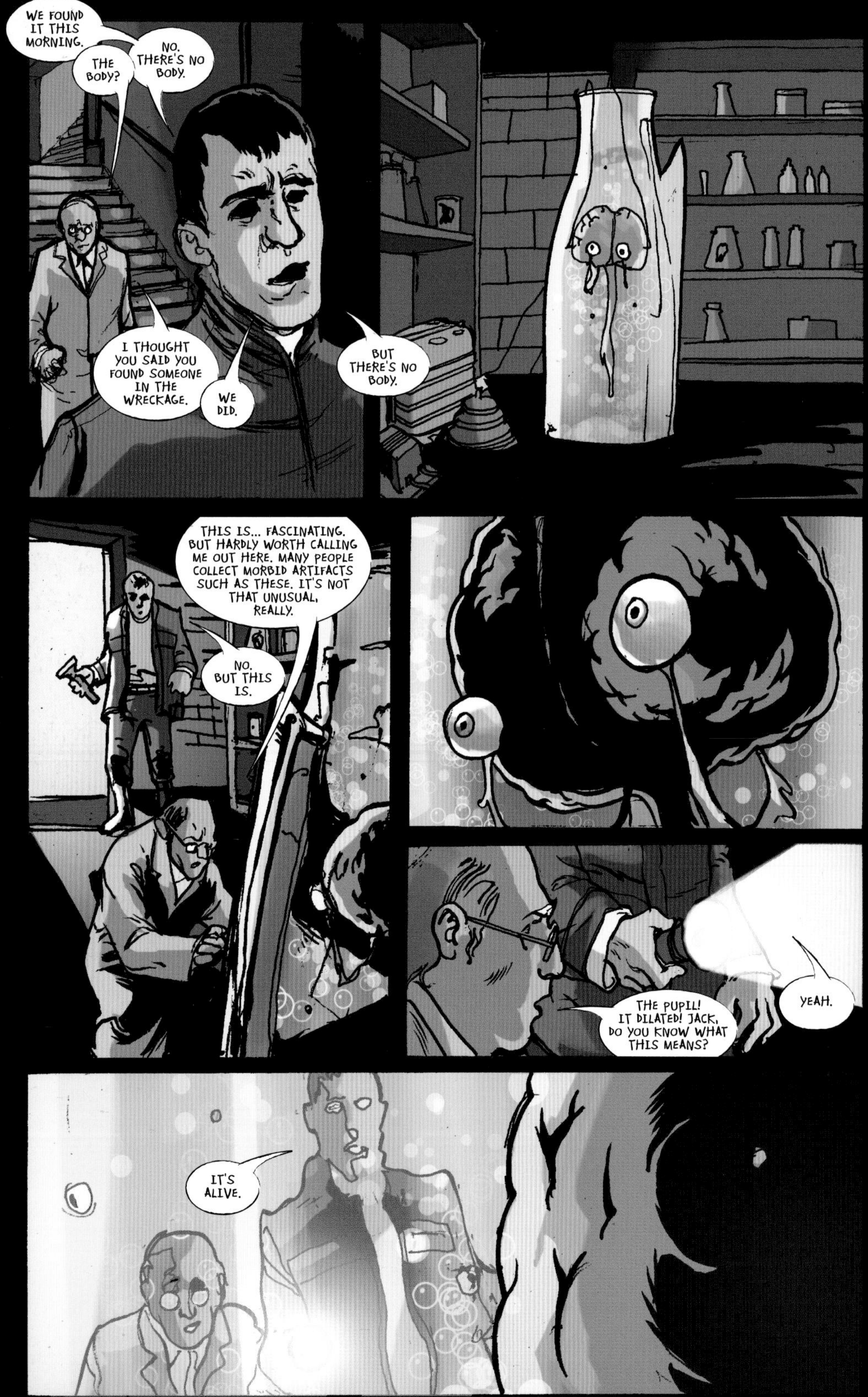
WE FOUND IT THIS MORNING.
THE BODY?
NO. THERE'S NO BODY.
I THOUGHT YOU SAID YOU FOUND SOMEONE IN THE WRECKAGE.
WE DID.
BUT THERE'S NO BODY.
THIS IS... FASCINATING. BUT HARDLY WORTH CALLING ME OUT HERE. MANY PEOPLE COLLECT MORBID ARTIFACTS SUCH AS THESE. IT'S NOT THAT UNUSUAL, REALLY.
NO. BUT THIS IS.
THE PUPIL! IT DILATED! JACK, DO YOU KNOW WHAT THIS MEANS?
YEAH.
IT'S ALIVE.

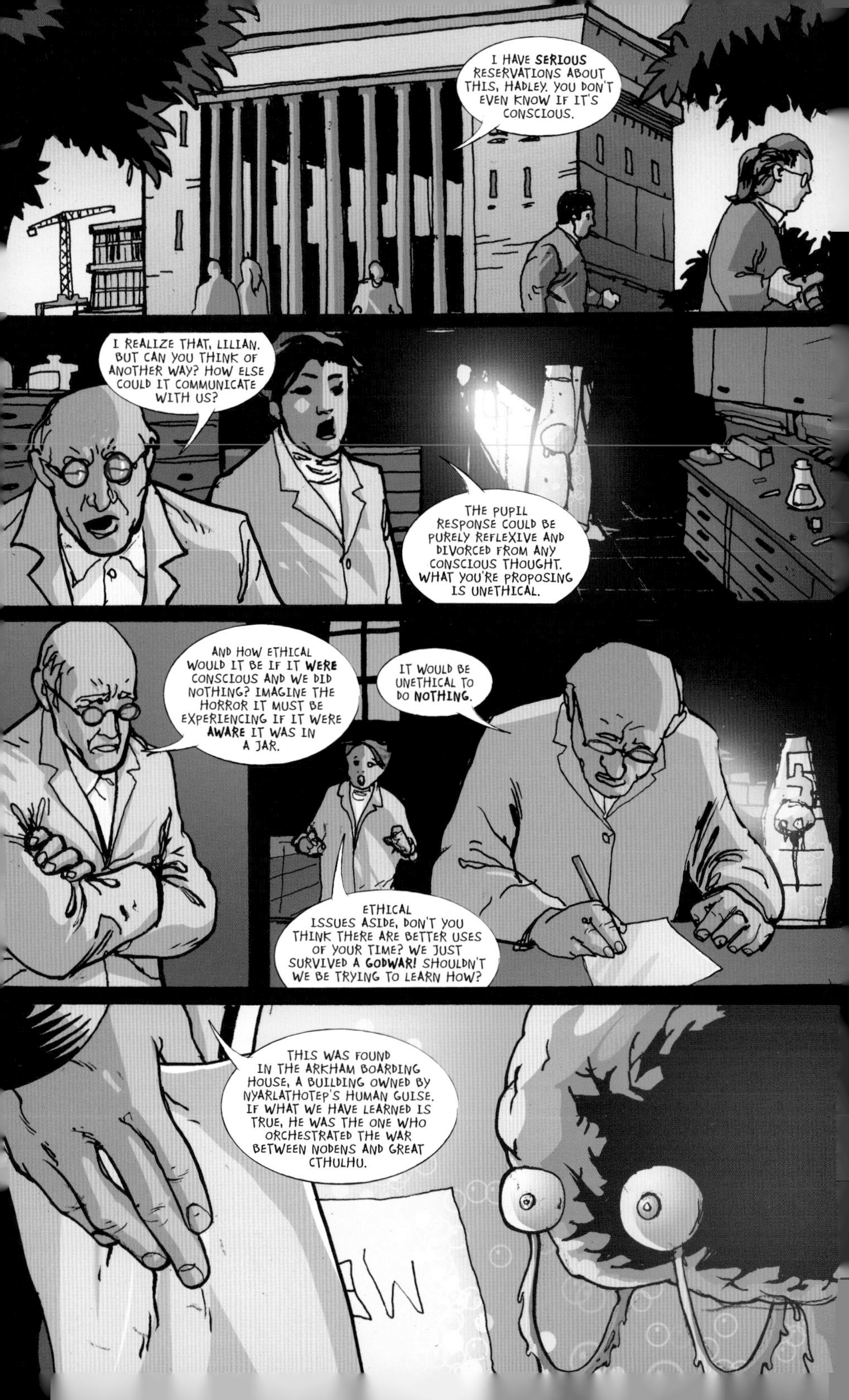
I HAVE SERIOUS RESERVATIONS ABOUT THIS, HADLEY. YOU DON'T EVEN KNOW IF IT'S CONSCIOUS.
I REALIZE THAT, LILLIAN. BUT CAN YOU THINK OF ANOTHER WAY? HOW ELSE COULD IT COMMUNICATE WITH US?
THE PUPIL RESPONSE COULD BE PURELY REFLEXIVE AND DIVORCED FROM ANY CONSCIOUS THOUGHT. WHAT YOU'RE PROPOSING IS UNETHICAL.
AND HOW ETHICAL WOULD IT BE IF IT WERE CONSCIOUS AND WE DID NOTHING? IMAGINE THE HORROR IT MUST BE EXPERIENCING IF IT WERE AWARE IT WAS IN A JAR.
IT WOULD BE UNETHICAL TO DO NOTHING.
ETHICAL ISSUES ASIDE, DON'T YOU THINK THERE ARE BETTER USES OF YOUR TIME? WE JUST SURVIVED A GODWAR! SHOULDN'T WE BE TRYING TO LEARN HOW?
THIS WAS FOUND IN THE ARKHAM BOARDING HOUSE, A BUILDING OWNED BY NYARLATHOTEP'S HUMAN GUISE. IF WHAT WE HAVE LEARNED IS TRUE, HE WAS THE ONE WHO ORCHESTRATED THE WAR BETWEEN NODENS AND GREAT CTHULHU.

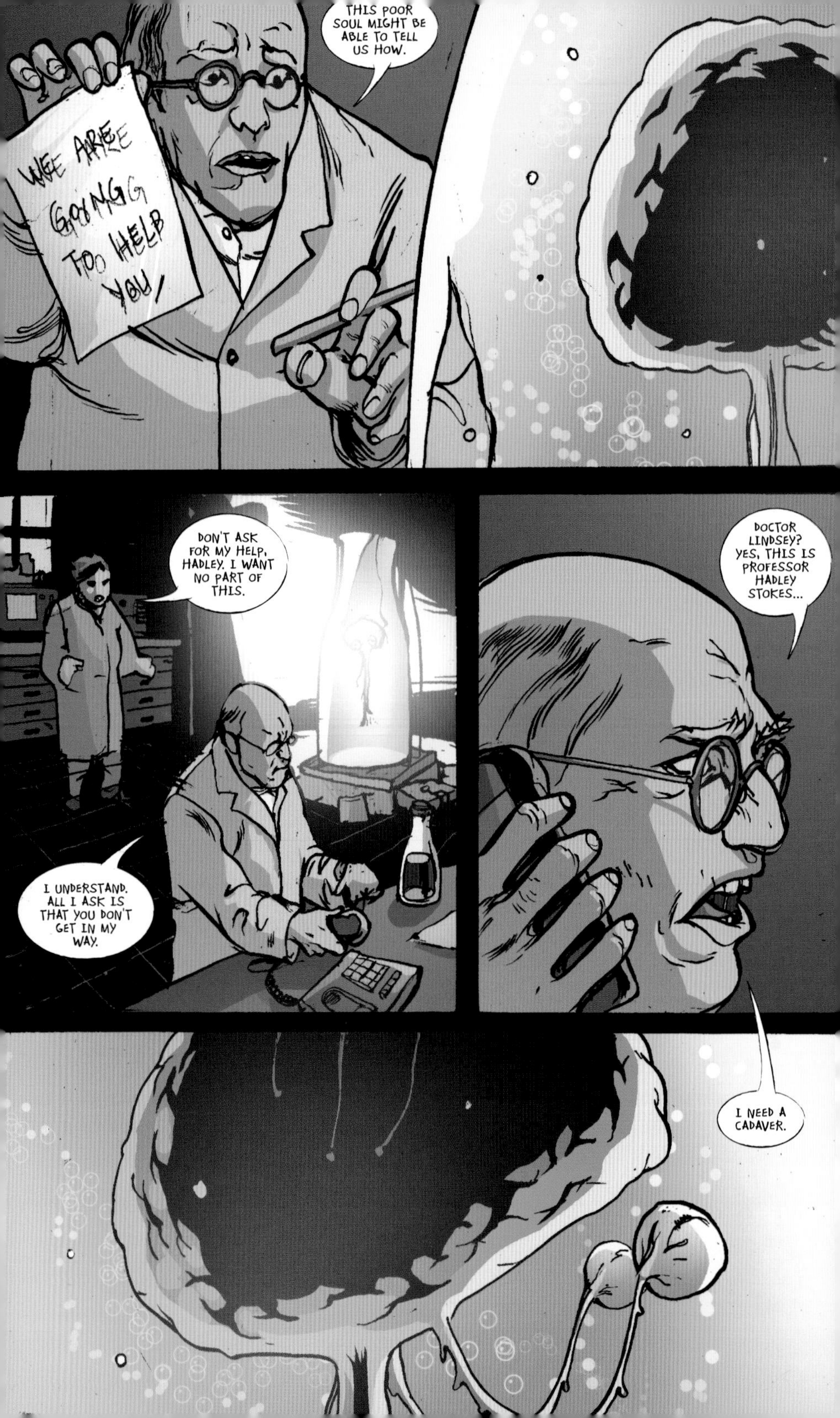
WE ARE GOING TO HELB YOU!
THIS POOR SOUL MIGHT BE ABLE TO TELL US HOW.
DON'T ASK FOR MY HELP, HADLEY. I WANT NO PART OF THIS.
I UNDERSTAND. ALL I ASK IS THAT YOU DON'T GET IN MY WAY.
DOCTOR LINDSEY? YES, THIS IS PROFESSOR HADLEY STOKES...
I NEED A CADAVER.

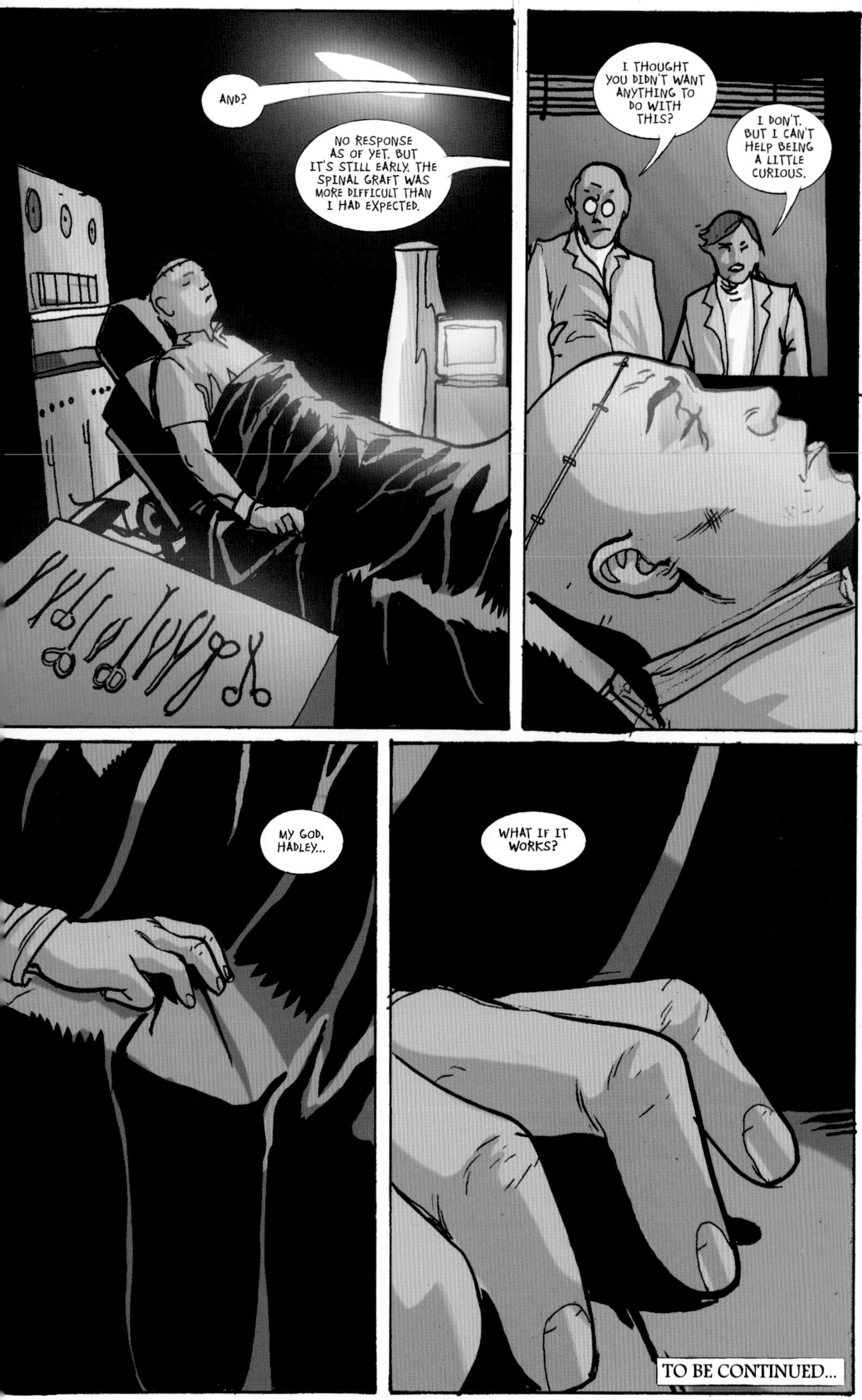
AND?
NO RESPONSE AS OF YET. BUT IT'S STILL EARLY. THE SPINAL GRAFT WAS MORE DIFFICULT THAN I HAD EXPECTED.
I THOUGHT YOU DIDN'T WANT ANYTHING TO DO WITH THIS?
I DON'T. BUT I CAN'T HELP BEING A LITTLE CURIOUS.
MY GOD, HADLEY...
WHAT IF IT WORKS?
TO BE CONTINUED...

INCORPORATION

STORY CHRISTOPHER SEQUEIRA
ART W. CHEWIE CHAN

THE INVENTION

STORY CHRISTINE BOYLAN
ART MILTON SOBREIRO

WHERE AM I? [PART 2]

STORY MICHAEL ALAN NELSON
ART ARITZ

SELECTIONS FROM H.P. LOVECRAFT'S BRIEF TENURE AS A CHOCOLATE SAMPLER COPYWRITER

WRITER LUKE BURNS
ARTIST ROGER LANGRIDGE

INCORPORATION

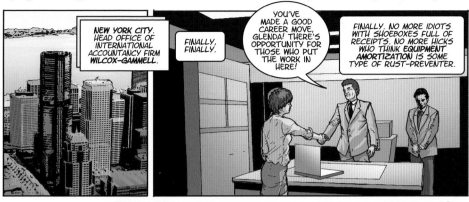

NEW YORK CITY. HEAD OFFICE OF INTERNATIONAL ACCOUNTANCY FIRM WILCOX-GAMMELL.

FINALLY, FINALLY.

YOU'VE MADE A GOOD CAREER MOVE, GLENDA! THERE'S OPPORTUNITY FOR THOSE WHO PUT THE WORK IN HERE!

FINALLY. NO MORE IDIOTS WITH SHOEBOXES FULL OF RECEIPTS. NO MORE HICKS WHO THINK EQUIPMENT AMORTIZATION IS SOME TYPE OF RUST-PREVENTER.

THANKS, MR PETERS. I FELT I WAS READY TO STEP INTO BIGGER ROLES, SO I'M KEEN TO PROVE THAT!

WONDERFUL! DEREK, HERE, WAS THE ASSISTANT TO YOUR PREDECESSOR. HE'LL POINT YOU ROUND!

OKAY. WELL, I'LL SHOW YOU WHERE THE LUNCH ROOM IS, AND YOU CAN MEET SOME OF THE SOCIAL CLU--

JUST TAKE ME TO MY OFFICE, DEREK. I'M NOT INTERESTED IN THE LOCAL BOTTOM-FEEDERS.

OH! SURE!

JOHN MORGAN HAD THIS OFFICE BEFORE HE LEFT. HE USED TO SAY IT GOT JUST THE RIGHT AMOUNT OF SUN IN THE SUMMER.

IT'S FINE. IT'S--

JOHN MUST HAVE LEFT THAT, BUT I DON'T REMEMBER SEEING IT. DO YOU WANT ME TO GET RID OF IT?

NO...I KINDA LIKE IT, I THINK! HA! A REAL MOUTH-BREATHER! REMINDS ME OF WHAT I DON'T WANT TO DEAL WITH!

Story: Christopher Sequeira   Art: W. Chewie Chan   Colors: Digikore Studios   Letters: Marshall Dillon

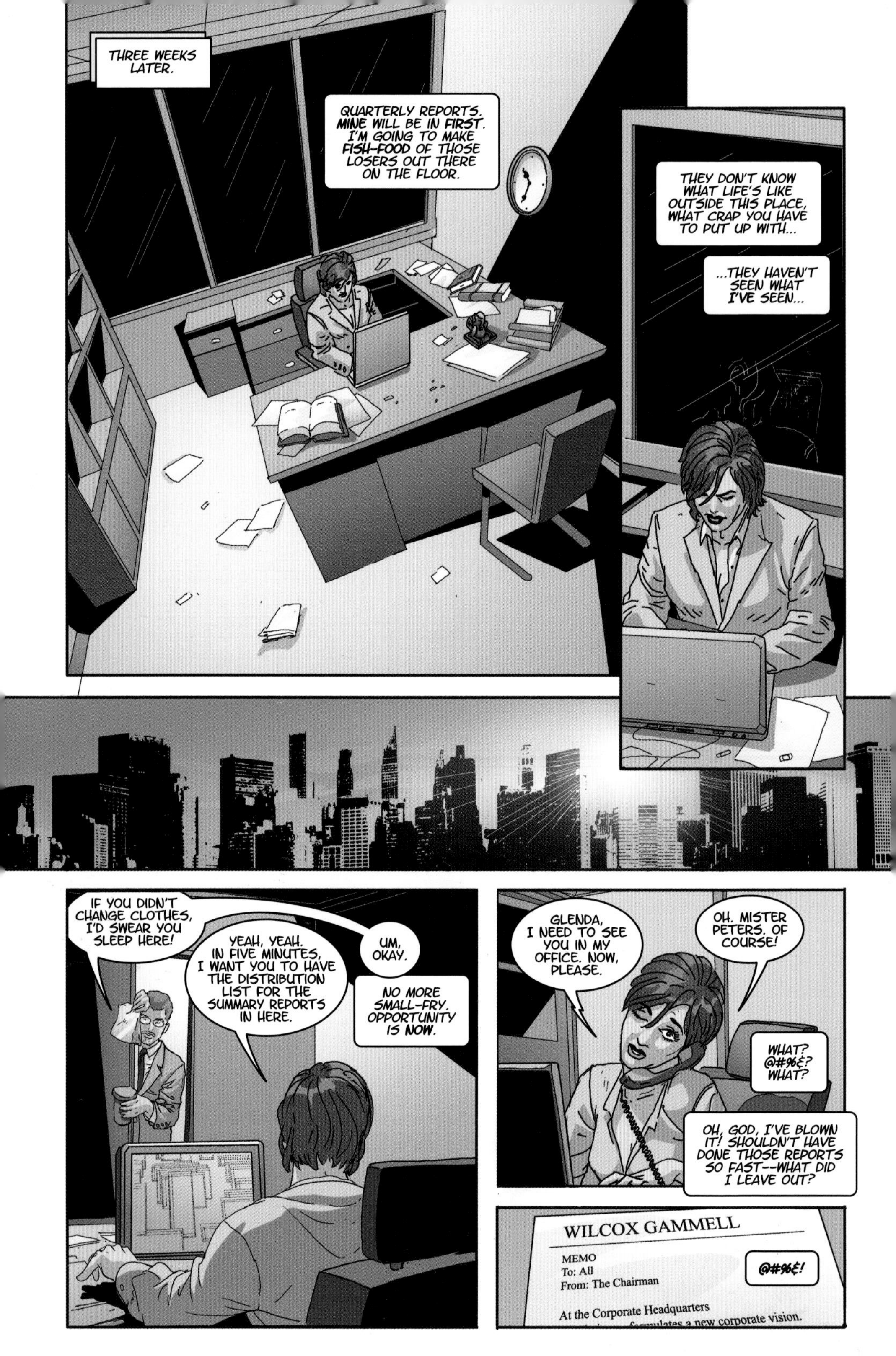
THREE WEEKS LATER.
QUARTERLY REPORTS. MINE WILL BE IN FIRST. I'M GOING TO MAKE FISH-FOOD OF THOSE LOSERS OUT THERE ON THE FLOOR.
THEY DON'T KNOW WHAT LIFE'S LIKE OUTSIDE THIS PLACE, WHAT CRAP YOU HAVE TO PUT UP WITH...
...THEY HAVEN'T SEEN WHAT I'VE SEEN...
IF YOU DIDN'T CHANGE CLOTHES, I'D SWEAR YOU SLEEP HERE!
YEAH, YEAH. IN FIVE MINUTES, I WANT YOU TO HAVE THE DISTRIBUTION LIST FOR THE SUMMARY REPORTS IN HERE.
UM, OKAY.
NO MORE SMALL-FRY. OPPORTUNITY IS NOW.
GLENDA, I NEED TO SEE YOU IN MY OFFICE. NOW, PLEASE.
OH. MISTER PETERS. OF COURSE!
WHAT? @#96₵? WHAT?
OH, GOD, I'VE BLOWN IT! SHOULDN'T HAVE DONE THOSE REPORTS SO FAST--WHAT DID I LEAVE OUT?
WILCOX GAMMELL
MEMO
To: All
From: The Chairman
At the Corporate Headquarters
formulates a new corporate vision.
@#96₵!

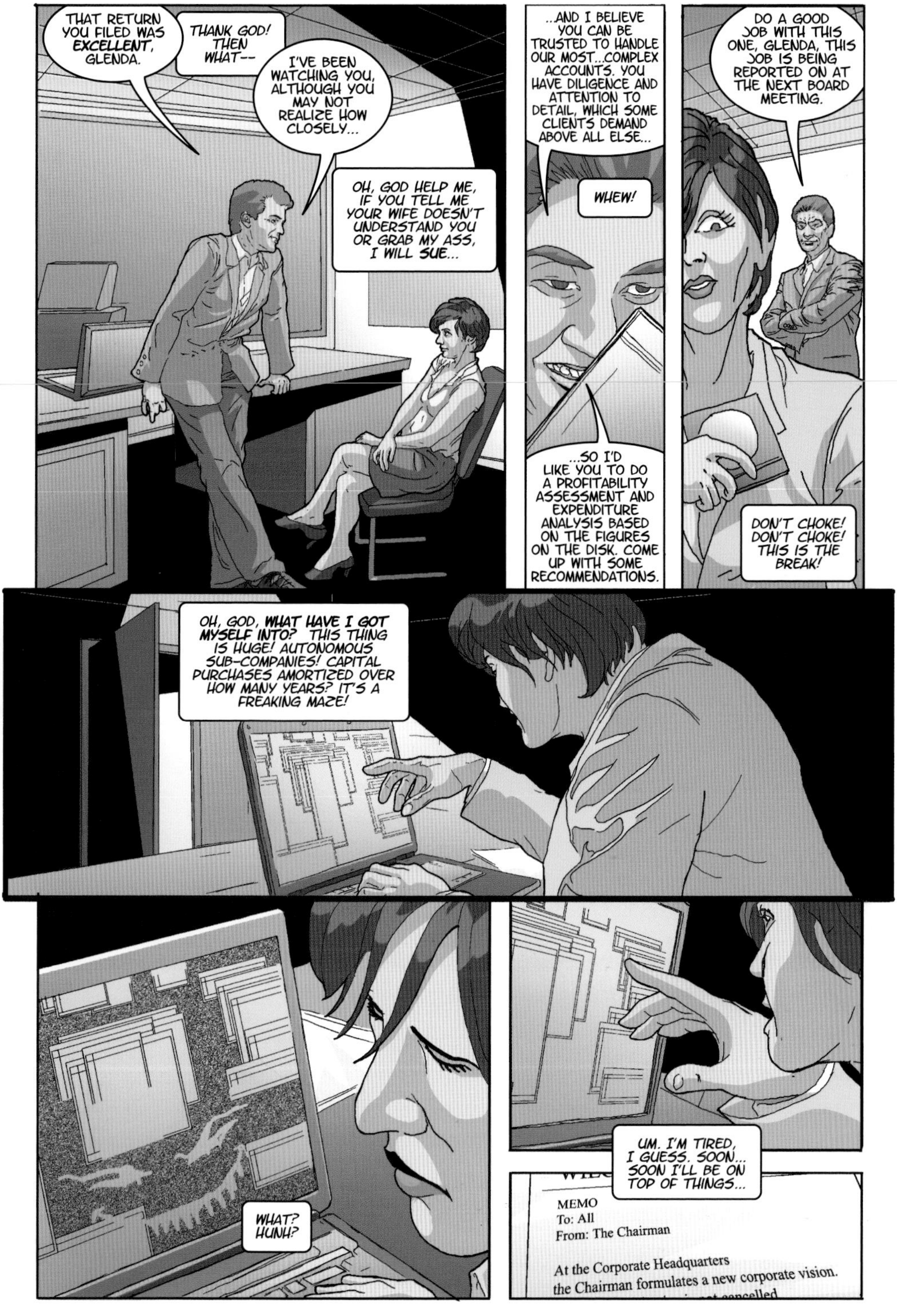
THAT RETURN YOU FILED WAS **EXCELLENT**, GLENDA.
THANK GOD! THEN WHAT--
I'VE BEEN WATCHING YOU, ALTHOUGH YOU MAY NOT REALIZE HOW CLOSELY...
OH, GOD HELP ME, IF YOU TELL ME YOUR WIFE DOESN'T UNDERSTAND YOU OR GRAB MY ASS, I WILL **SUE**...
...AND I BELIEVE YOU CAN BE TRUSTED TO HANDLE OUR MOST...COMPLEX ACCOUNTS. YOU HAVE DILIGENCE AND ATTENTION TO DETAIL, WHICH SOME CLIENTS DEMAND ABOVE ALL ELSE...
WHEW!
...SO I'D LIKE YOU TO DO A PROFITABILITY ASSESSMENT AND EXPENDITURE ANALYSIS BASED ON THE FIGURES ON THE DISK. COME UP WITH SOME RECOMMENDATIONS.
DO A GOOD JOB WITH THIS ONE, GLENDA, THIS JOB IS BEING REPORTED ON AT THE NEXT BOARD MEETING.
DON'T CHOKE! DON'T CHOKE! THIS IS THE BREAK!
OH, GOD, **WHAT HAVE I GOT MYSELF INTO?** THIS THING IS HUGE! AUTONOMOUS SUB-COMPANIES! CAPITAL PURCHASES AMORTIZED OVER HOW MANY YEARS? IT'S A FREAKING MAZE!
WHAT? HUNH?
UM. I'M TIRED, I GUESS. SOON... SOON I'LL BE ON TOP OF THINGS...
MEMO
To: All
From: The Chairman
At the Corporate Headquarters
the Chairman formulates a new corporate vision.

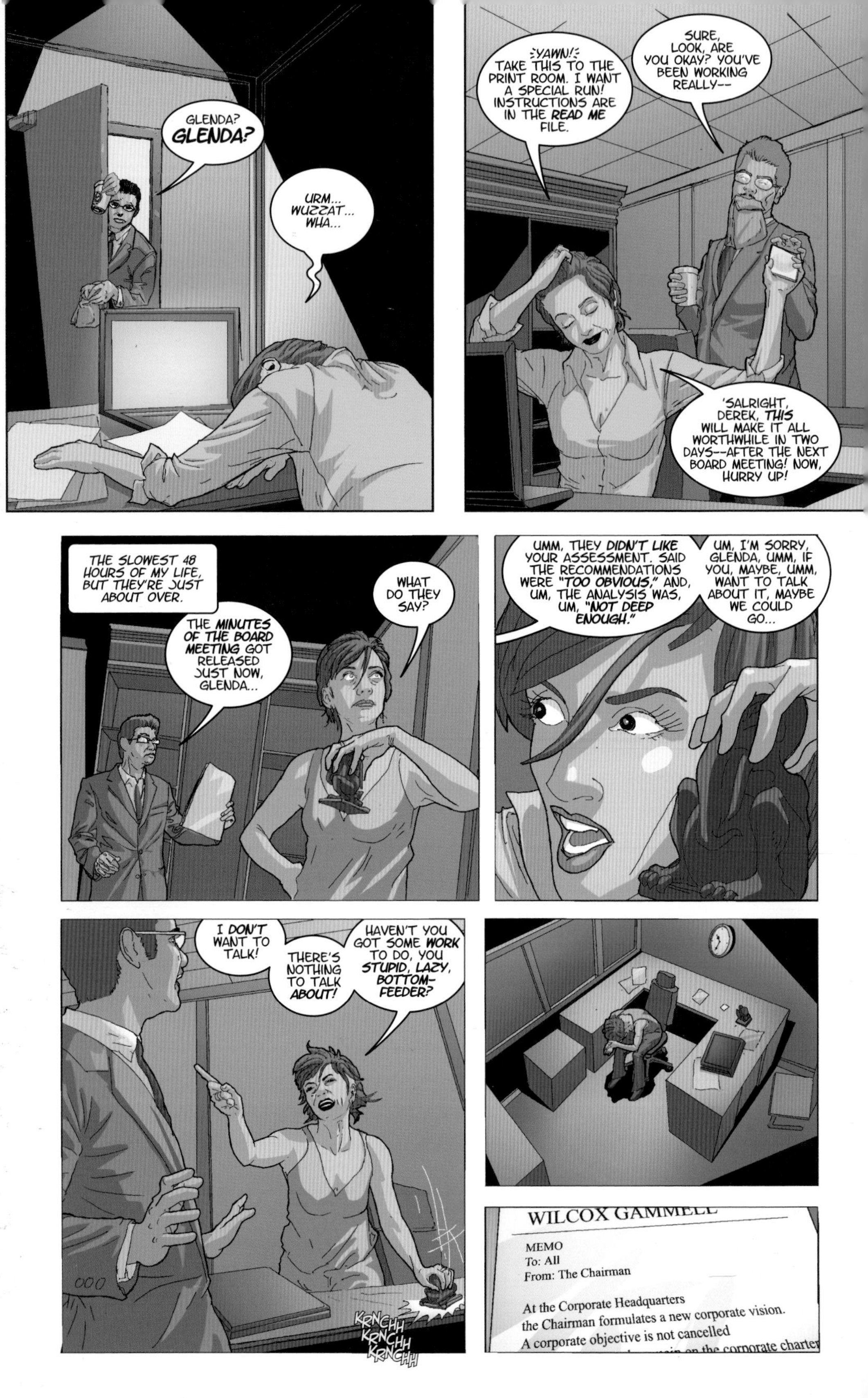
GLENDA? GLENDA?
URM... WUZZAT... WHA...
YAWN! TAKE THIS TO THE PRINT ROOM. I WANT A SPECIAL RUN! INSTRUCTIONS ARE IN THE READ ME FILE.
SURE, LOOK, ARE YOU OKAY? YOU'VE BEEN WORKING REALLY--
'SALRIGHT, DEREK, THIS WILL MAKE IT ALL WORTHWHILE IN TWO DAYS--AFTER THE NEXT BOARD MEETING! NOW, HURRY UP!
THE SLOWEST 48 HOURS OF MY LIFE, BUT THEY'RE JUST ABOUT OVER.
THE MINUTES OF THE BOARD MEETING GOT RELEASED JUST NOW, GLENDA...
WHAT DO THEY SAY?
UMM, THEY DIDN'T LIKE YOUR ASSESSMENT. SAID THE RECOMMENDATIONS WERE "TOO OBVIOUS," AND, UM, THE ANALYSIS WAS, UM, "NOT DEEP ENOUGH."
UM, I'M SORRY, GLENDA, UMM, IF YOU, MAYBE, UMM, WANT TO TALK ABOUT IT, MAYBE WE COULD GO...
I DON'T WANT TO TALK!
THERE'S NOTHING TO TALK ABOUT!
HAVEN'T YOU GOT SOME WORK TO DO, YOU STUPID, LAZY, BOTTOM-FEEDER?
KRNCHH KRNCHH KRNCHH
WILCOX GAMMELL
MEMO
To: All
From: The Chairman
At the Corporate Headquarters
the Chairman formulates a new corporate vision.
A corporate objective is not cancelled

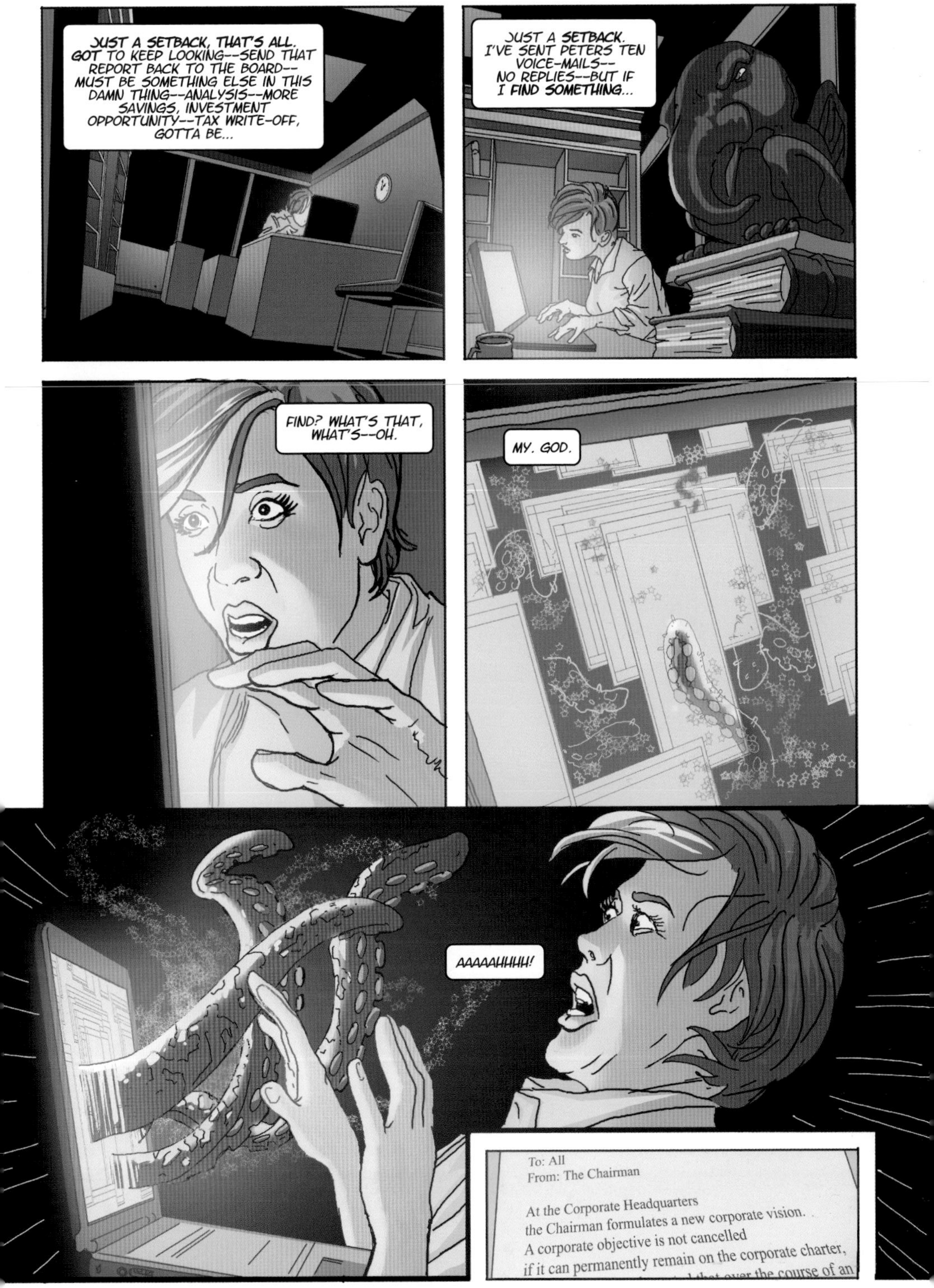
JUST A SETBACK, THAT'S ALL. GOT TO KEEP LOOKING--SEND THAT REPORT BACK TO THE BOARD--MUST BE SOMETHING ELSE IN THIS DAMN THING--ANALYSIS--MORE SAVINGS, INVESTMENT OPPORTUNITY--TAX WRITE-OFF, GOTTA BE...
JUST A SETBACK. I'VE SENT PETERS TEN VOICE-MAILS--NO REPLIES--BUT IF I FIND SOMETHING...
FIND? WHAT'S THAT, WHAT'S--OH.
MY. GOD.
AAAAAHHHH!
To: All
From: The Chairman
At the Corporate Headquarters
the Chairman formulates a new corporate vision.
A corporate objective is not cancelled
if it can permanently remain on the corporate charter,

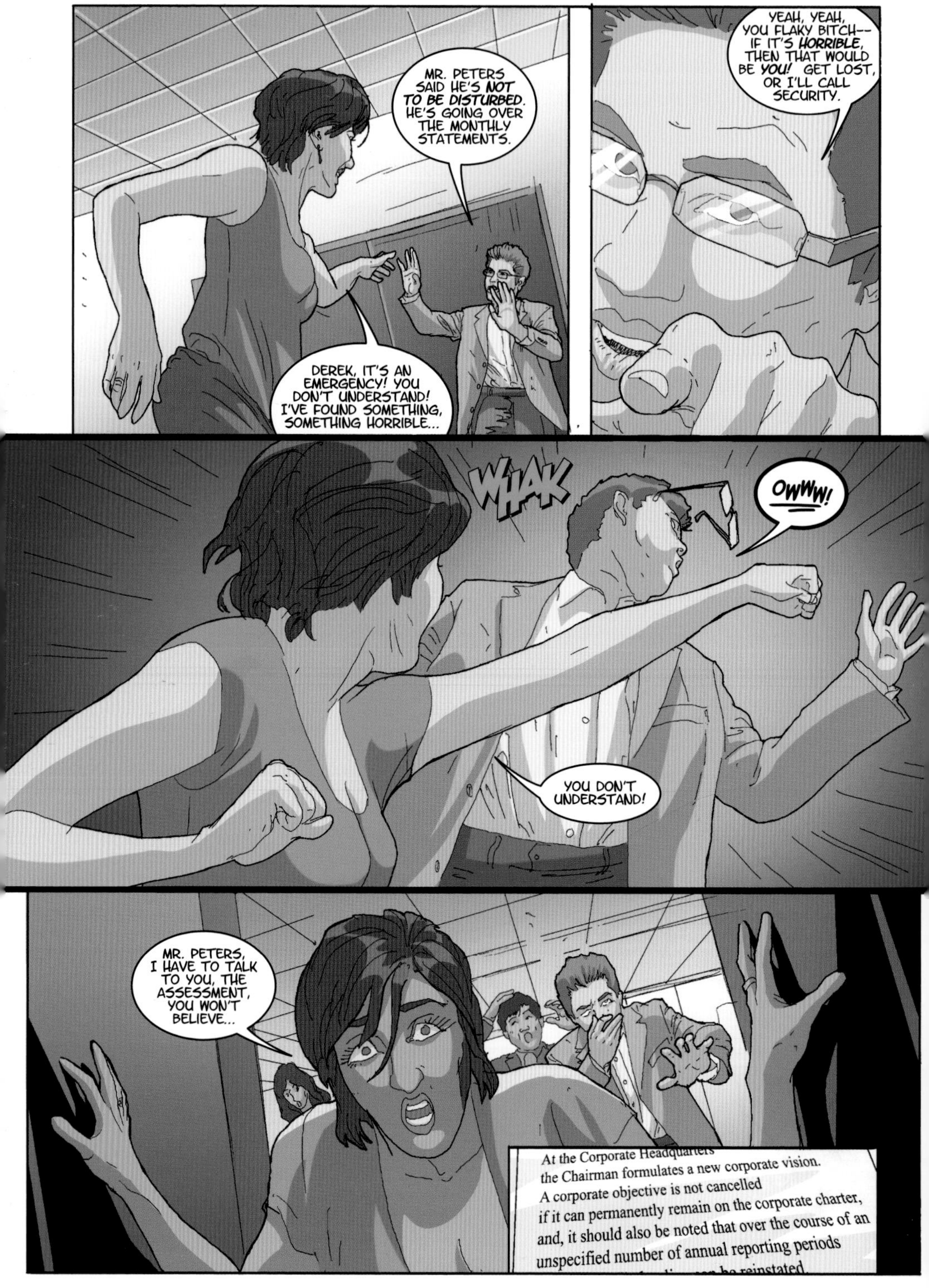
MR. PETERS SAID HE'S NOT TO BE DISTURBED. HE'S GOING OVER THE MONTHLY STATEMENTS.
DEREK, IT'S AN EMERGENCY! YOU DON'T UNDERSTAND! I'VE FOUND SOMETHING, SOMETHING HORRIBLE...
YEAH, YEAH, YOU FLAKY BITCH-- IF IT'S HORRIBLE, THEN THAT WOULD BE YOU! GET LOST, OR I'LL CALL SECURITY.
WHAK
OWWW!
YOU DON'T UNDERSTAND!
MR. PETERS, I HAVE TO TALK TO YOU, THE ASSESSMENT, YOU WON'T BELIEVE...
At the Corporate Headquarters
the Chairman formulates a new corporate vision.
A corporate objective is not cancelled
if it can permanently remain on the corporate charter,
and, it should also be noted that over the course of an
unspecified number of annual reporting periods

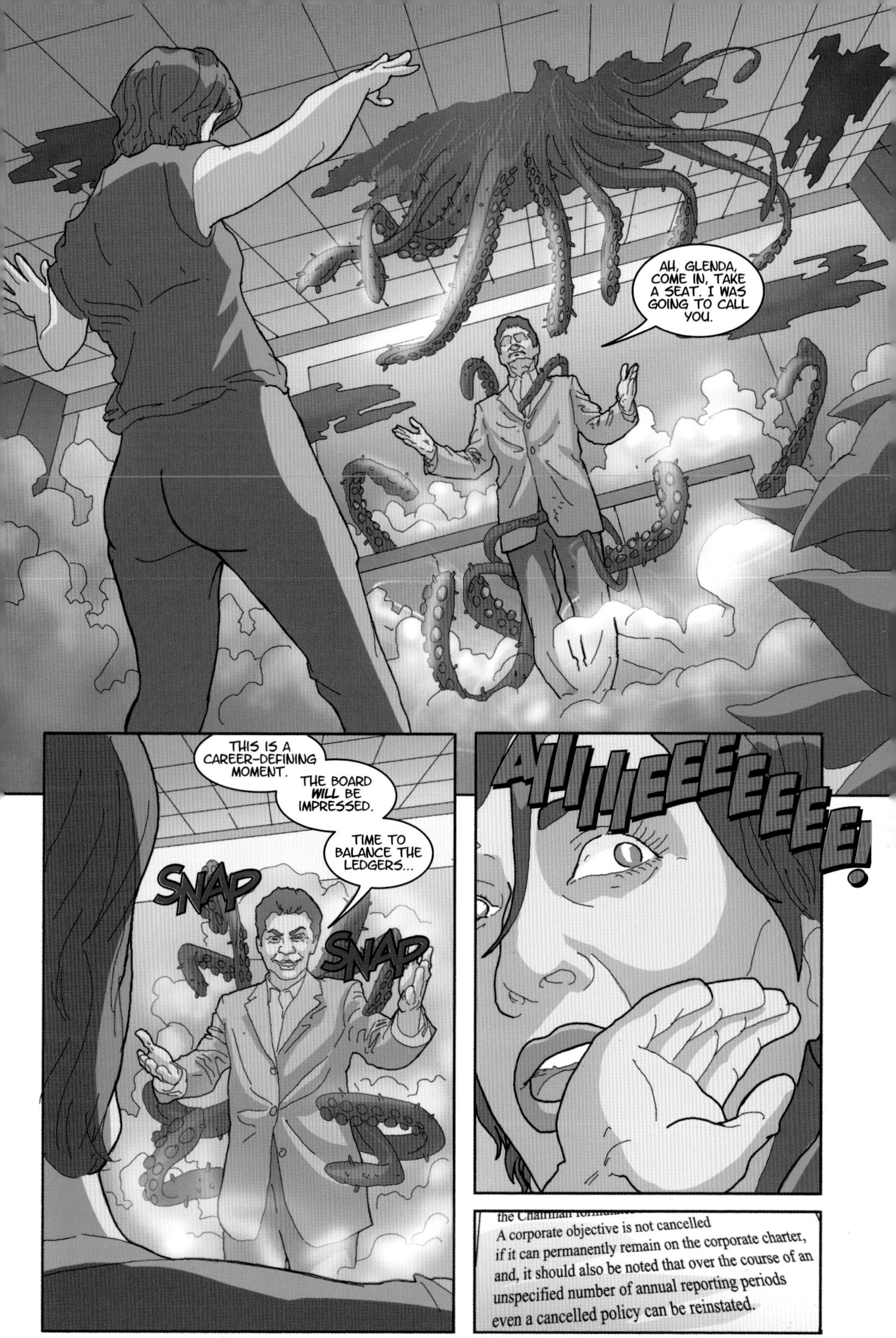
AH, GLENDA, COME IN, TAKE A SEAT. I WAS GOING TO CALL YOU.
THIS IS A CAREER-DEFINING MOMENT.
THE BOARD WILL BE IMPRESSED.
TIME TO BALANCE THE LEDGERS...
SNAP
SNAP
AIIIIEEEEEEEE!
the Chairman
A corporate objective is not cancelled
if it can permanently remain on the corporate charter,
and, it should also be noted that over the course of an
unspecified number of annual reporting periods
even a cancelled policy can be reinstated.

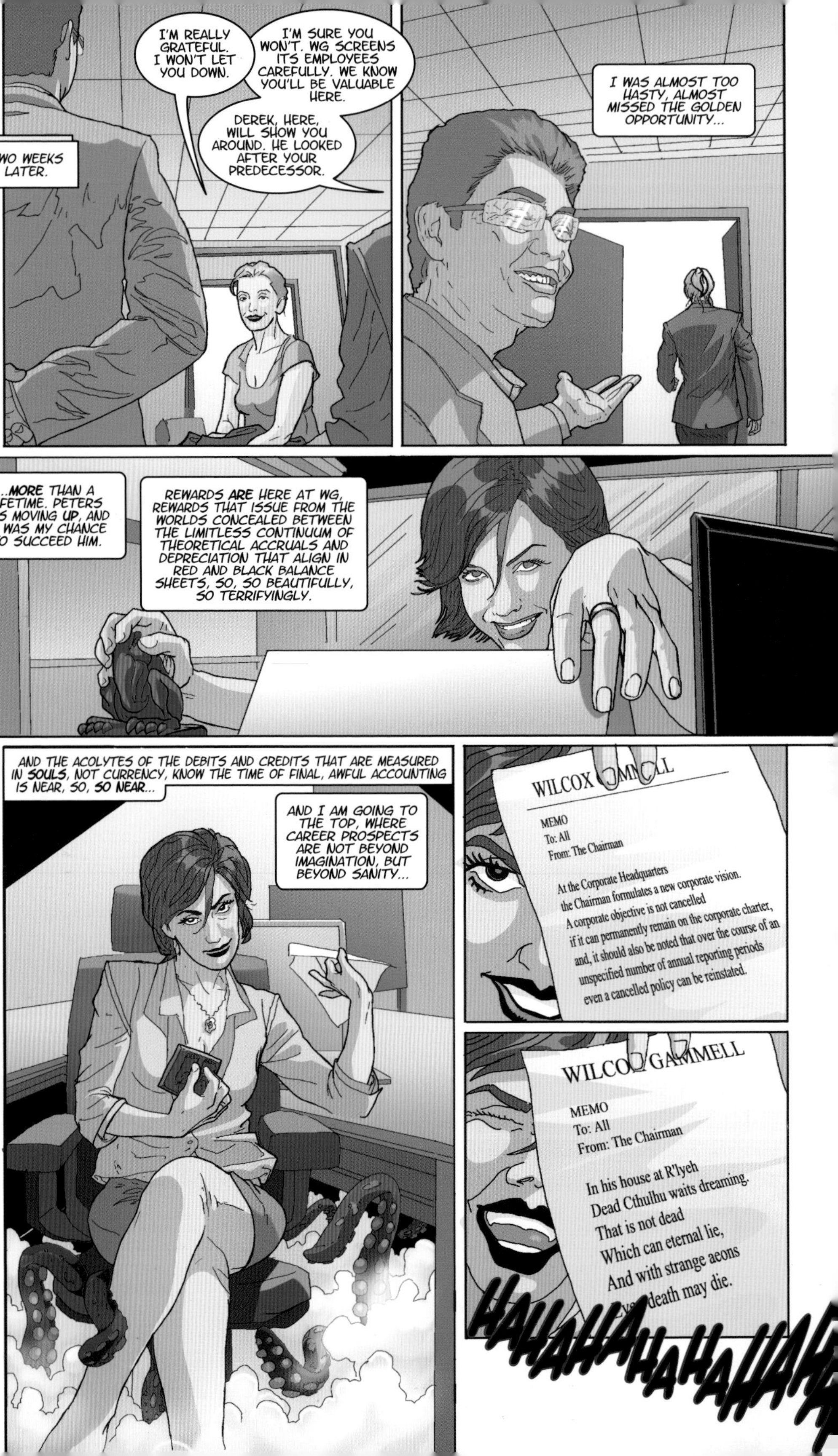

TWO WEEKS LATER.
I'M REALLY GRATEFUL. I WON'T LET YOU DOWN.
I'M SURE YOU WON'T. WG SCREENS ITS EMPLOYEES CAREFULLY. WE KNOW YOU'LL BE VALUABLE HERE.
DEREK, HERE, WILL SHOW YOU AROUND. HE LOOKED AFTER YOUR PREDECESSOR.
I WAS ALMOST TOO HASTY, ALMOST MISSED THE GOLDEN OPPORTUNITY...
...MORE THAN A LIFETIME. PETERS WAS MOVING UP, AND IT WAS MY CHANCE TO SUCCEED HIM.
REWARDS ARE HERE AT WG, REWARDS THAT ISSUE FROM THE WORLDS CONCEALED BETWEEN THE LIMITLESS CONTINUUM OF THEORETICAL ACCRUALS AND DEPRECIATION THAT ALIGN IN RED AND BLACK BALANCE SHEETS, SO, SO BEAUTIFULLY, SO TERRIFYINGLY.
AND THE ACOLYTES OF THE DEBITS AND CREDITS THAT ARE MEASURED IN SOULS, NOT CURRENCY, KNOW THE TIME OF FINAL, AWFUL ACCOUNTING IS NEAR, SO, SO NEAR...
AND I AM GOING TO THE TOP, WHERE CAREER PROSPECTS ARE NOT BEYOND IMAGINATION, BUT BEYOND SANITY...
WILCOX
MEMO
To: All
From: The Chairman
At the Corporate Headquarters
the Chairman formulates a new corporate vision.
A corporate objective is not cancelled
if it can permanently remain on the corporate charter,
and, it should also be noted that over the course of an
unspecified number of annual reporting periods
even a cancelled policy can be reinstated.
GAMMELL
MEMO
To: All
From: The Chairman
In his house at R'lyeh
Dead Cthulhu waits dreaming.
That is not dead
Which can eternal lie,
And with strange aeons
death may die.
HAHAHAHAHAHAHAHA

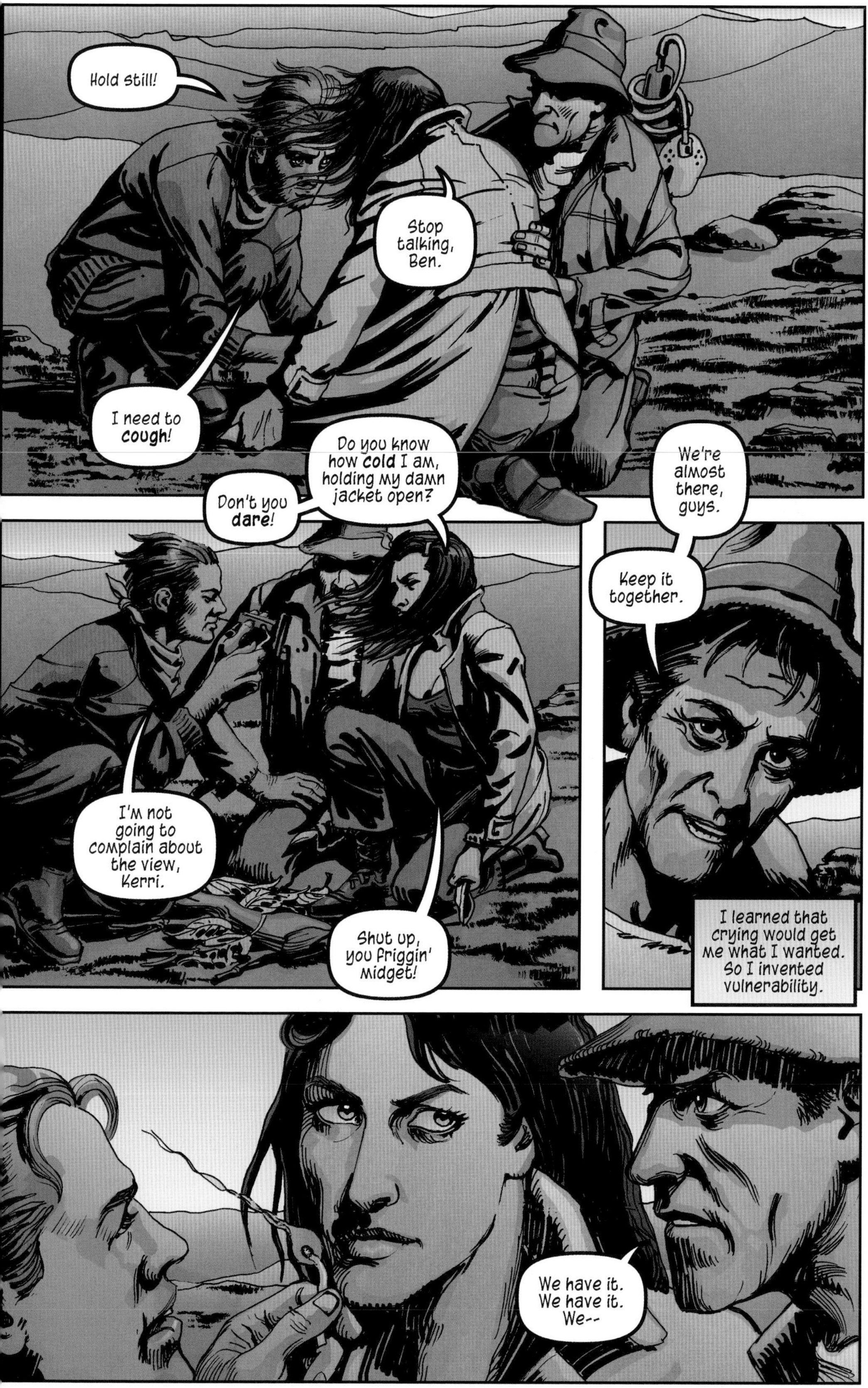
Hold still!
Stop talking, Ben.
I need to cough!
Do you know how cold I am, holding my damn jacket open?
Don't you dare!
We're almost there, guys.
Keep it together.
I'm not going to complain about the view, Kerri.
Shut up, you friggin' midget!
I learned that crying would get me what I wanted. So I invented vulnerability.
We have it. We have it. We--

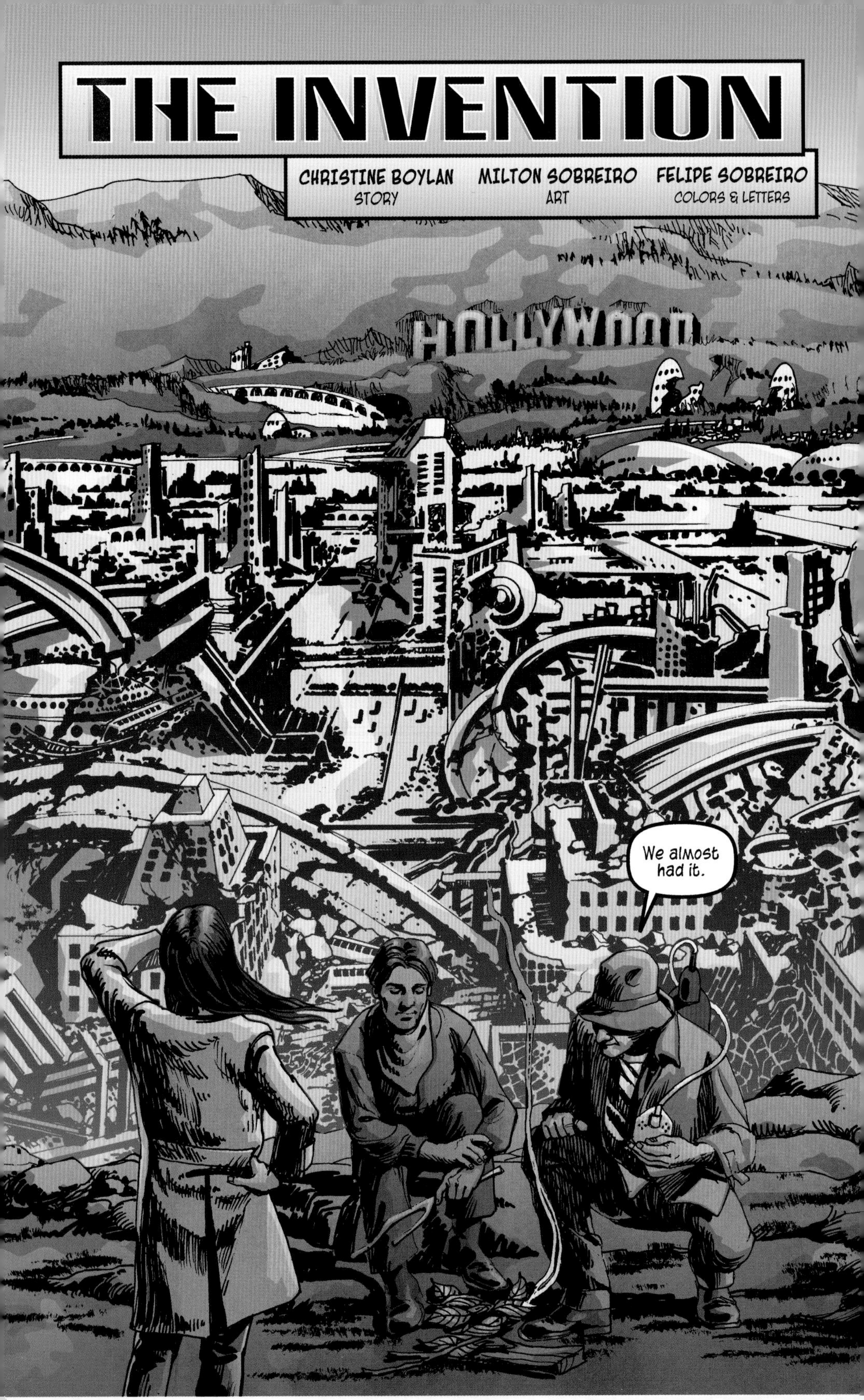
THE INVENTION
CHRISTINE BOYLAN
STORY
MILTON SOBREIRO
ART
FELIPE SOBREIRO
COLORS & LETTERS
HOLLYWOOD
We almost had it.

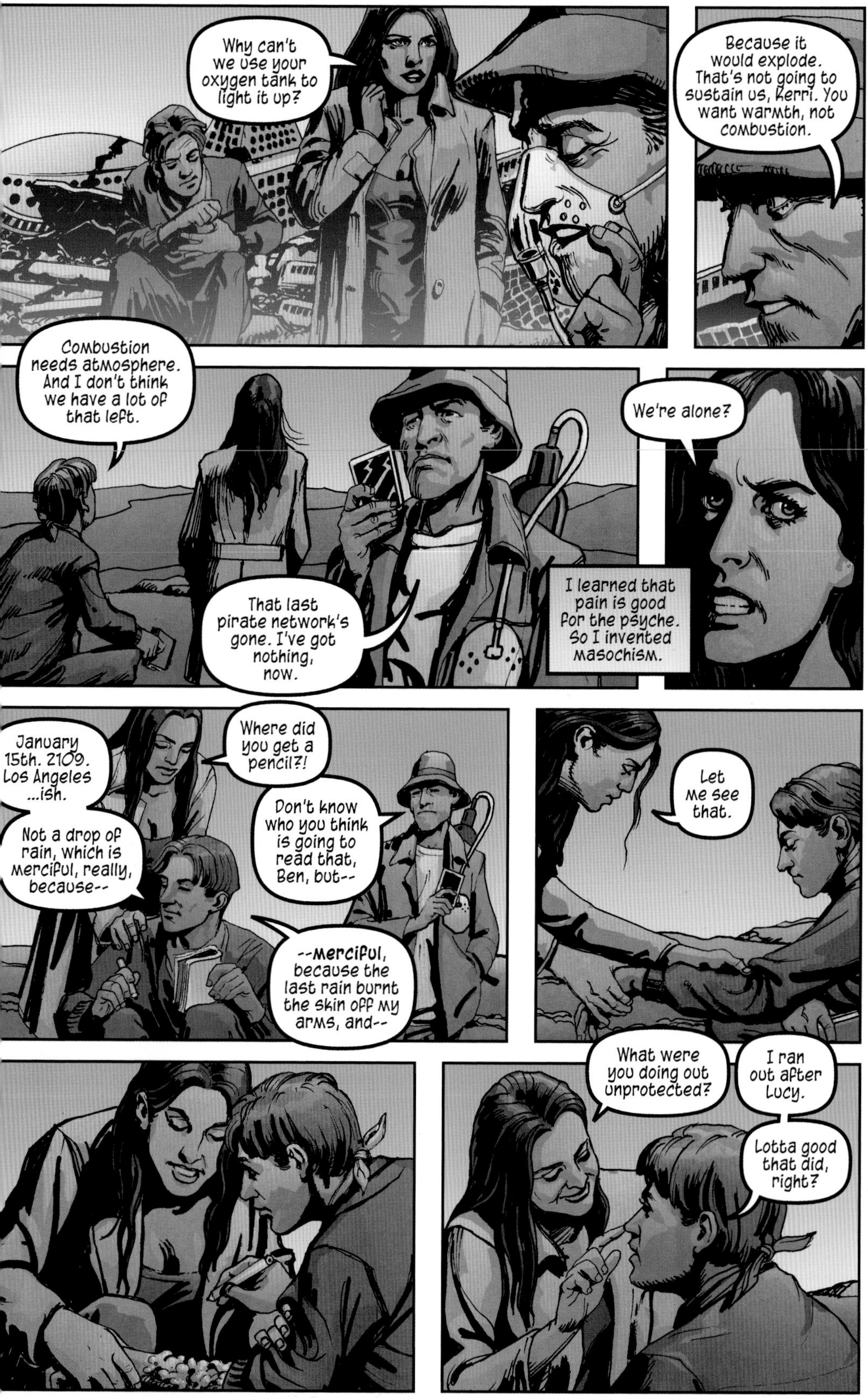
Why can't we use your oxygen tank to light it up?
Because it would explode. That's not going to sustain us, Kerri. You want warmth, not combustion.
Combustion needs atmosphere. And I don't think we have a lot of that left.
That last pirate network's gone. I've got nothing, now.
We're alone?
I learned that pain is good for the psyche. So I invented masochism.
January 15th. 2109. Los Angeles ...ish.
Not a drop of rain, which is merciful, really, because--
Where did you get a pencil?!
Don't know who you think is going to read that, Ben, but--
--Merciful, because the last rain burnt the skin off my arms, and--
Let me see that.
What were you doing out unprotected?
I ran out after Lucy.
Lotta good that did, right?

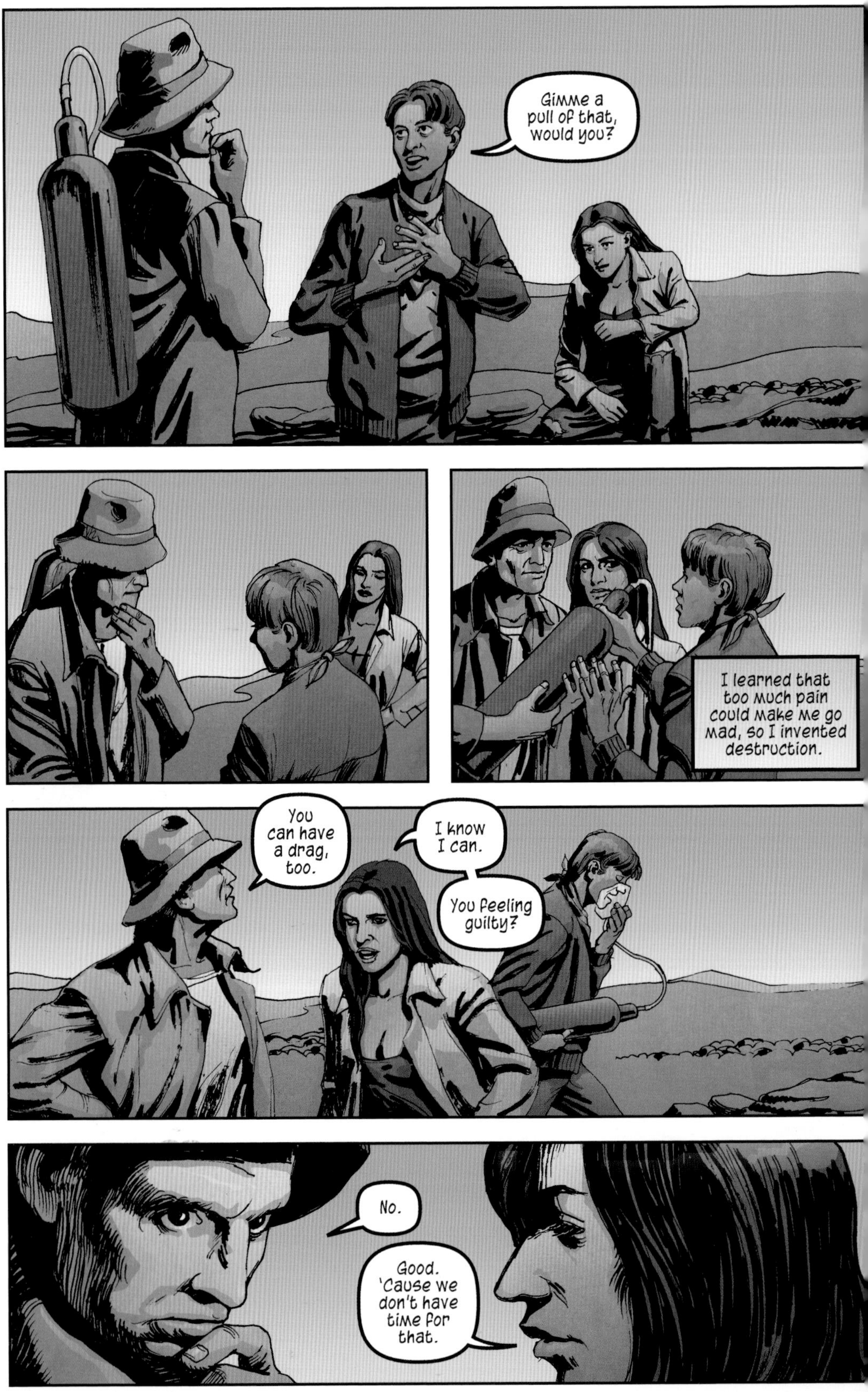
Gimme a pull of that, would you?
I learned that too much pain could make me go mad, so I invented destruction.
You can have a drag, too.
I know I can.
You feeling guilty?
No.
Good. 'Cause we don't have time for that.

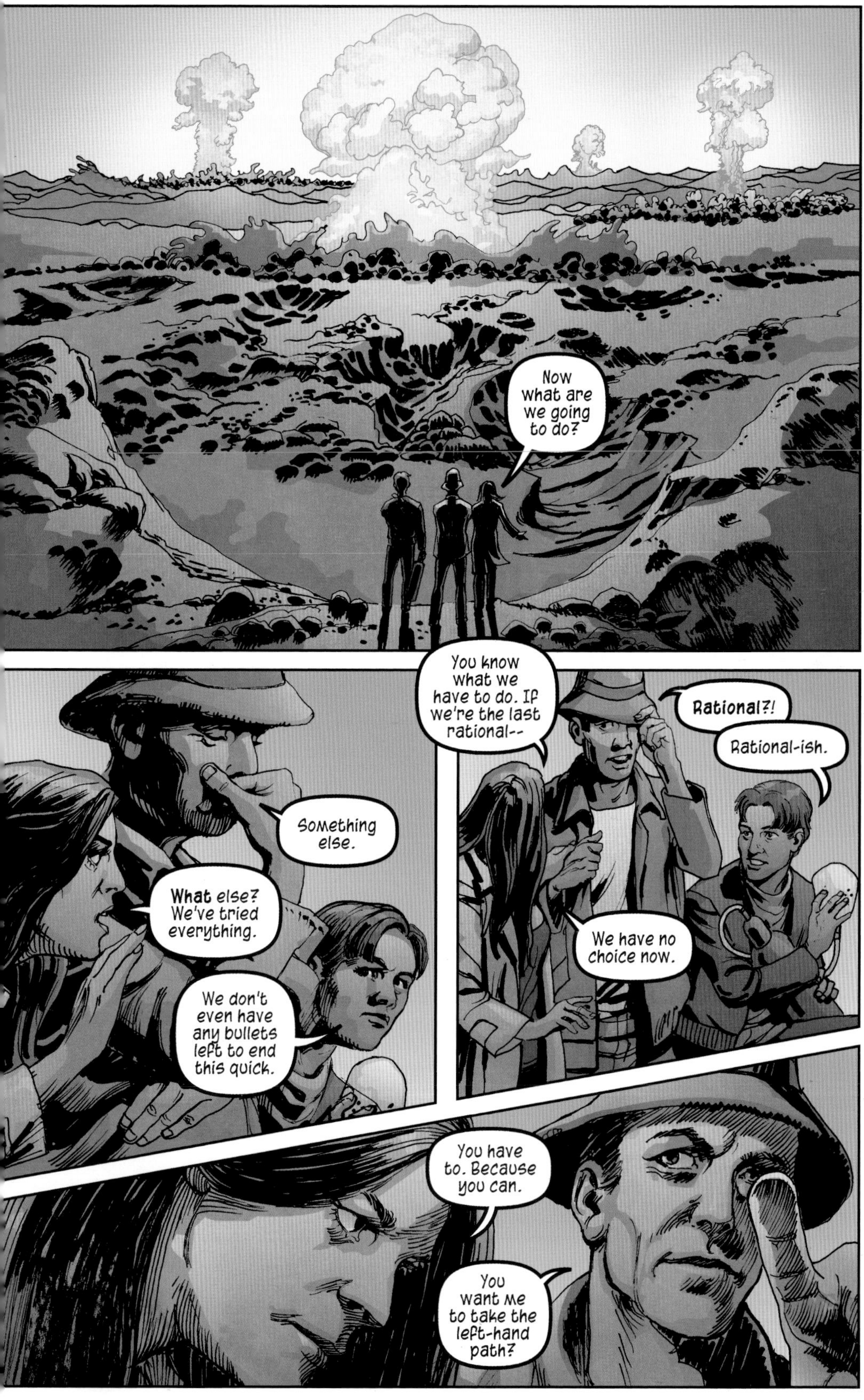
Now what are we going to do?
Something else.
What else? We've tried everything.
We don't even have any bullets left to end this quick.
You know what we have to do. If we're the last rational--
Rational?!
Rational-ish.
We have no choice now.
You have to. Because you can.
You want me to take the left-hand path?

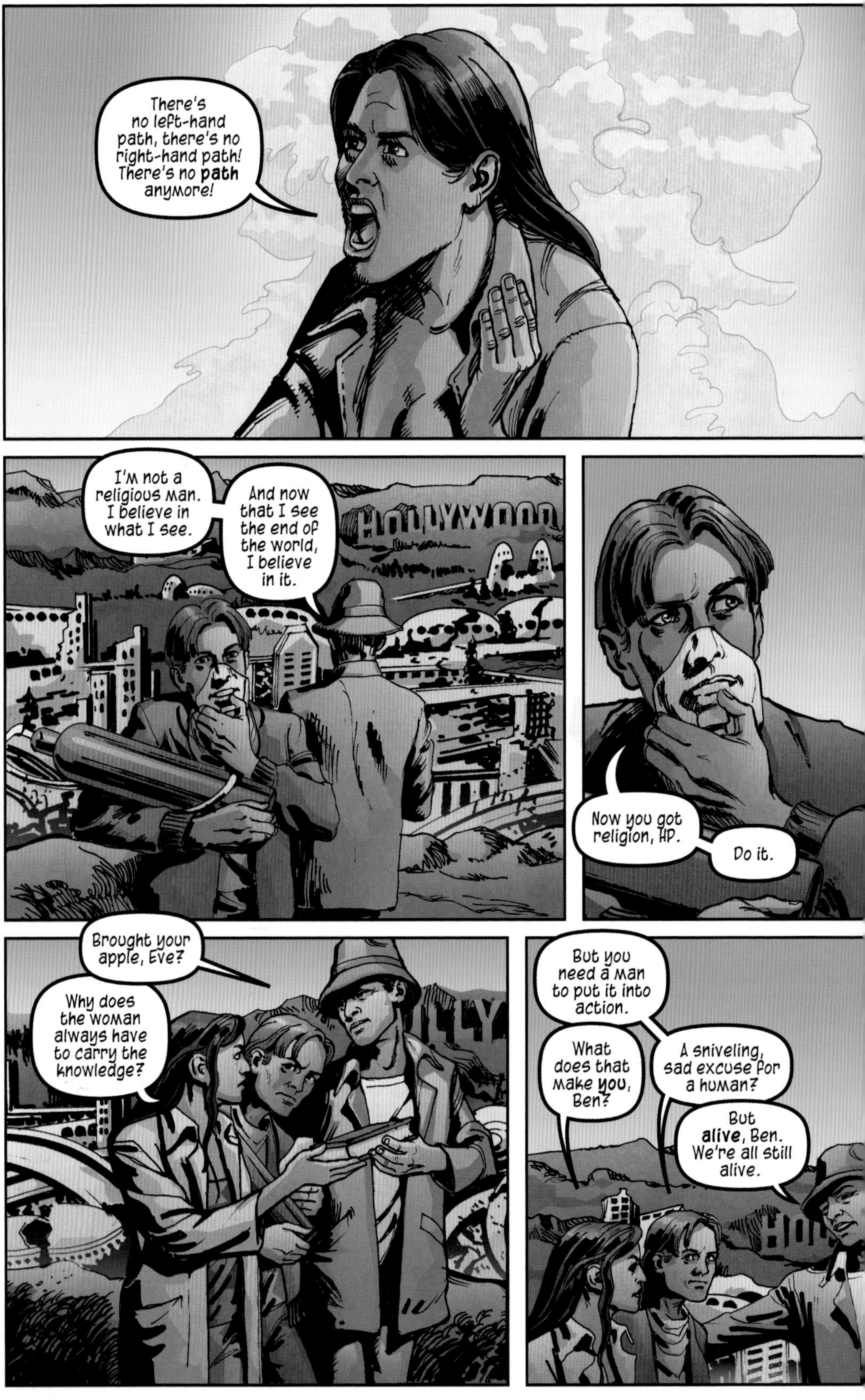

There's no left-hand path, there's no right-hand path! There's no **path** anymore!
I'm not a religious man. I believe in what I see.
And now that I see the end of the world, I believe in it.
HOLLYWOOD
Now you got religion, HP.
Do it.
Brought your apple, Eve?
Why does the woman always have to carry the knowledge?
But you need a man to put it into action.
What does that make **you**, Ben?
A sniveling, sad excuse for a human?
But **alive**, Ben. We're all still alive.

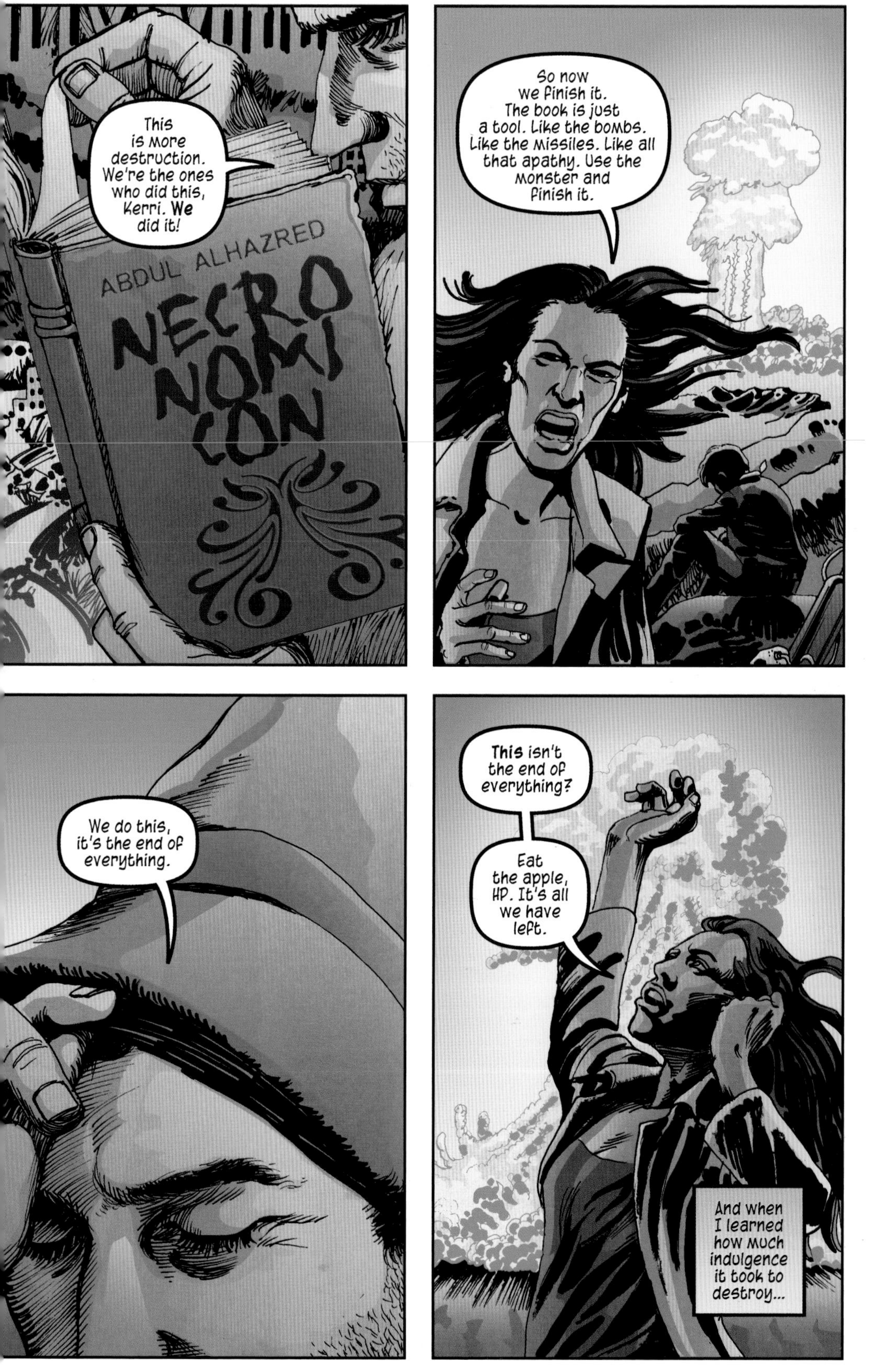
This is more destruction. We're the ones who did this, Kerri. We did it!
ABDUL ALHAZRED
NECRONOMICON
So now we finish it. The book is just a tool. Like the bombs. Like the missiles. Like all that apathy. Use the monster and finish it.
We do this, it's the end of everything.
This isn't the end of everything?
Eat the apple, HP. It's all we have left.
And when I learned how much indulgence it took to destroy...

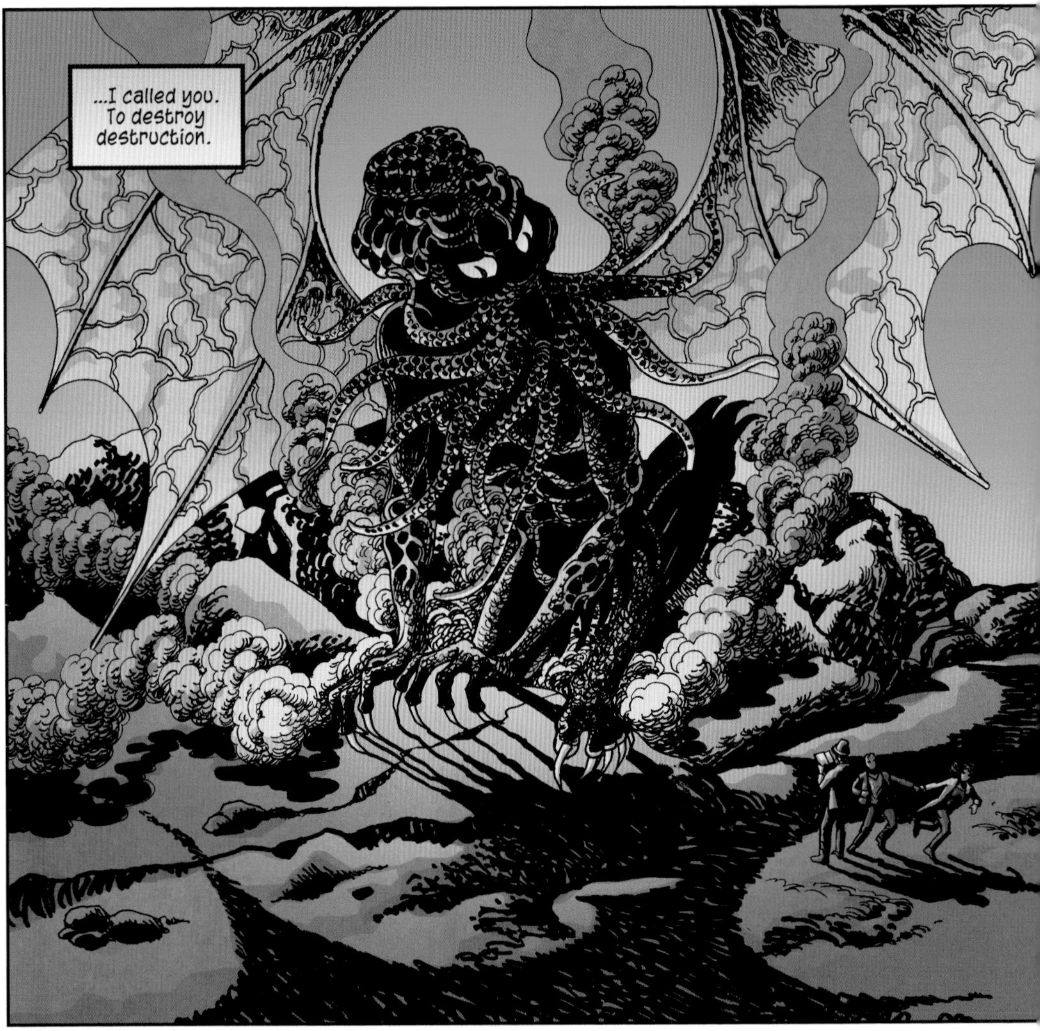
...I called you. To destroy destruction.

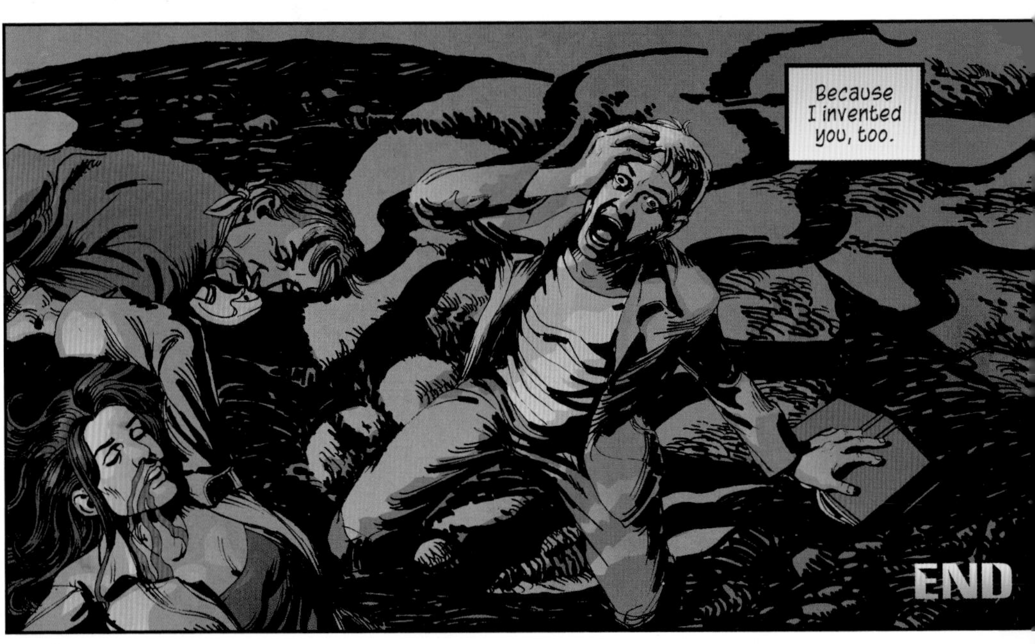
Because I invented you, too.
END

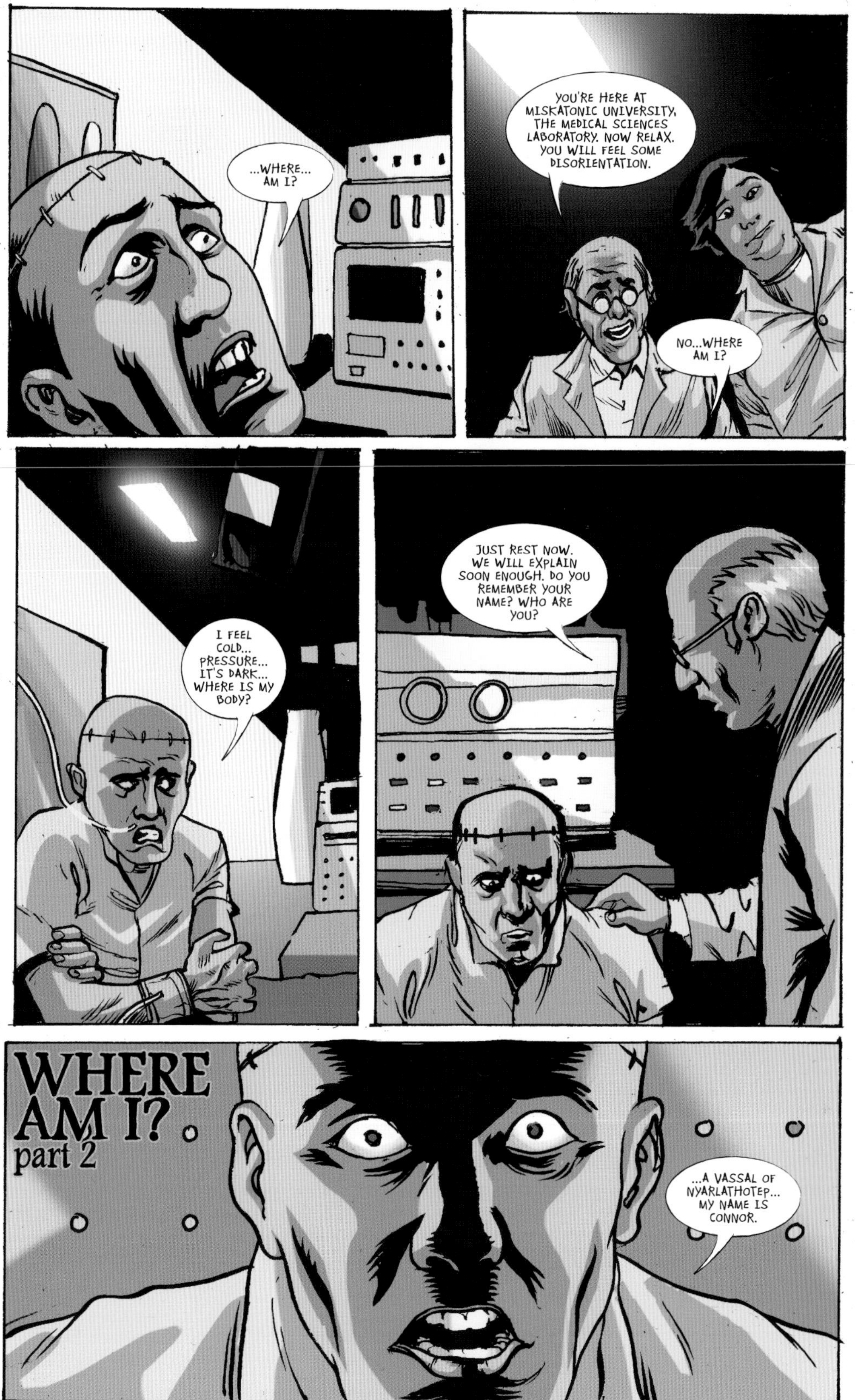

...WHERE... AM I?
YOU'RE HERE AT MISKATONIC UNIVERSITY, THE MEDICAL SCIENCES LABORATORY. NOW RELAX. YOU WILL FEEL SOME DISORIENTATION.
NO...WHERE AM I?
I FEEL COLD... PRESSURE... IT'S DARK... WHERE IS MY BODY?
JUST REST NOW. WE WILL EXPLAIN SOON ENOUGH. DO YOU REMEMBER YOUR NAME? WHO ARE YOU?
WHERE AM I? part 2
...A VASSAL OF NYARLATHOTEP... MY NAME IS CONNOR.

Michael Alan Nelson, story   Aritz Eiguren, art   Digikore Studios, colors   Marshall Dillon, letters

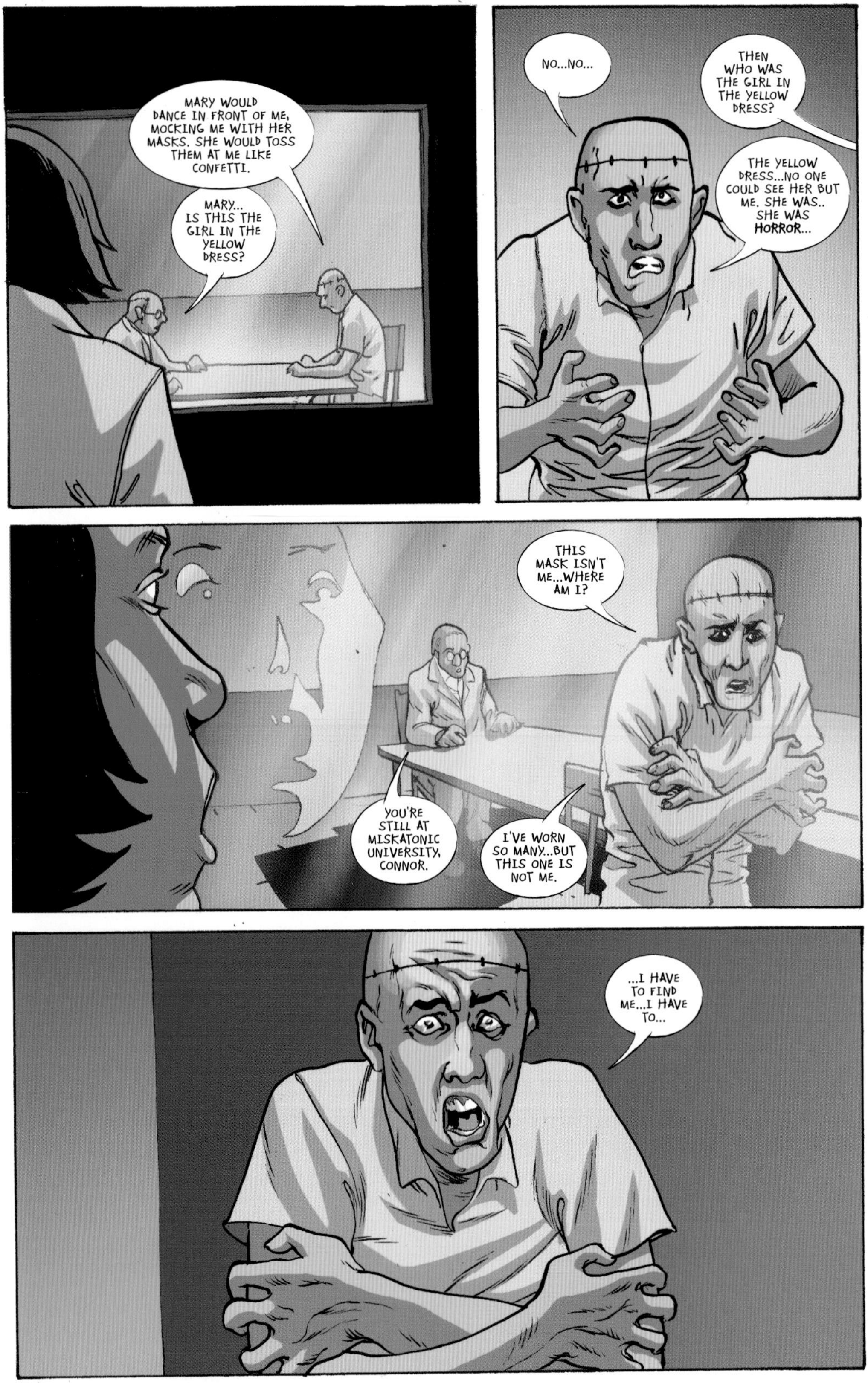
MARY WOULD DANCE IN FRONT OF ME, MOCKING ME WITH HER MASKS. SHE WOULD TOSS THEM AT ME LIKE CONFETTI.
MARY... IS THIS THE GIRL IN THE YELLOW DRESS?
NO...NO...
THEN WHO WAS THE GIRL IN THE YELLOW DRESS?
THE YELLOW DRESS...NO ONE COULD SEE HER BUT ME. SHE WAS.. SHE WAS **HORROR**...
THIS MASK ISN'T ME...WHERE AM I?
YOU'RE STILL AT MISKATONIC UNIVERSITY, CONNOR.
I'VE WORN SO MANY...BUT THIS ONE IS NOT ME.
...I HAVE TO FIND ME...I HAVE TO...

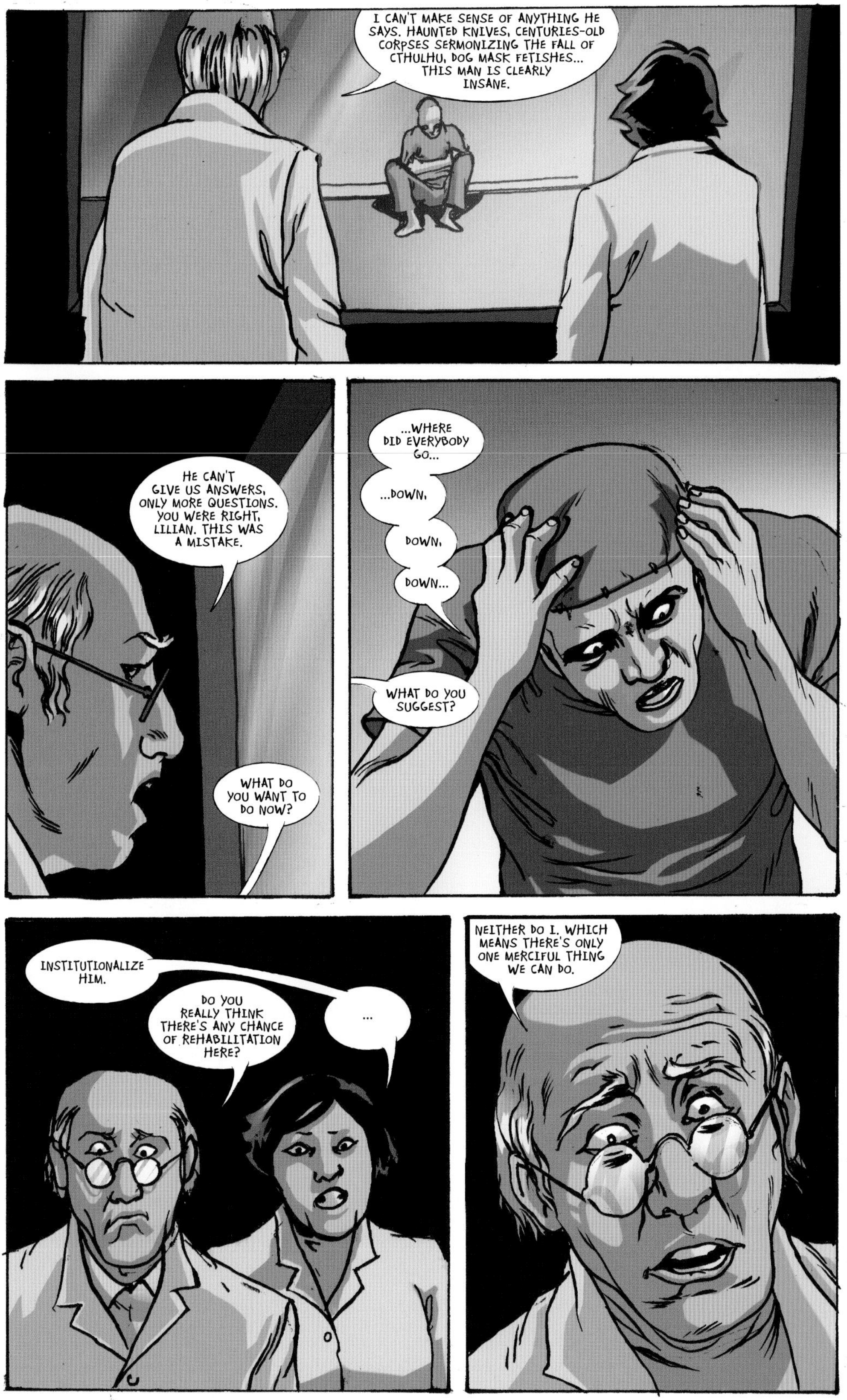
I CAN'T MAKE SENSE OF ANYTHING HE SAYS. HAUNTED KNIVES, CENTURIES-OLD CORPSES SERMONIZING THE FALL OF CTHULHU, DOG MASK FETISHES... THIS MAN IS CLEARLY INSANE.
HE CAN'T GIVE US ANSWERS, ONLY MORE QUESTIONS. YOU WERE RIGHT, LILIAN. THIS WAS A MISTAKE.
WHAT DO YOU WANT TO DO NOW?
...WHERE DID EVERYBODY GO...
...DOWN,
DOWN,
DOWN...
WHAT DO YOU SUGGEST?
INSTITUTIONALIZE HIM.
DO YOU REALLY THINK THERE'S ANY CHANCE OF REHABILITATION HERE?
...
NEITHER DO I. WHICH MEANS THERE'S ONLY ONE MERCIFUL THING WE CAN DO.

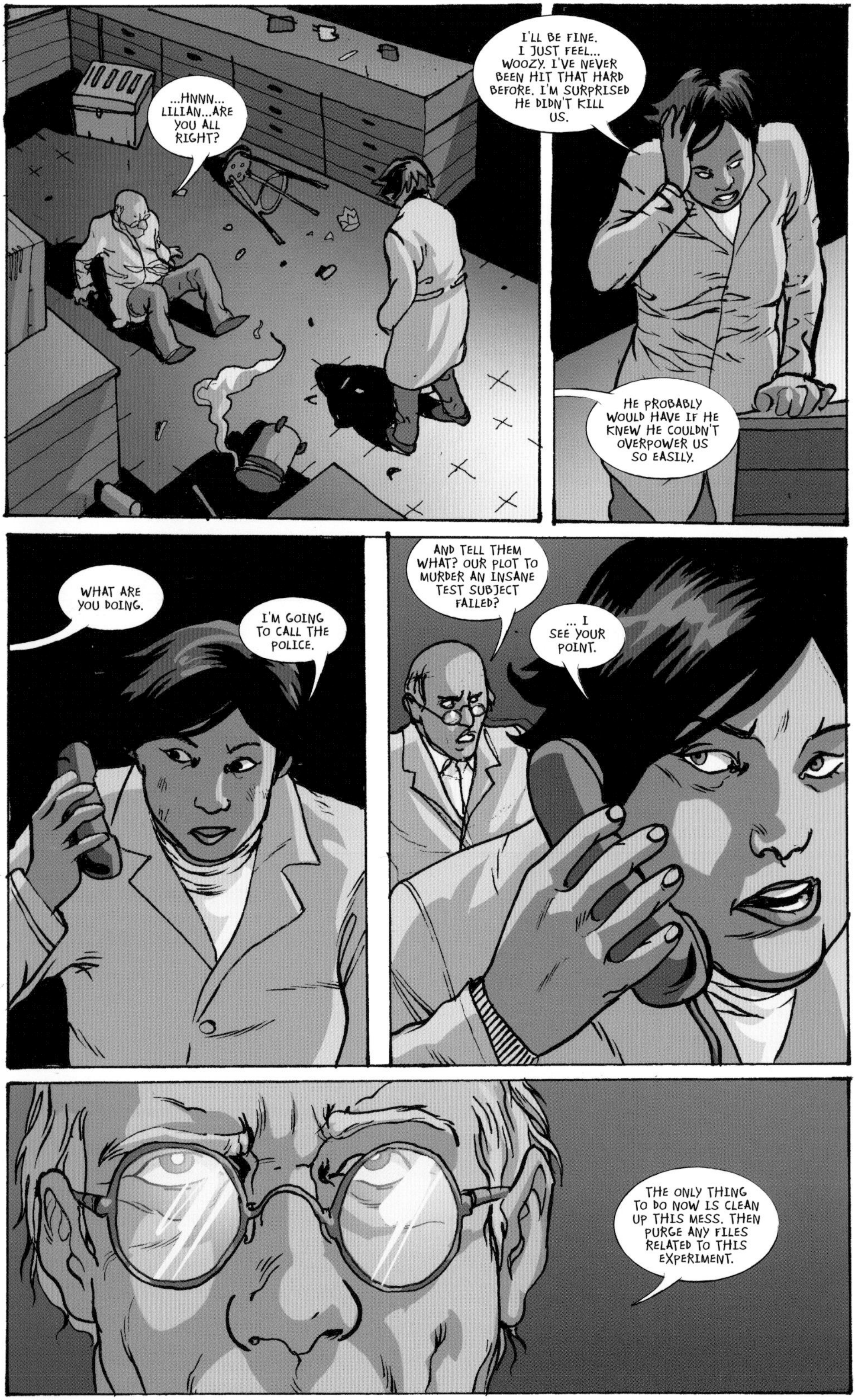
...HNNN... LILIAN...ARE YOU ALL RIGHT?
I'LL BE FINE. I JUST FEEL... WOOZY. I'VE NEVER BEEN HIT THAT HARD BEFORE. I'M SURPRISED HE DIDN'T KILL US.
HE PROBABLY WOULD HAVE IF HE KNEW HE COULDN'T OVERPOWER US SO EASILY.
WHAT ARE YOU DOING.
I'M GOING TO CALL THE POLICE.
AND TELL THEM WHAT? OUR PLOT TO MURDER AN INSANE TEST SUBJECT FAILED?
... I SEE YOUR POINT.
THE ONLY THING TO DO NOW IS CLEAN UP THIS MESS. THEN PURGE ANY FILES RELATED TO THIS EXPERIMENT.

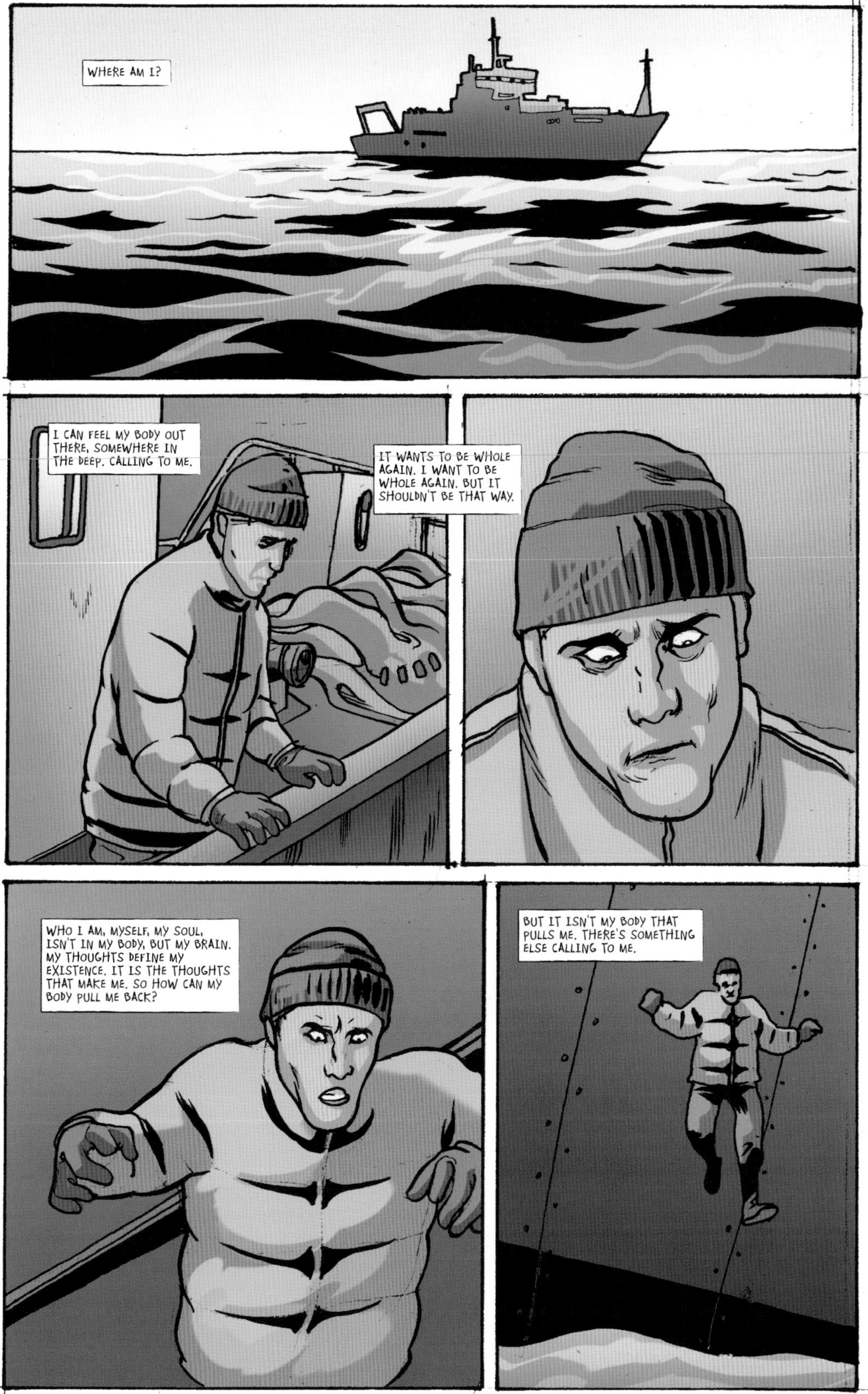
WHERE AM I?
I CAN FEEL MY BODY OUT THERE, SOMEWHERE IN THE DEEP. CALLING TO ME.
IT WANTS TO BE WHOLE AGAIN. I WANT TO BE WHOLE AGAIN. BUT IT SHOULDN'T BE THAT WAY.
WHO I AM, MYSELF, MY SOUL, ISN'T IN MY BODY, BUT MY BRAIN. MY THOUGHTS DEFINE MY EXISTENCE. IT IS THE THOUGHTS THAT MAKE ME. SO HOW CAN MY BODY PULL ME BACK?
BUT IT ISN'T MY BODY THAT PULLS ME. THERE'S SOMETHING ELSE CALLING TO ME.

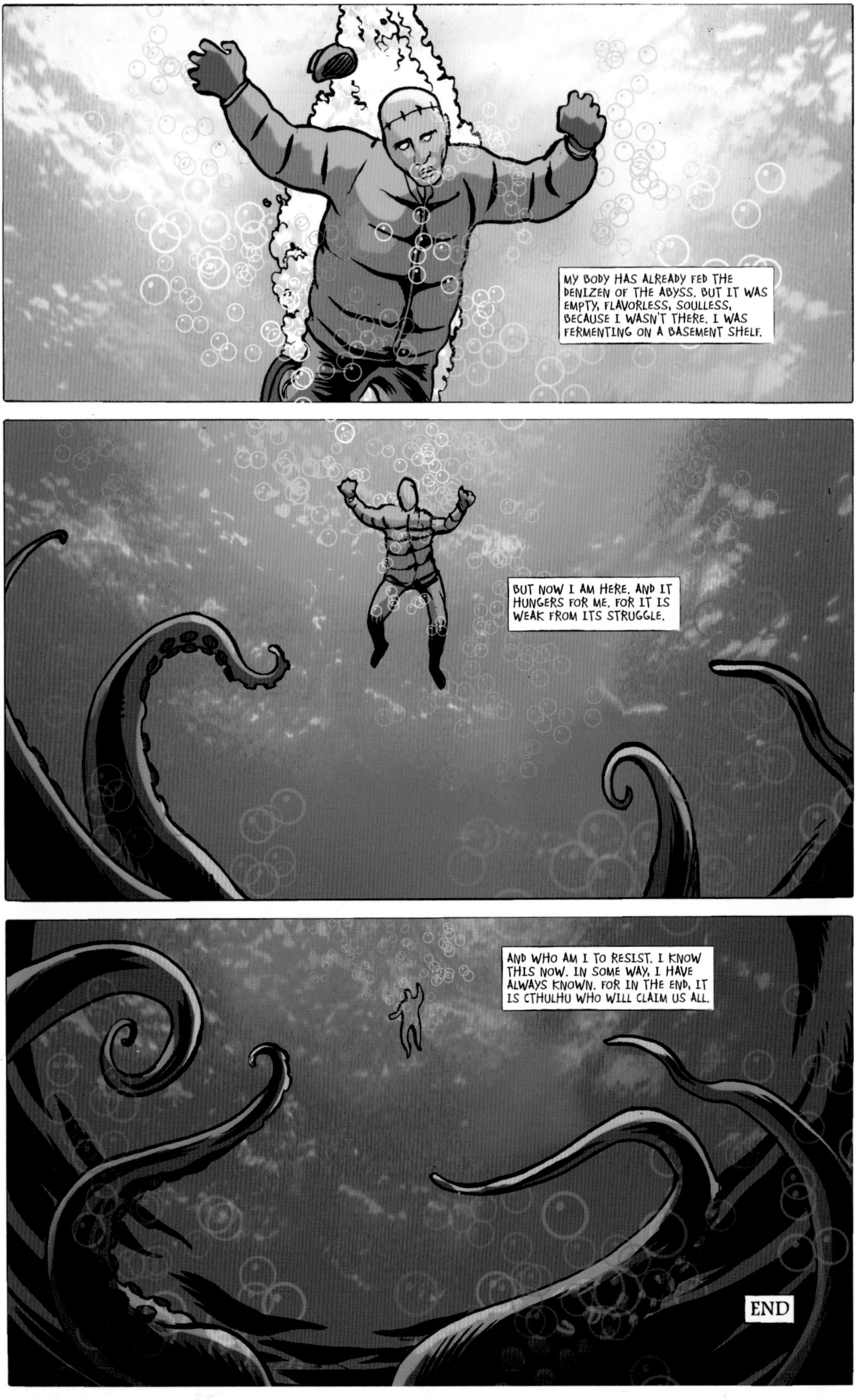
MY BODY HAS ALREADY FED THE DENIZEN OF THE ABYSS. BUT IT WAS EMPTY, FLAVORLESS, SOULLESS, BECAUSE I WASN'T THERE. I WAS FERMENTING ON A BASEMENT SHELF.
BUT NOW I AM HERE. AND IT HUNGERS FOR ME. FOR IT IS WEAK FROM ITS STRUGGLE.
AND WHO AM I TO RESIST. I KNOW THIS NOW. IN SOME WAY, I HAVE ALWAYS KNOWN. FOR IN THE END, IT IS CTHULHU WHO WILL CLAIM US ALL.
END

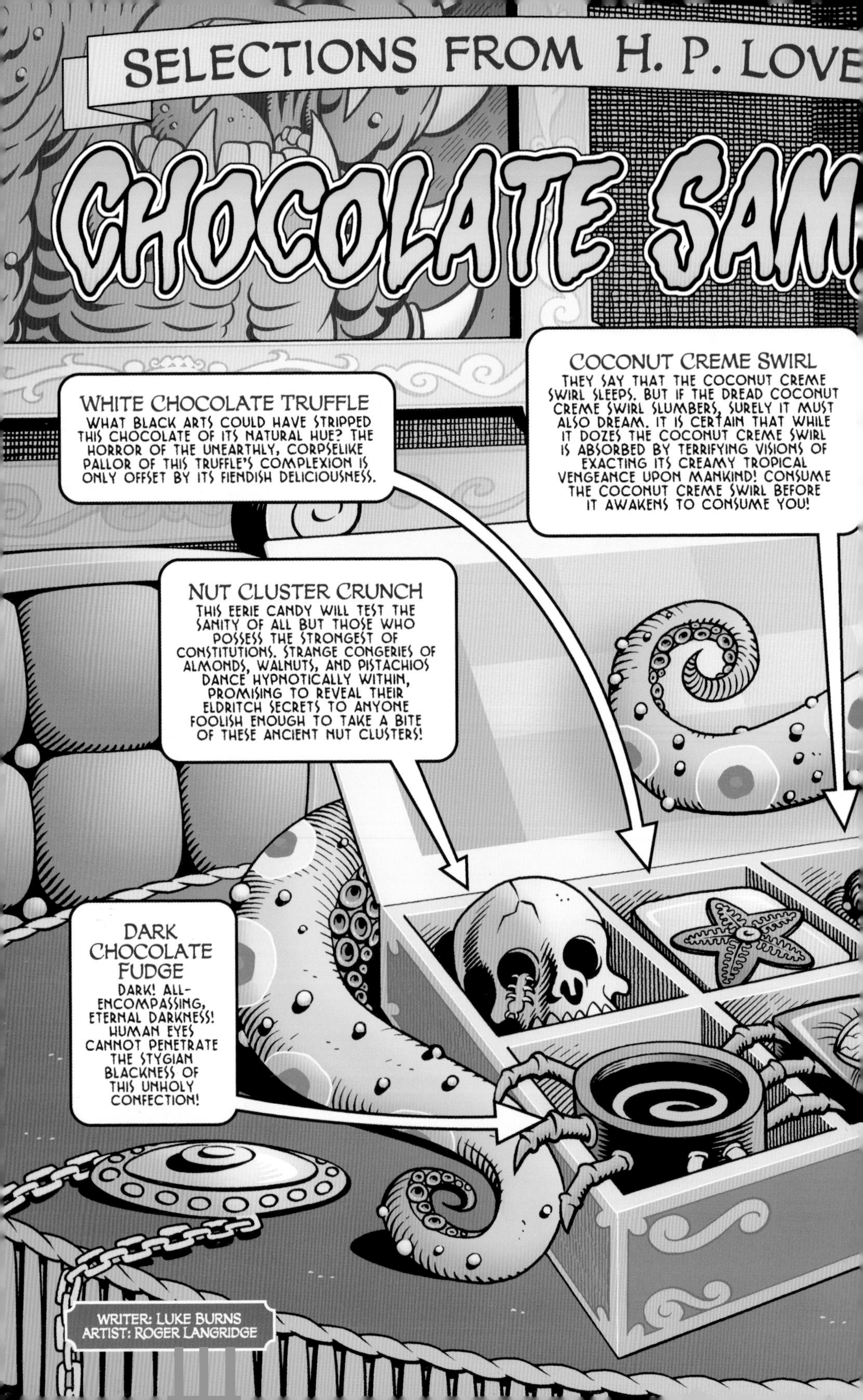
SELECTIONS FROM H. P. LOVE
CHOCOLATE SAM
WHITE CHOCOLATE TRUFFLE
WHAT BLACK ARTS COULD HAVE STRIPPED THIS CHOCOLATE OF ITS NATURAL HUE? THE HORROR OF THE UNEARTHLY, CORPSELIKE PALLOR OF THIS TRUFFLE'S COMPLEXION IS ONLY OFFSET BY ITS FIENDISH DELICIOUSNESS.
COCONUT CREME SWIRL
THEY SAY THAT THE COCONUT CREME SWIRL SLEEPS. BUT IF THE DREAD COCONUT CREME SWIRL SLUMBERS, SURELY IT MUST ALSO DREAM. IT IS CERTAIN THAT WHILE IT DOZES THE COCONUT CREME SWIRL IS ABSORBED BY TERRIFYING VISIONS OF EXACTING ITS CREAMY TROPICAL VENGEANCE UPON MANKIND! CONSUME THE COCONUT CREME SWIRL BEFORE IT AWAKENS TO CONSUME YOU!
NUT CLUSTER CRUNCH
THIS EERIE CANDY WILL TEST THE SANITY OF ALL BUT THOSE WHO POSSESS THE STRONGEST OF CONSTITUTIONS. STRANGE CONGERIES OF ALMONDS, WALNUTS, AND PISTACHIOS DANCE HYPNOTICALLY WITHIN, PROMISING TO REVEAL THEIR ELDRITCH SECRETS TO ANYONE FOOLISH ENOUGH TO TAKE A BITE OF THESE ANCIENT NUT CLUSTERS!
DARK CHOCOLATE FUDGE
DARK! ALL-ENCOMPASSING, ETERNAL DARKNESS! HUMAN EYES CANNOT PENETRATE THE STYGIAN BLACKNESS OF THIS UNHOLY CONFECTION!
WRITER: LUKE BURNS
ARTIST: ROGER LANGRIDGE

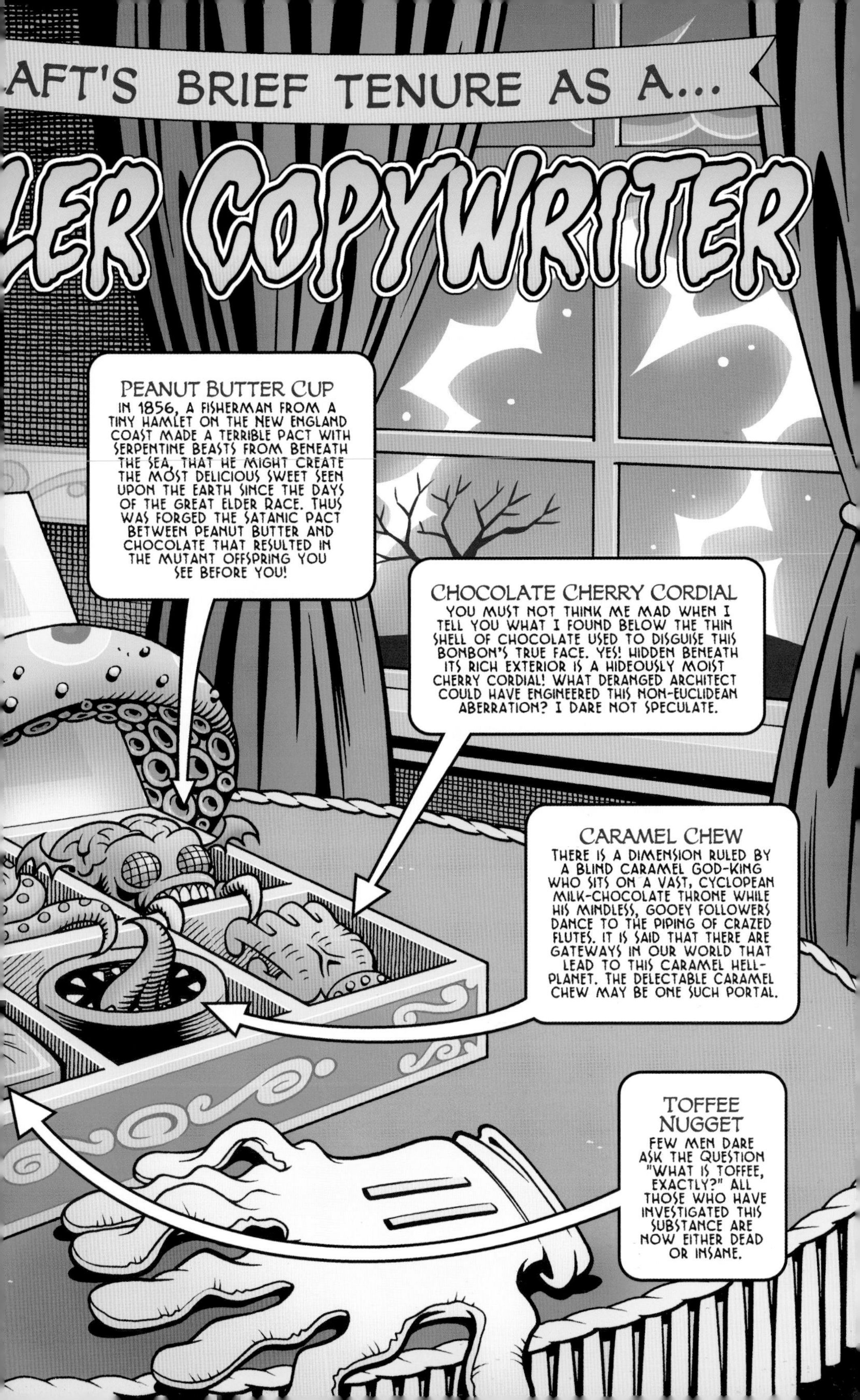
AFT'S BRIEF TENURE AS A...
LER COPYWRITER
PEANUT BUTTER CUP
IN 1856, A FISHERMAN FROM A TINY HAMLET ON THE NEW ENGLAND COAST MADE A TERRIBLE PACT WITH SERPENTINE BEASTS FROM BENEATH THE SEA, THAT HE MIGHT CREATE THE MOST DELICIOUS SWEET SEEN UPON THE EARTH SINCE THE DAYS OF THE GREAT ELDER RACE. THUS WAS FORGED THE SATANIC PACT BETWEEN PEANUT BUTTER AND CHOCOLATE THAT RESULTED IN THE MUTANT OFFSPRING YOU SEE BEFORE YOU!
CHOCOLATE CHERRY CORDIAL
YOU MUST NOT THINK ME MAD WHEN I TELL YOU WHAT I FOUND BELOW THE THIN SHELL OF CHOCOLATE USED TO DISGUISE THIS BONBON'S TRUE FACE. YES! HIDDEN BENEATH ITS RICH EXTERIOR IS A HIDEOUSLY MOIST CHERRY CORDIAL! WHAT DERANGED ARCHITECT COULD HAVE ENGINEERED THIS NON-EUCLIDEAN ABERRATION? I DARE NOT SPECULATE.
CARAMEL CHEW
THERE IS A DIMENSION RULED BY A BLIND CARAMEL GOD-KING WHO SITS ON A VAST, CYCLOPEAN MILK-CHOCOLATE THRONE WHILE HIS MINDLESS, GOOEY FOLLOWERS DANCE TO THE PIPING OF CRAZED FLUTES. IT IS SAID THAT THERE ARE GATEWAYS IN OUR WORLD THAT LEAD TO THIS CARAMEL HELL-PLANET. THE DELECTABLE CARAMEL CHEW MAY BE ONE SUCH PORTAL.
TOFFEE NUGGET
FEW MEN DARE ASK THE QUESTION "WHAT IS TOFFEE, EXACTLY?" ALL THOSE WHO HAVE INVESTIGATED THIS SUBSTANCE ARE NOW EITHER DEAD OR INSANE.

ARKHAM SVU

STORY WILLIAM MESSNER–LOEBS

ART ANDREW RITCHIE

A WHISTLE
FOR THE DEEP

STORY SHANE OAKLEY

ART DAVID HITCHCOCK

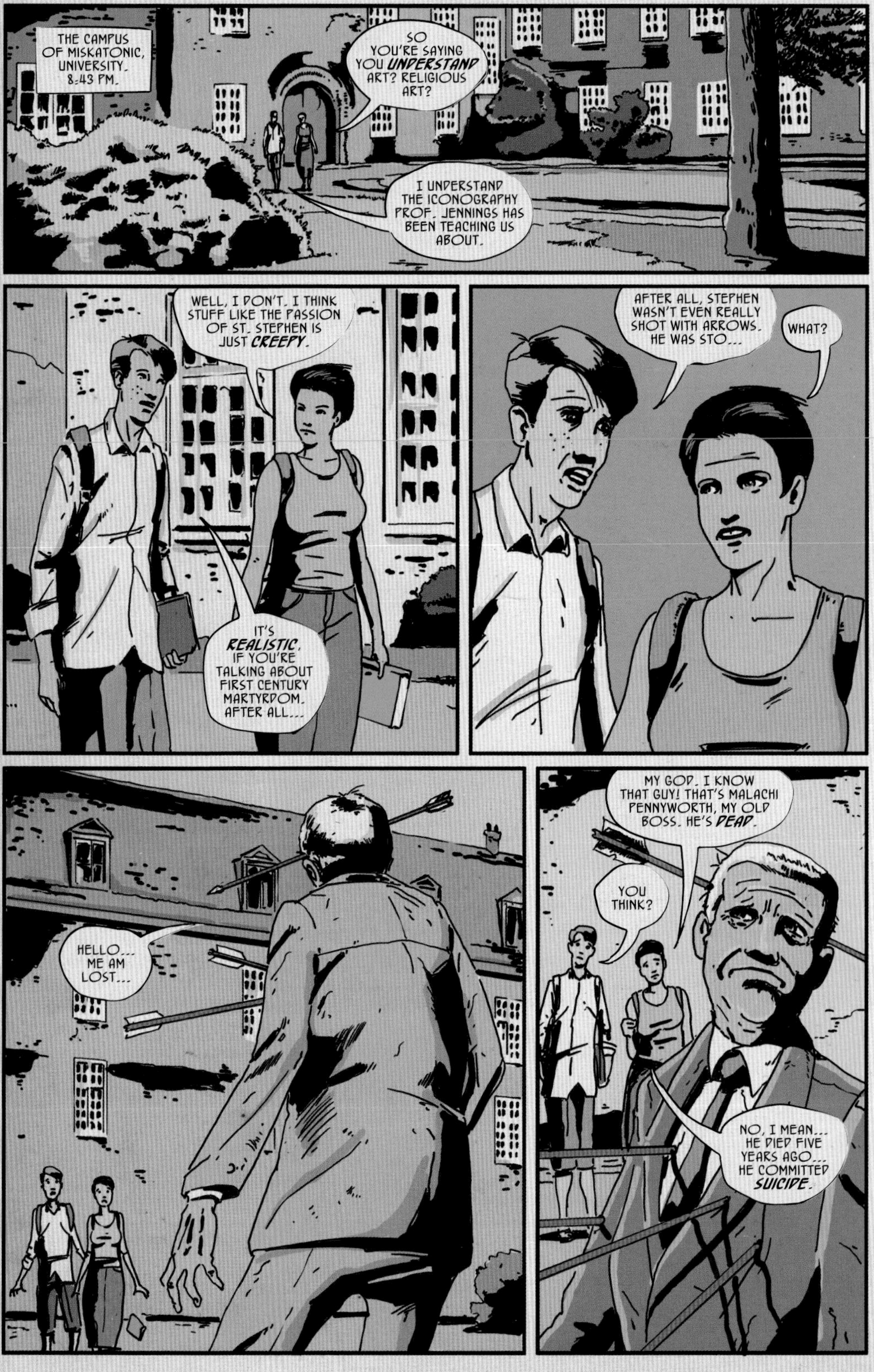
THE CAMPUS OF MISKATONIC UNIVERSITY. 8:43 PM.
SO YOU'RE SAYING YOU UNDERSTAND ART? RELIGIOUS ART?
I UNDERSTAND THE ICONOGRAPHY PROF. JENNINGS HAS BEEN TEACHING US ABOUT.
WELL, I DON'T. I THINK STUFF LIKE THE PASSION OF ST. STEPHEN IS JUST CREEPY.
IT'S REALISTIC, IF YOU'RE TALKING ABOUT FIRST CENTURY MARTYRDOM. AFTER ALL...
AFTER ALL, STEPHEN WASN'T EVEN REALLY SHOT WITH ARROWS. HE WAS STO...
WHAT?
HELLO... ME AM LOST...
MY GOD. I KNOW THAT GUY! THAT'S MALACHI PENNYWORTH, MY OLD BOSS. HE'S DEAD.
YOU THINK?
NO, I MEAN... HE DIED FIVE YEARS AGO... HE COMMITTED SUICIDE.

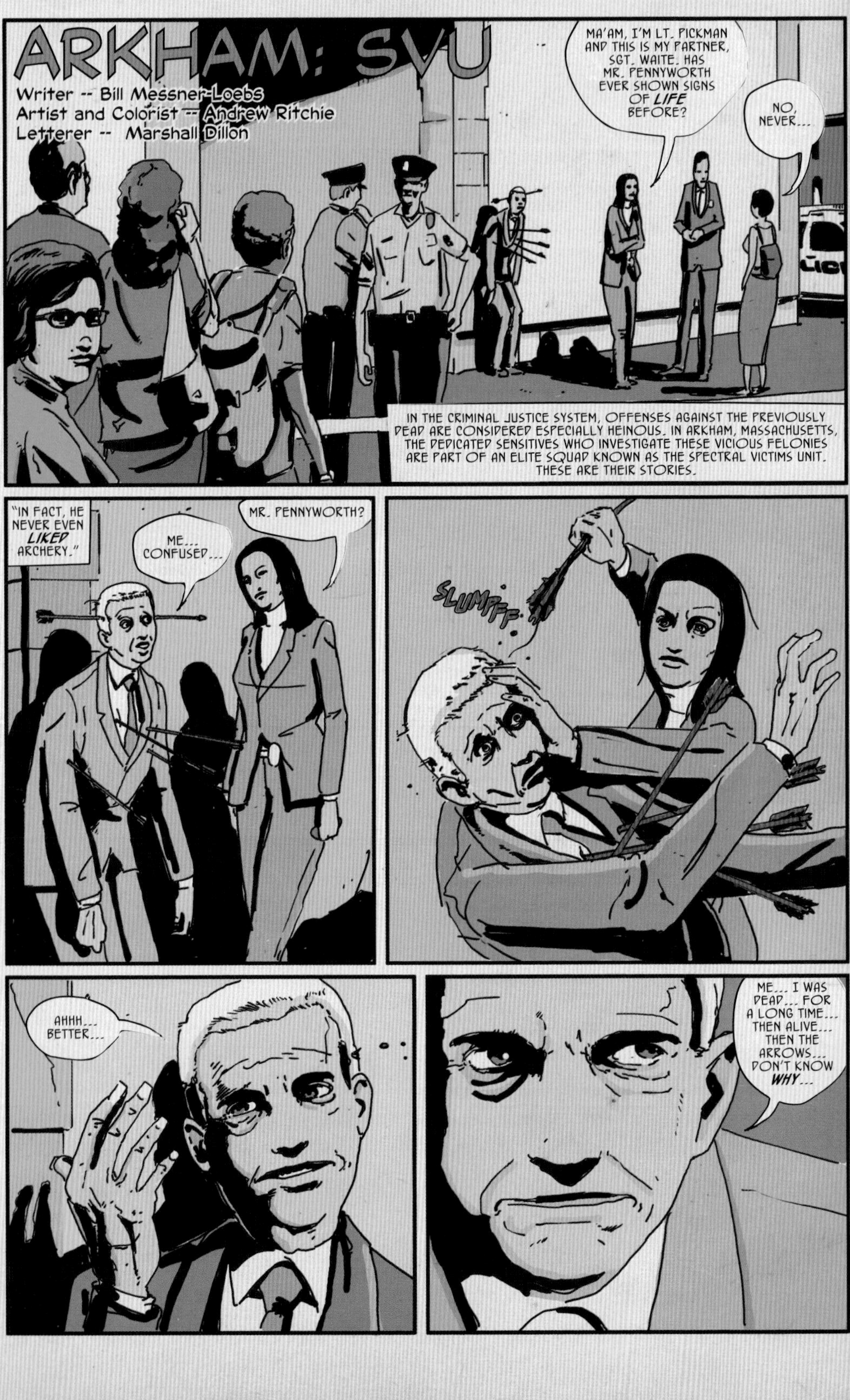
ARKHAM: SVU
Writer -- Bill Messner-Loebs
Artist and Colorist -- Andrew Ritchie
Letterer -- Marshall Dillon
MA'AM, I'M LT. PICKMAN AND THIS IS MY PARTNER, SGT. WAITE. HAS MR. PENNYWORTH EVER SHOWN SIGNS OF LIFE BEFORE?
NO, NEVER...
IN THE CRIMINAL JUSTICE SYSTEM, OFFENSES AGAINST THE PREVIOUSLY DEAD ARE CONSIDERED ESPECIALLY HEINOUS. IN ARKHAM, MASSACHUSETTS, THE DEDICATED SENSITIVES WHO INVESTIGATE THESE VICIOUS FELONIES ARE PART OF AN ELITE SQUAD KNOWN AS THE SPECTRAL VICTIMS UNIT. THESE ARE THEIR STORIES.
"IN FACT, HE NEVER EVEN LIKED ARCHERY."
ME... CONFUSED...
MR. PENNYWORTH?
SLUMPFF
AHHH... BETTER...
ME... I WAS DEAD... FOR A LONG TIME... THEN ALIVE... THEN THE ARROWS... DON'T KNOW WHY...

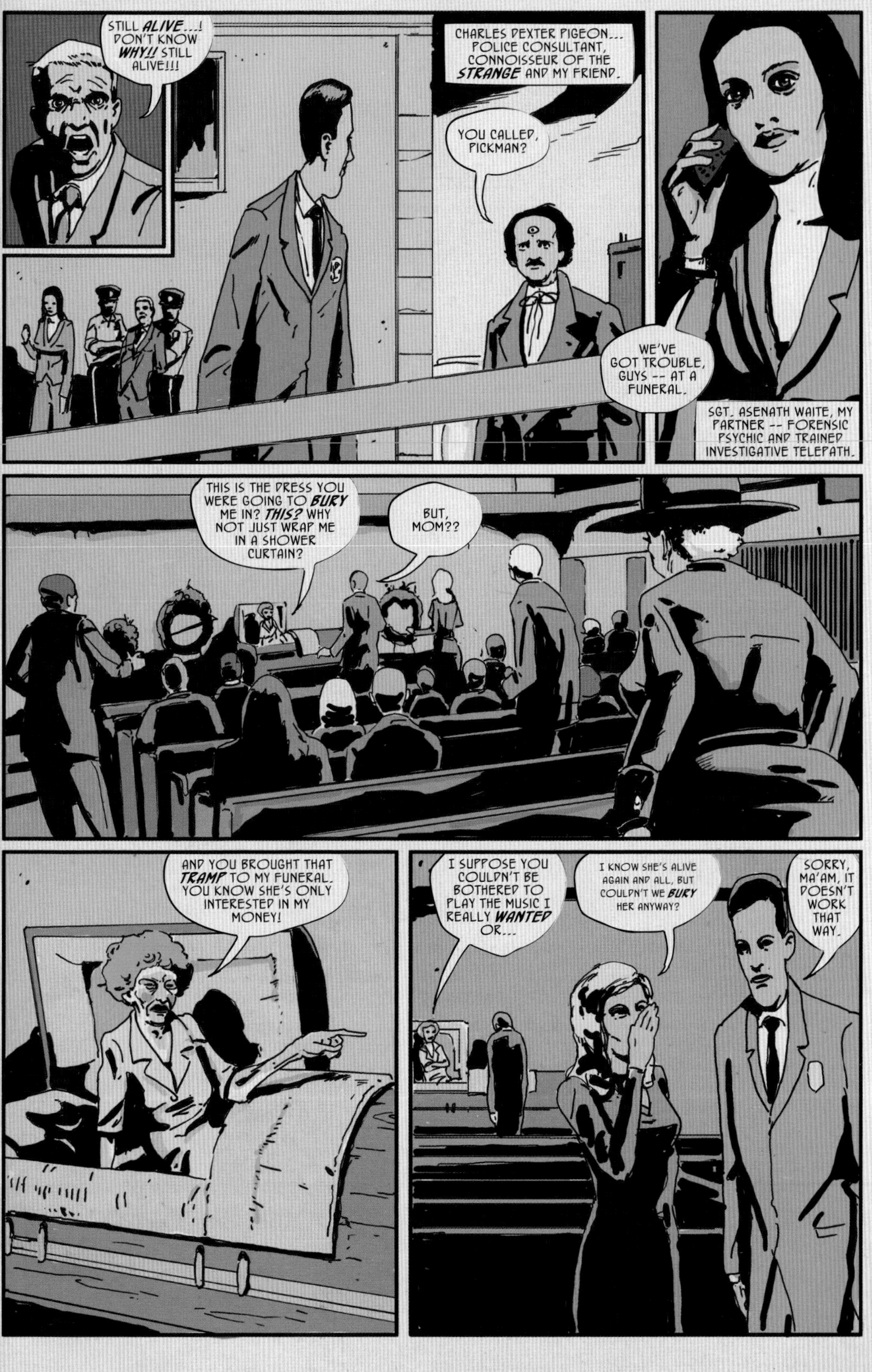
STILL ALIVE...! DON'T KNOW WHY!! STILL ALIVE!!!
CHARLES DEXTER PIGEON... POLICE CONSULTANT, CONNOISSEUR OF THE STRANGE AND MY FRIEND.
YOU CALLED, PICKMAN?
WE'VE GOT TROUBLE, GUYS -- AT A FUNERAL.
SGT. ASENATH WAITE, MY PARTNER -- FORENSIC PSYCHIC AND TRAINED INVESTIGATIVE TELEPATH.
THIS IS THE DRESS YOU WERE GOING TO BURY ME IN? THIS? WHY NOT JUST WRAP ME IN A SHOWER CURTAIN?
BUT, MOM??
AND YOU BROUGHT THAT TRAMP TO MY FUNERAL. YOU KNOW SHE'S ONLY INTERESTED IN MY MONEY!
I SUPPOSE YOU COULDN'T BE BOTHERED TO PLAY THE MUSIC I REALLY WANTED OR...
I KNOW SHE'S ALIVE AGAIN AND ALL, BUT COULDN'T WE BURY HER ANYWAY?
SORRY, MA'AM, IT DOESN'T WORK THAT WAY.

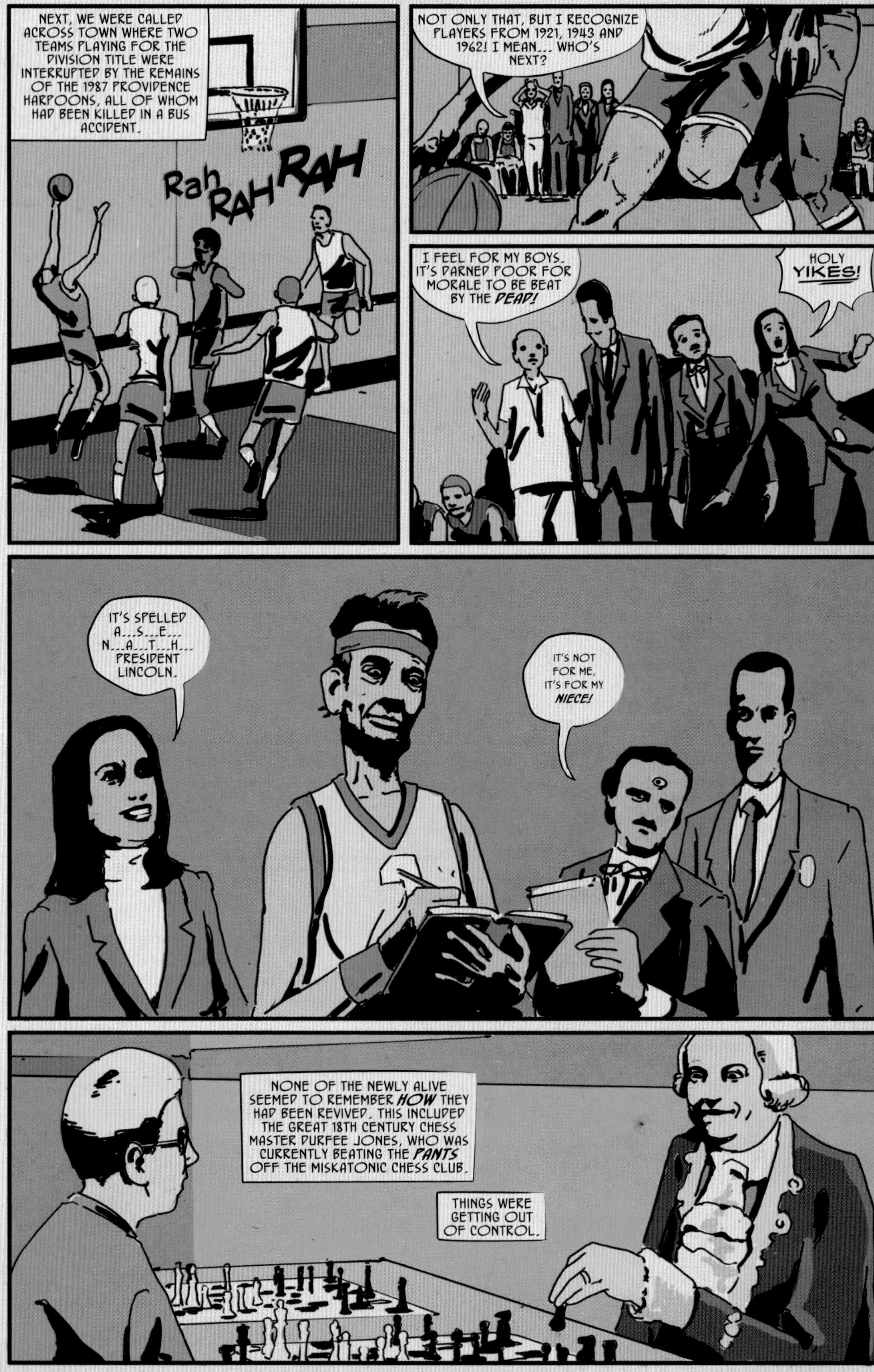
NEXT, WE WERE CALLED ACROSS TOWN WHERE TWO TEAMS PLAYING FOR THE DIVISION TITLE WERE INTERRUPTED BY THE REMAINS OF THE 1987 PROVIDENCE HARPOONS, ALL OF WHOM HAD BEEN KILLED IN A BUS ACCIDENT.
Rah RAH RAH
NOT ONLY THAT, BUT I RECOGNIZE PLAYERS FROM 1921, 1943 AND 1962! I MEAN... WHO'S NEXT?
I FEEL FOR MY BOYS. IT'S DARNED POOR FOR MORALE TO BE BEAT BY THE *DEAD!*
HOLY YIKES!
IT'S SPELLED A...S...E... N...A...T...H... PRESIDENT LINCOLN.
IT'S NOT FOR ME, IT'S FOR MY *NIECE!*
NONE OF THE NEWLY ALIVE SEEMED TO REMEMBER *HOW* THEY HAD BEEN REVIVED. THIS INCLUDED THE GREAT 18TH CENTURY CHESS MASTER DURFEE JONES, WHO WAS CURRENTLY BEATING THE *PANTS* OFF THE MISKATONIC CHESS CLUB.
THINGS WERE GETTING OUT OF CONTROL.

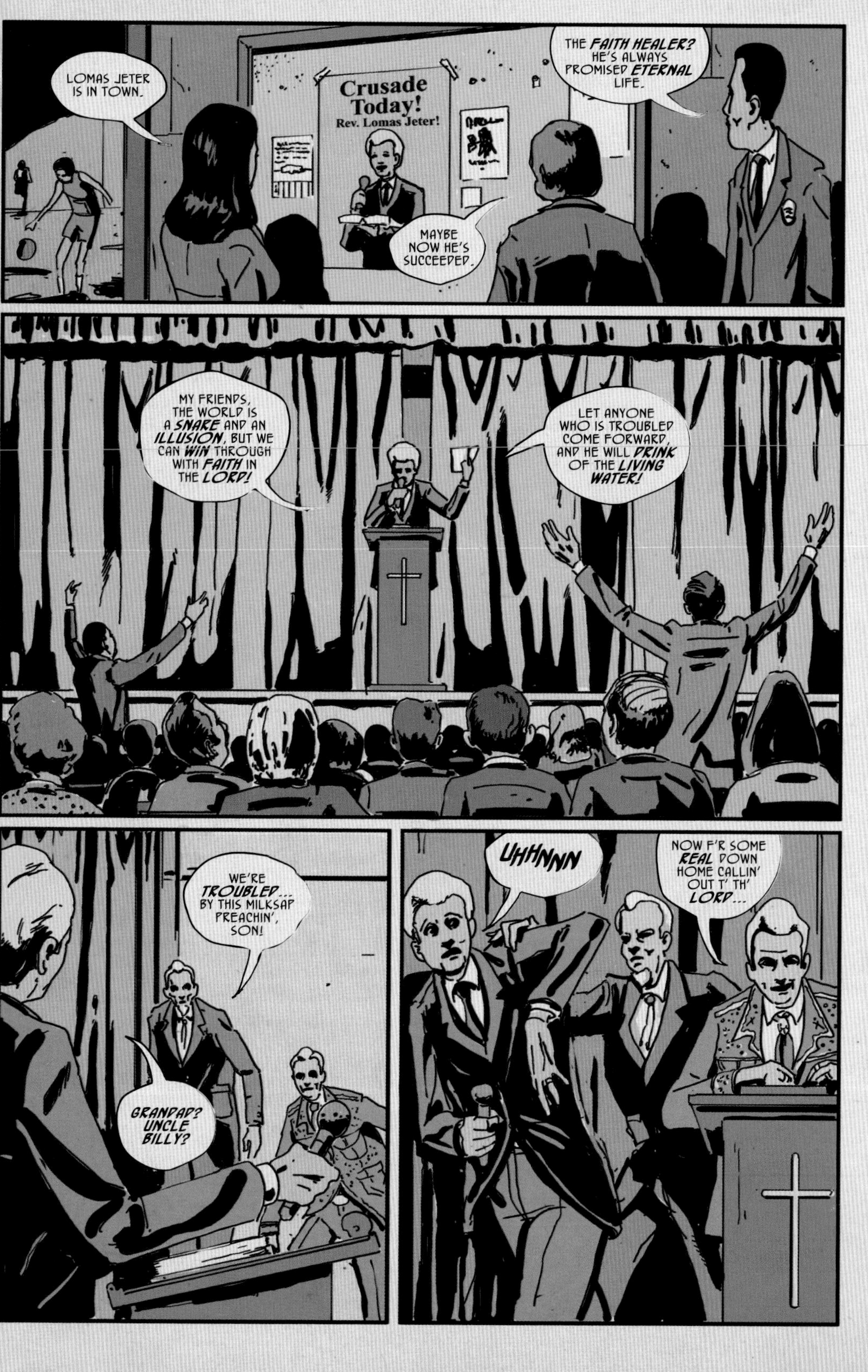
LOMAS JETER IS IN TOWN.
Crusade Today!
Rev. Lomas Jeter!
THE FAITH HEALER? HE'S ALWAYS PROMISED ETERNAL LIFE.
MAYBE NOW HE'S SUCCEEDED.
MY FRIENDS, THE WORLD IS A SNARE AND AN ILLUSION, BUT WE CAN WIN THROUGH WITH FAITH IN THE LORD!
LET ANYONE WHO IS TROUBLED COME FORWARD, AND HE WILL DRINK OF THE LIVING WATER!
WE'RE TROUBLED... BY THIS MILKSAP PREACHIN', SON!
GRANDAD? UNCLE BILLY?
UHHNNN
NOW F'R SOME REAL DOWN HOME CALLIN' OUT T' TH' LORD...

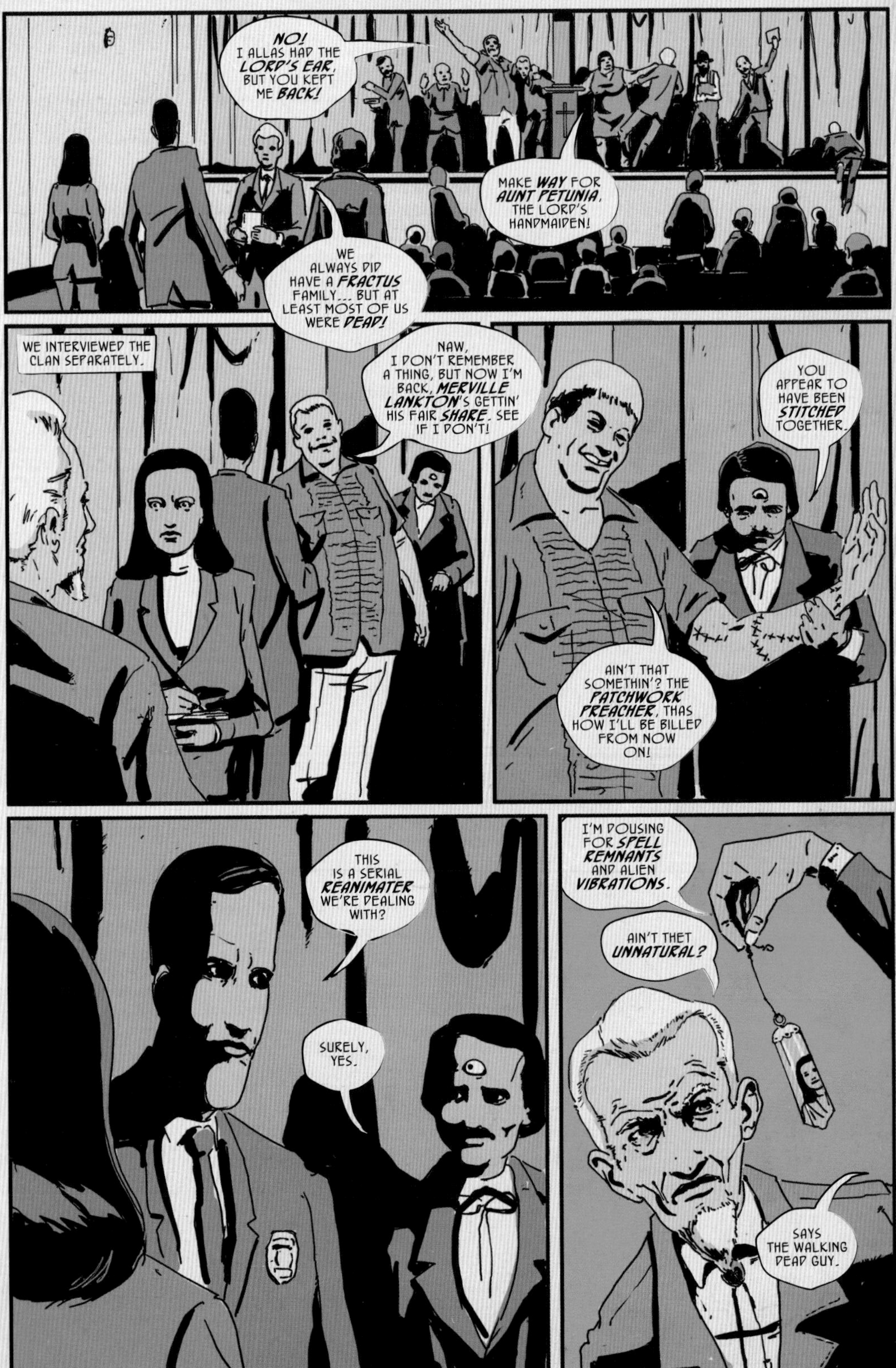
NO! I ALLAS HAD THE LORD'S EAR, BUT YOU KEPT ME BACK!
MAKE WAY FOR AUNT PETUNIA, THE LORD'S HANDMAIDEN!
WE ALWAYS DID HAVE A FRACTUS FAMILY... BUT AT LEAST MOST OF US WERE DEAD!
WE INTERVIEWED THE CLAN SEPARATELY.
NAW, I DON'T REMEMBER A THING, BUT NOW I'M BACK, MERVILLE LANKTON'S GETTIN' HIS FAIR SHARE. SEE IF I DON'T!
YOU APPEAR TO HAVE BEEN STITCHED TOGETHER.
AIN'T THAT SOMETHIN'? THE PATCHWORK PREACHER, THAS HOW I'LL BE BILLED FROM NOW ON!
THIS IS A SERIAL REANIMATER WE'RE DEALING WITH?
SURELY, YES.
I'M DOUSING FOR SPELL REMNANTS AND ALIEN VIBRATIONS.
AIN'T THET UNNATURAL?
SAYS THE WALKING DEAD GUY.

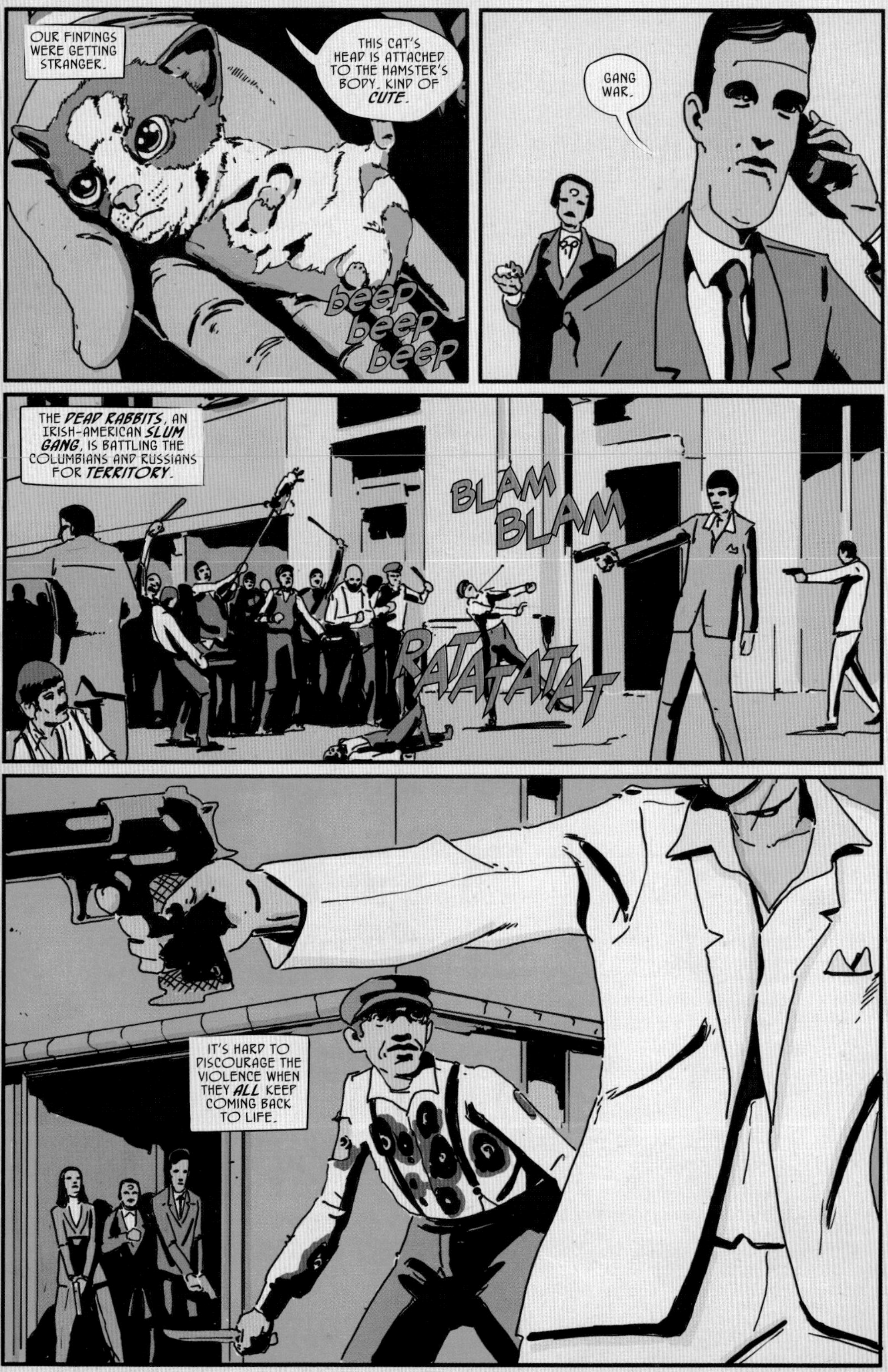
OUR FINDINGS WERE GETTING STRANGER.
THIS CAT'S HEAD IS ATTACHED TO THE HAMSTER'S BODY. KIND OF CUTE.
beep beep beep
GANG WAR.
THE DEAD RABBITS, AN IRISH-AMERICAN SLUM GANG, IS BATTLING THE COLUMBIANS AND RUSSIANS FOR TERRITORY.
BLAM BLAM
RATATATAT
IT'S HARD TO DISCOURAGE THE VIOLENCE WHEN THEY ALL KEEP COMING BACK TO LIFE.

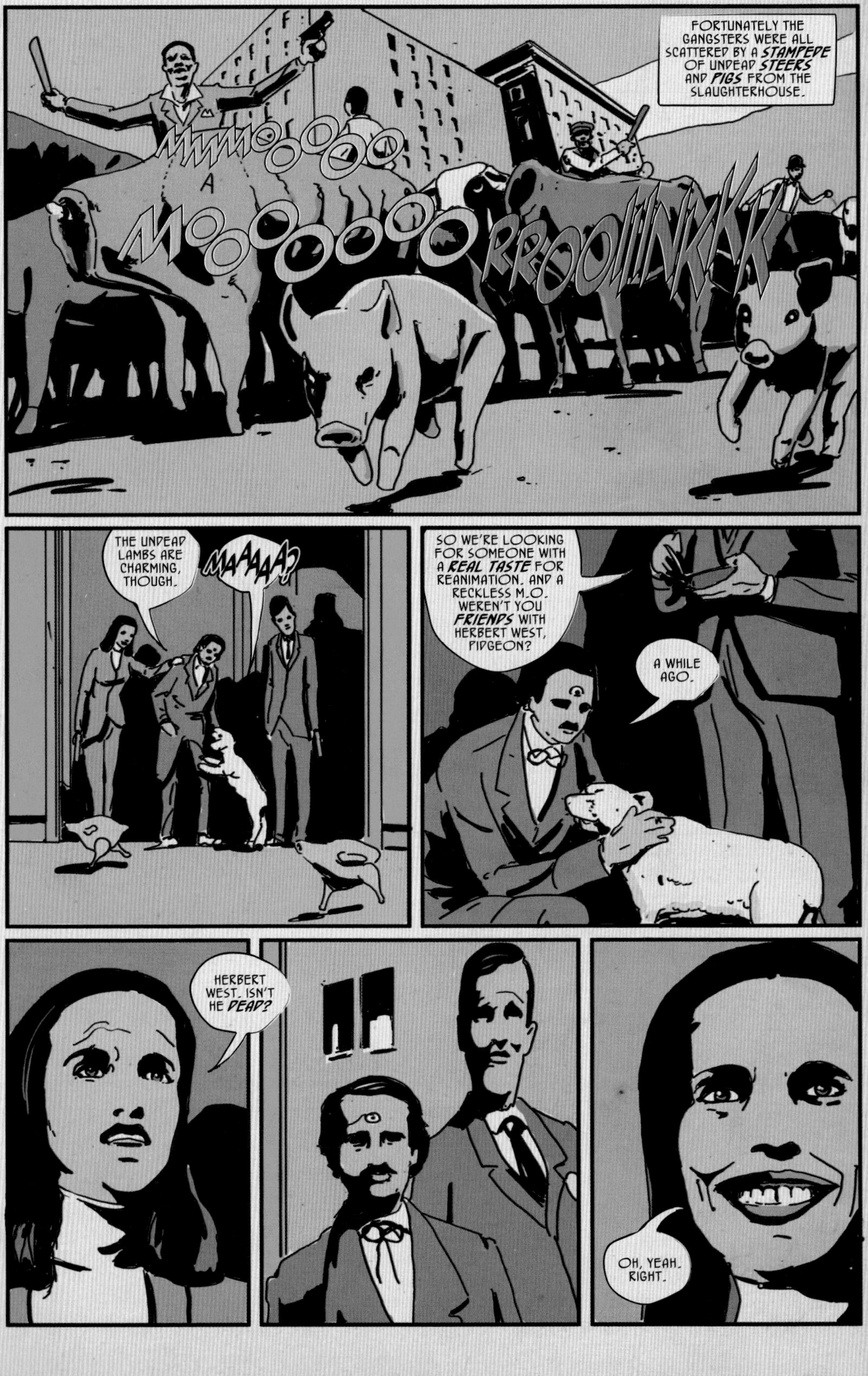
FORTUNATELY THE GANGSTERS WERE ALL SCATTERED BY A *STAMPEDE* OF UNDEAD *STEERS* AND *PIGS* FROM THE SLAUGHTERHOUSE.
MMMOOOOOO
A
MOOOOOOOO
RROOIIINKKK
THE UNDEAD LAMBS ARE CHARMING, THOUGH.
MAAAAA?
SO WE'RE LOOKING FOR SOMEONE WITH A *REAL TASTE* FOR REANIMATION. AND A RECKLESS M.O. WEREN'T YOU *FRIENDS* WITH HERBERT WEST, PIDGEON?
A WHILE AGO.
HERBERT WEST. ISN'T HE *DEAD?*
OH, YEAH. RIGHT.

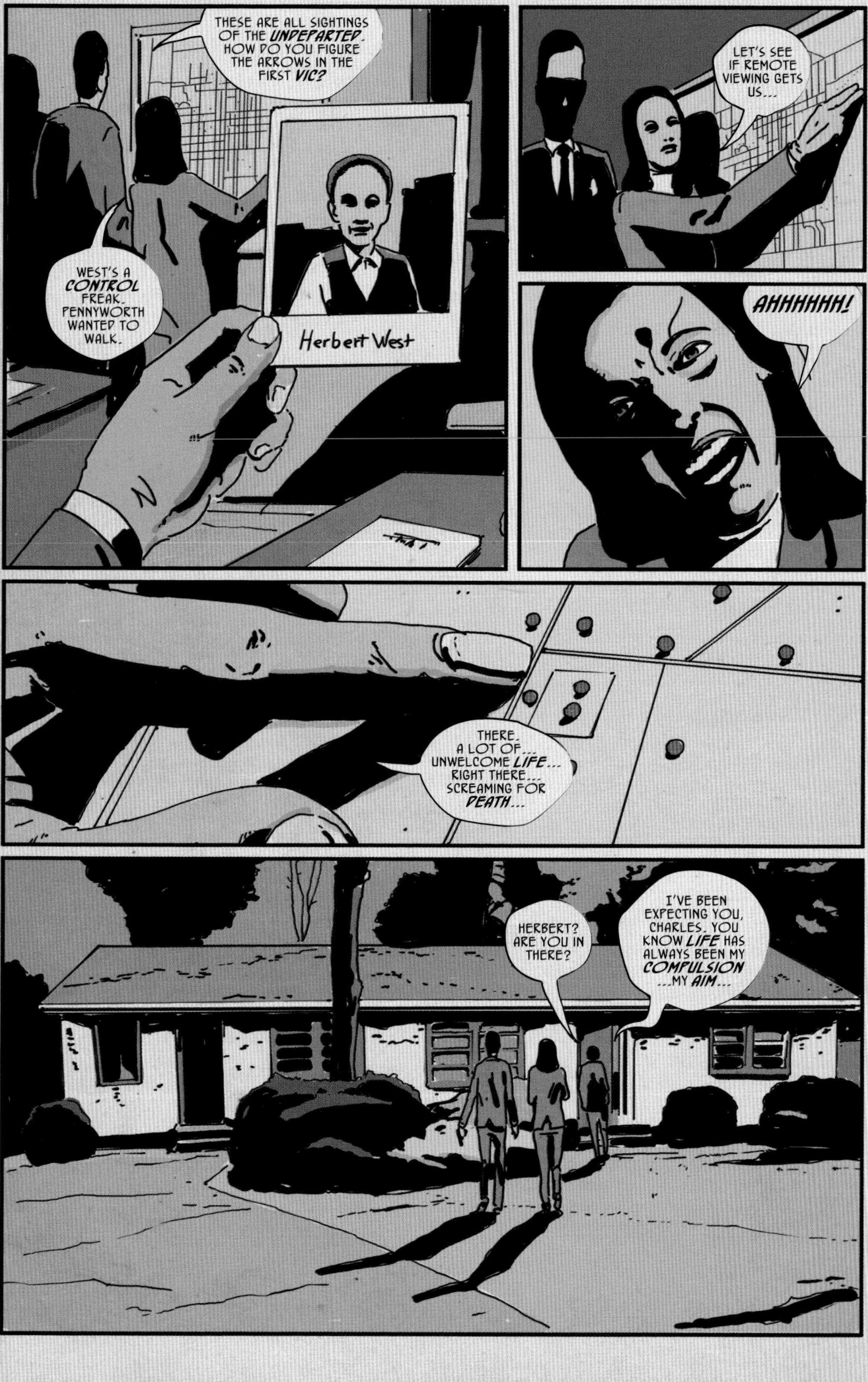
THESE ARE ALL SIGHTINGS OF THE UNDEPARTED. HOW DO YOU FIGURE THE ARROWS IN THE FIRST VIC?
WEST'S A CONTROL FREAK. PENNYWORTH WANTED TO WALK.
Herbert West
LET'S SEE IF REMOTE VIEWING GETS US...
AHHHHHH!
THERE. A LOT OF... UNWELCOME LIFE... RIGHT THERE... SCREAMING FOR DEATH...
HERBERT? ARE YOU IN THERE?
I'VE BEEN EXPECTING YOU, CHARLES. YOU KNOW LIFE HAS ALWAYS BEEN MY COMPULSION ...MY AIM...

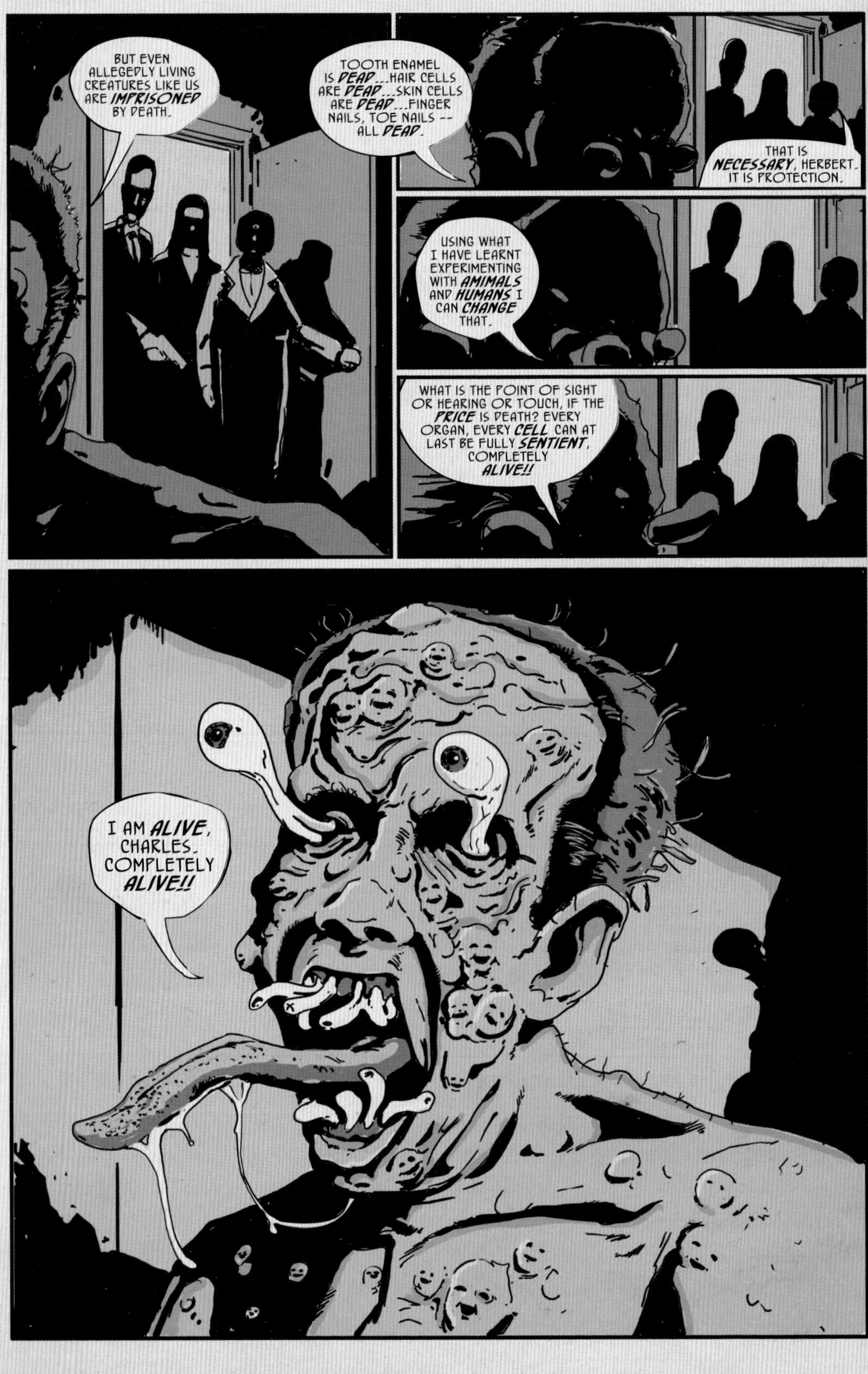
BUT EVEN ALLEGEDLY LIVING CREATURES LIKE US ARE IMPRISONED BY DEATH.
TOOTH ENAMEL IS DEAD... HAIR CELLS ARE DEAD... SKIN CELLS ARE DEAD... FINGER NAILS, TOE NAILS -- ALL DEAD.
THAT IS NECESSARY, HERBERT. IT IS PROTECTION.
USING WHAT I HAVE LEARNT EXPERIMENTING WITH ANIMALS AND HUMANS I CAN CHANGE THAT.
WHAT IS THE POINT OF SIGHT OR HEARING OR TOUCH, IF THE PRICE IS DEATH? EVERY ORGAN, EVERY CELL CAN AT LAST BE FULLY SENTIENT, COMPLETELY ALIVE!!
I AM ALIVE, CHARLES. COMPLETELY ALIVE!!

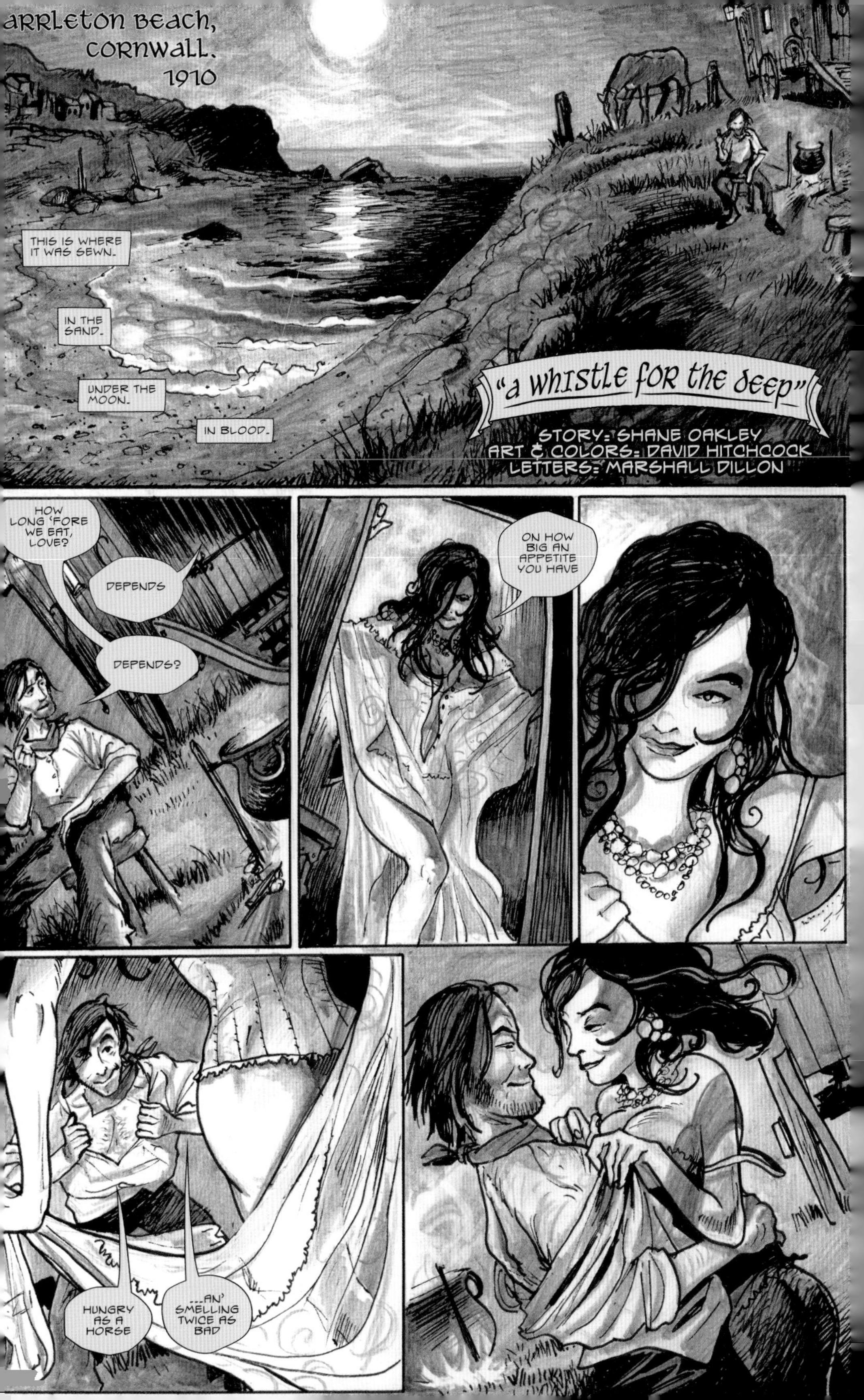

ARRLETON BEACH, CORNWALL. 1910
THIS IS WHERE IT WAS SEWN.
IN THE SAND.
UNDER THE MOON.
IN BLOOD.
"A WHISTLE FOR THE DEEP"
STORY: SHANE OAKLEY
ART & COLORS: DAVID HITCHCOCK
LETTERS: MARSHALL DILLON
HOW LONG 'FORE WE EAT, LOVE?
DEPENDS
DEPENDS?
ON HOW BIG AN APPETITE YOU HAVE
HUNGRY AS A HORSE
...AN' SMELLING TWICE AS BAD

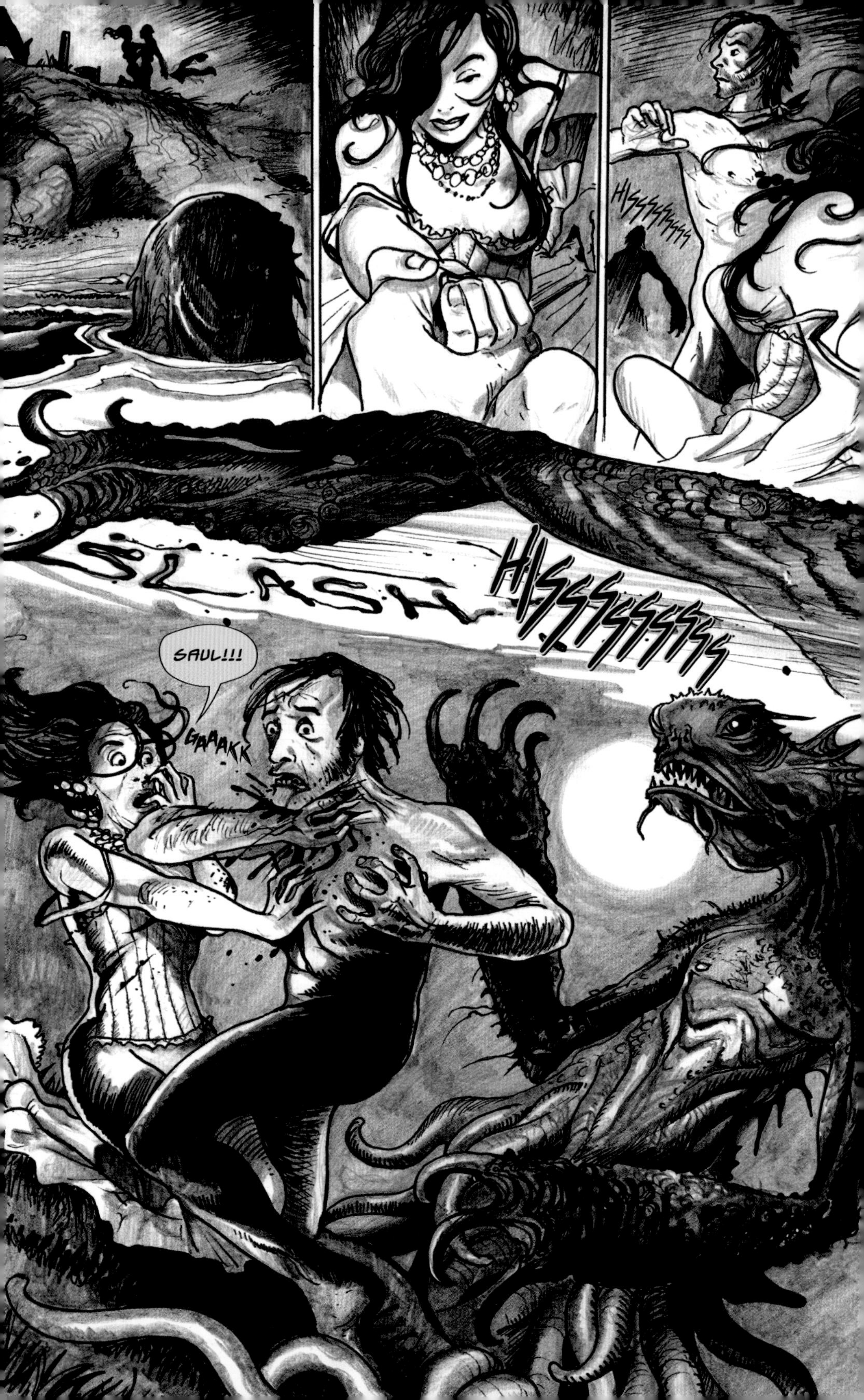
HISSSSSSSS
SLASH
HISSSSSSSSS
SAUL!!!
GAAAKK

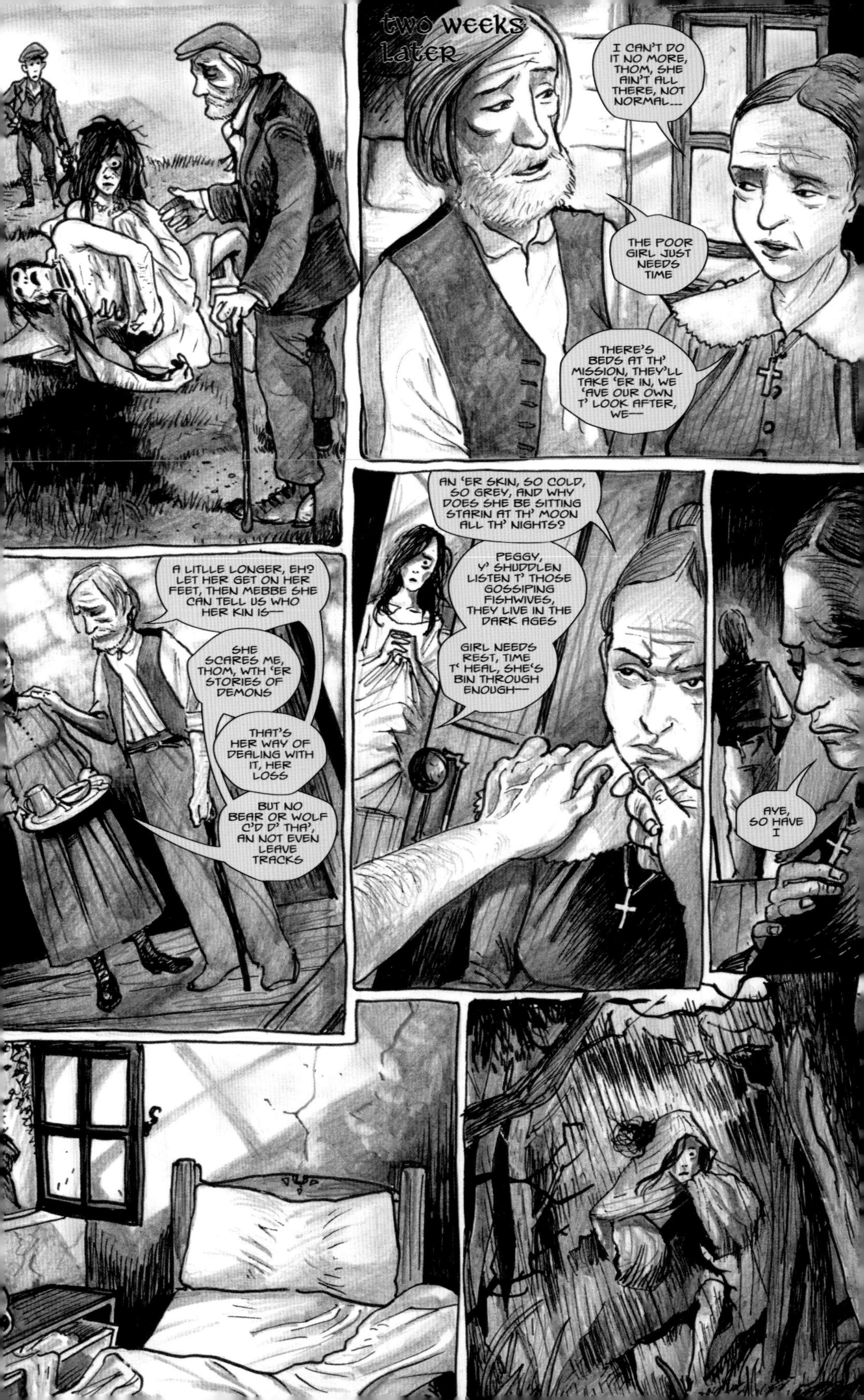
two weeks later
I CAN'T DO IT NO MORE, THOM, SHE AIN'T ALL THERE, NOT NORMAL---
THE POOR GIRL JUST NEEDS TIME
THERE'S BEDS AT TH' MISSION, THEY'LL TAKE 'ER IN, WE 'AVE OUR OWN T' LOOK AFTER, WE---
A LITLLE LONGER, EH? LET HER GET ON HER FEET, THEN MEBBE SHE CAN TELL US WHO HER KIN IS---
SHE SCARES ME, THOM, WTH 'ER STORIES OF DEMONS
THAT'S HER WAY OF DEALING WITH IT, HER LOSS
BUT NO BEAR OR WOLF C'D D' THA', AN NOT EVEN LEAVE TRACKS
AN 'ER SKIN, SO COLD, SO GREY, AND WHY DOES SHE BE SITTING STARIN AT TH' MOON ALL TH' NIGHTS?
PEGGY, Y' SHUDDLEN LISTEN T' THOSE GOSSIPING FISHWIVES, THEY LIVE IN THE DARK AGES
GIRL NEEDS REST, TIME T' HEAL, SHE'S BIN THROUGH ENOUGH---
AYE, SO HAVE I

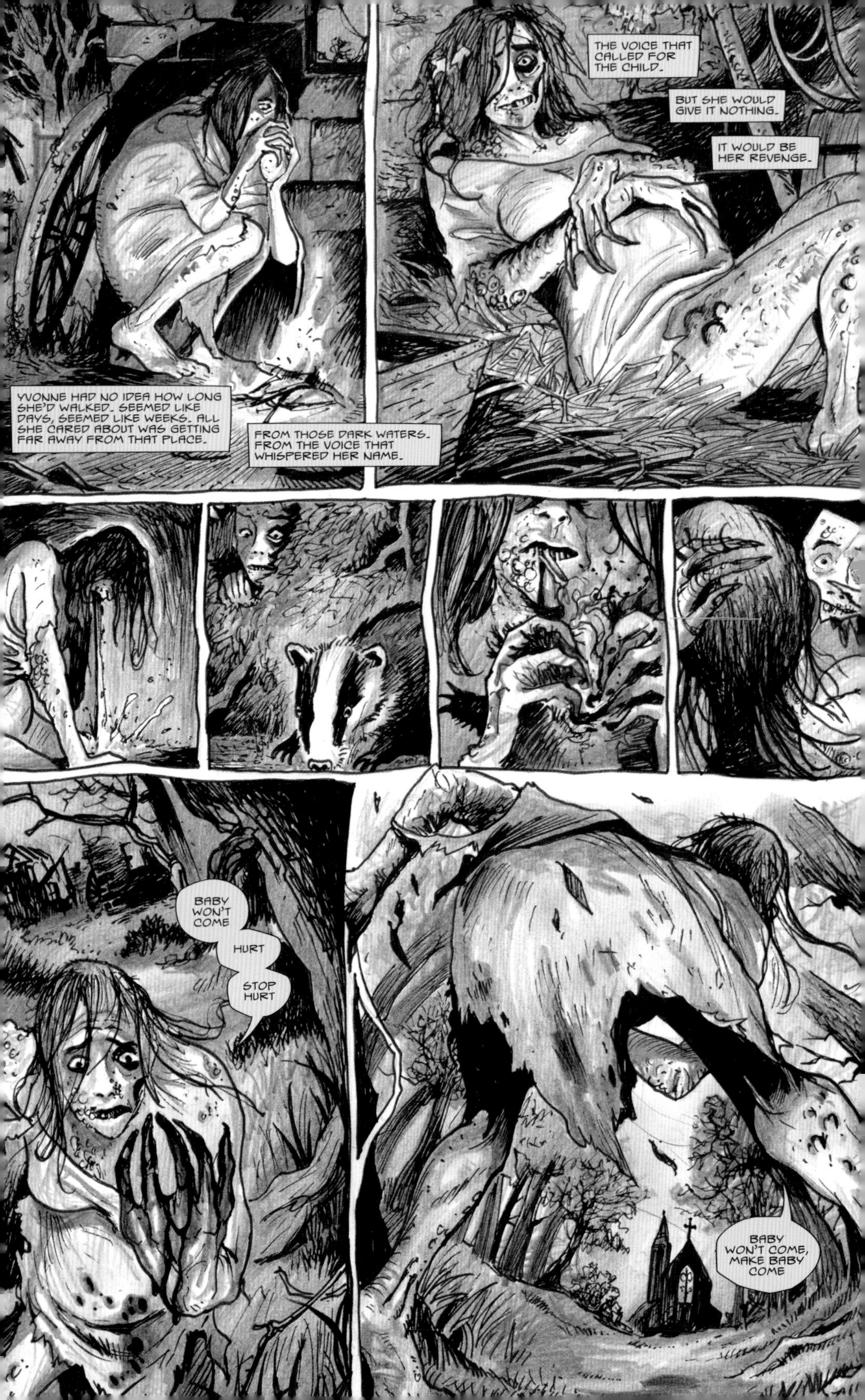
YVONNE HAD NO IDEA HOW LONG SHE'D WALKED. SEEMED LIKE DAYS, SEEMED LIKE WEEKS. ALL SHE CARED ABOUT WAS GETTING FAR AWAY FROM THAT PLACE.
FROM THOSE DARK WATERS. FROM THE VOICE THAT WHISPERED HER NAME.
THE VOICE THAT CALLED FOR THE CHILD.
BUT SHE WOULD GIVE IT NOTHING.
IT WOULD BE HER REVENGE.
BABY WON'T COME
HURT
STOP HURT
BABY WON'T COME, MAKE BABY COME

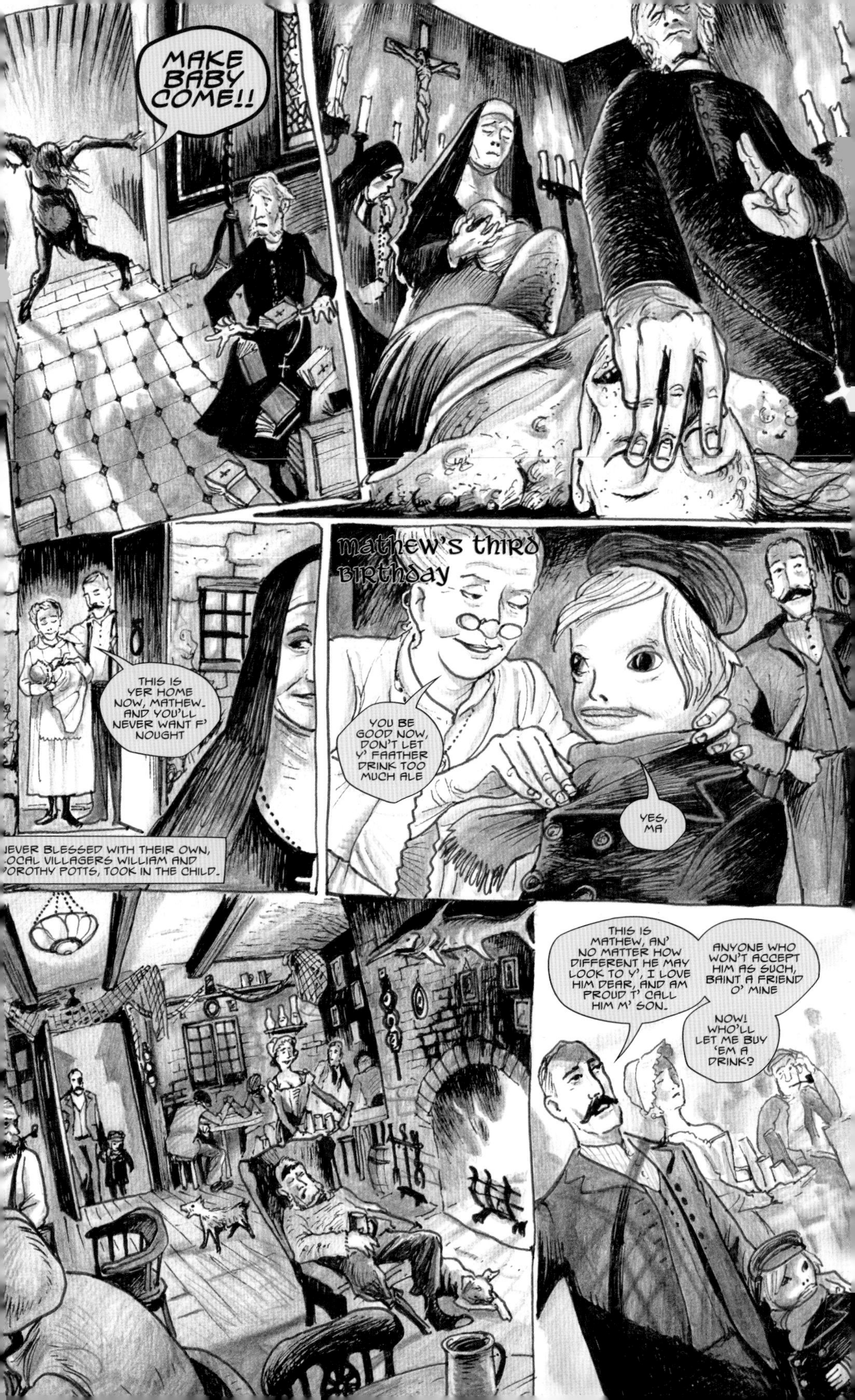
MAKE BABY COME!!
mathew's third BIRTHday
THIS IS YER HOME NOW, MATHEW. AND YOU'LL NEVER WANT F' NOUGHT
NEVER BLESSED WITH THEIR OWN, LOCAL VILLAGERS WILLIAM AND DOROTHY POTTS, TOOK IN THE CHILD.
YOU BE GOOD NOW, DON'T LET Y' FAATHER DRINK TOO MUCH ALE
YES, MA
THIS IS MATHEW, AN' NO MATTER HOW DIFFERENT HE MAY LOOK TO Y', I LOVE HIM DEAR, AND AM PROUD T' CALL HIM M' SON.
ANYONE WHO WON'T ACCEPT HIM AS SUCH, BAINT A FRIEND O' MINE
NOW! WHO'LL LET ME BUY 'EM A DRINK?

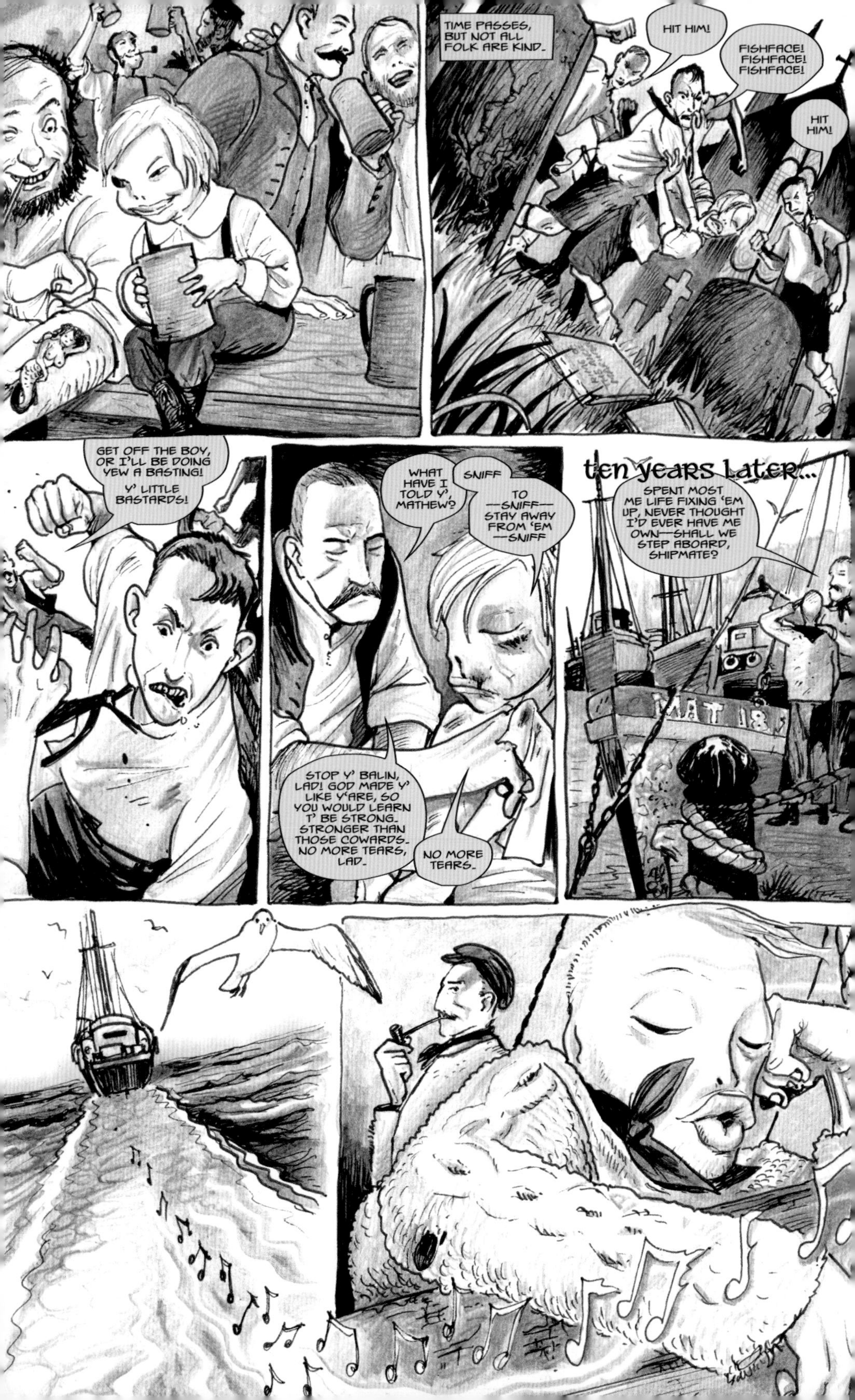
TIME PASSES, BUT NOT ALL FOLK ARE KIND.
HIT HIM!
FISHFACE! FISHFACE! FISHFACE!
HIT HIM!
GET OFF THE BOY, OR I'LL BE DOING YEW A BASTING!
Y' LITTLE BASTARDS!
WHAT HAVE I TOLD Y', MATHEW?
SNIFF
TO —SNIFF— STAY AWAY FROM 'EM —SNIFF
STOP Y' BALIN, LAD! GOD MADE Y' LIKE Y'ARE, SO YOU WOULD LEARN T' BE STRONG. STRONGER THAN THOSE COWARDS. NO MORE TEARS, LAD.
NO MORE TEARS.
ten years later...
SPENT MOST ME LIFE FIXING 'EM UP, NEVER THOUGHT I'D EVER HAVE ME OWN—SHALL WE STEP ABOARD, SHIPMATE?
MAT 18

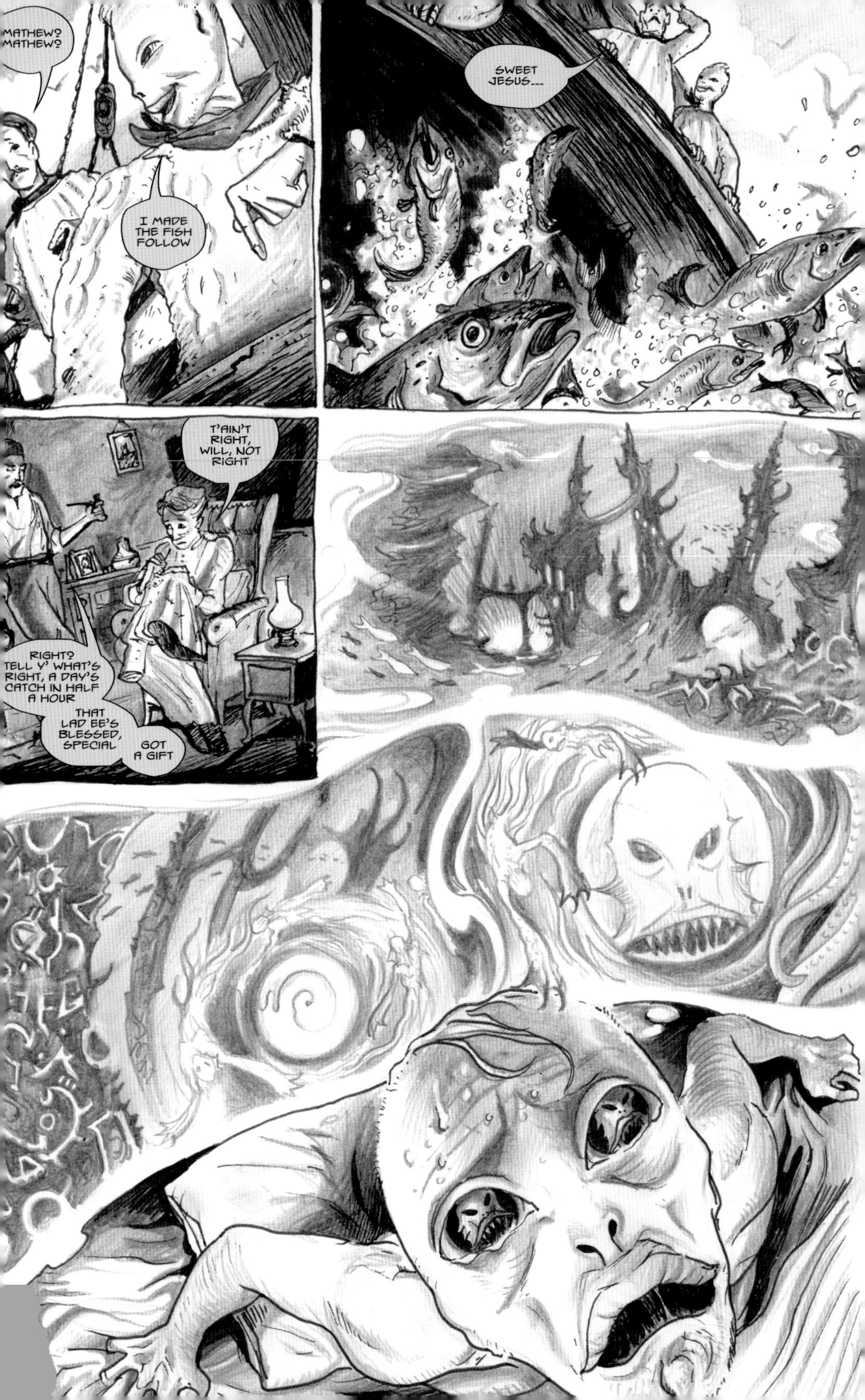
MATHEW? MATHEW?
I MADE THE FISH FOLLOW
SWEET JESUS...
T'AIN'T RIGHT, WILL, NOT RIGHT
RIGHT? TELL Y' WHAT'S RIGHT, A DAY'S CATCH IN HALF A HOUR
THAT LAD BE'S BLESSED, SPECIAL
GOT A GIFT

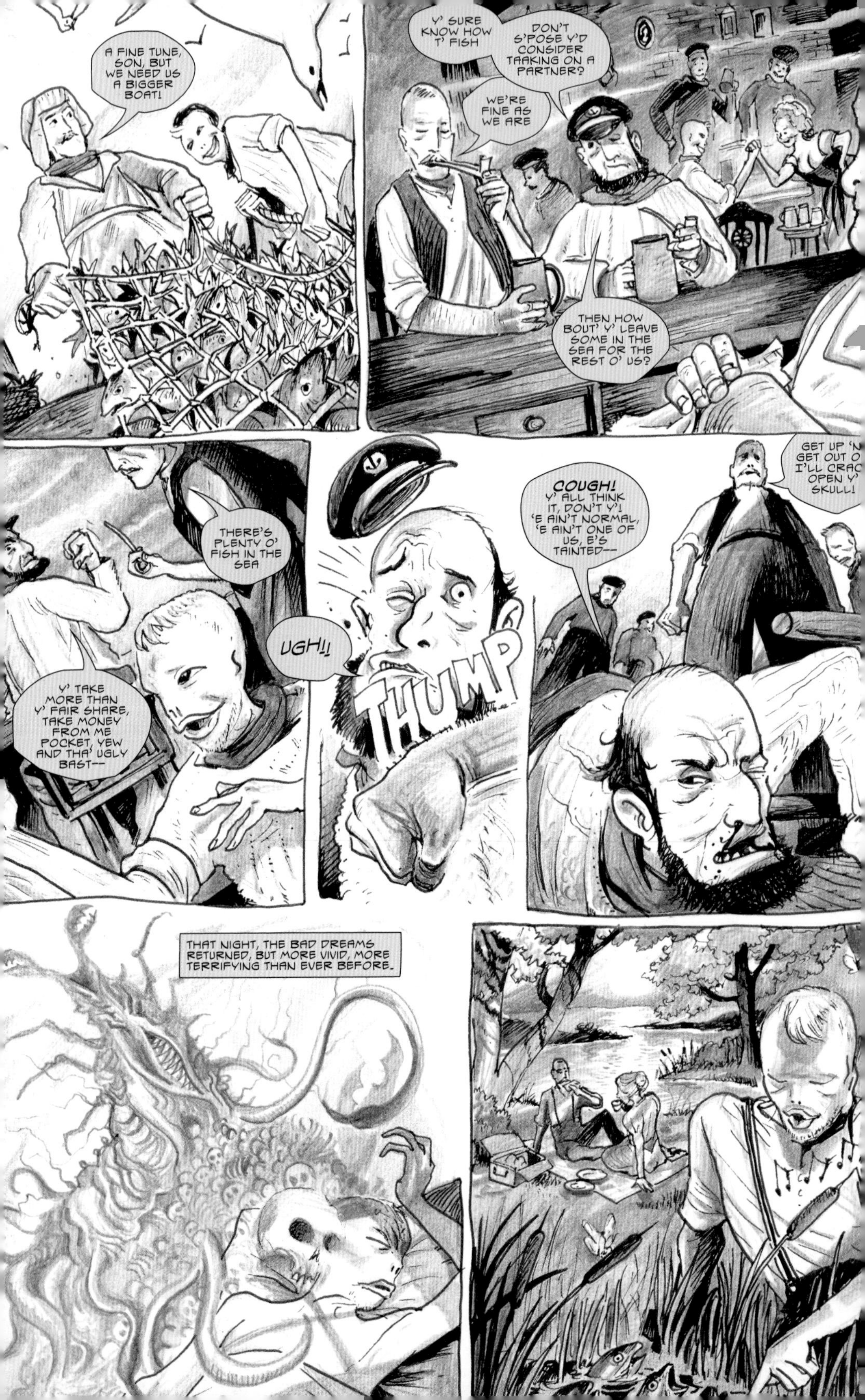
A FINE TUNE, SON, BUT WE NEED US A BIGGER BOAT!
Y' SURE KNOW HOW T' FISH
DON'T S'POSE Y'D CONSIDER TAAKING ON A PARTNER?
WE'RE FINE AS WE ARE
THEN HOW BOUT' Y' LEAVE SOME IN THE SEA FOR THE REST O' US?
THERE'S PLENTY O' FISH IN THE SEA
Y' TAKE MORE THAN Y' FAIR SHARE, TAKE MONEY FROM ME POCKET, YEW AND THA' UGLY BAST--
UGH!!
THUMP
COUGH! Y' ALL THINK IT, DON'T Y'! 'E AIN'T NORMAL, 'E AIN'T ONE OF US, E'S TAINTED--
THAT NIGHT, THE BAD DREAMS RETURNED, BUT MORE VIVID, MORE TERRIFYING THAN EVER BEFORE.

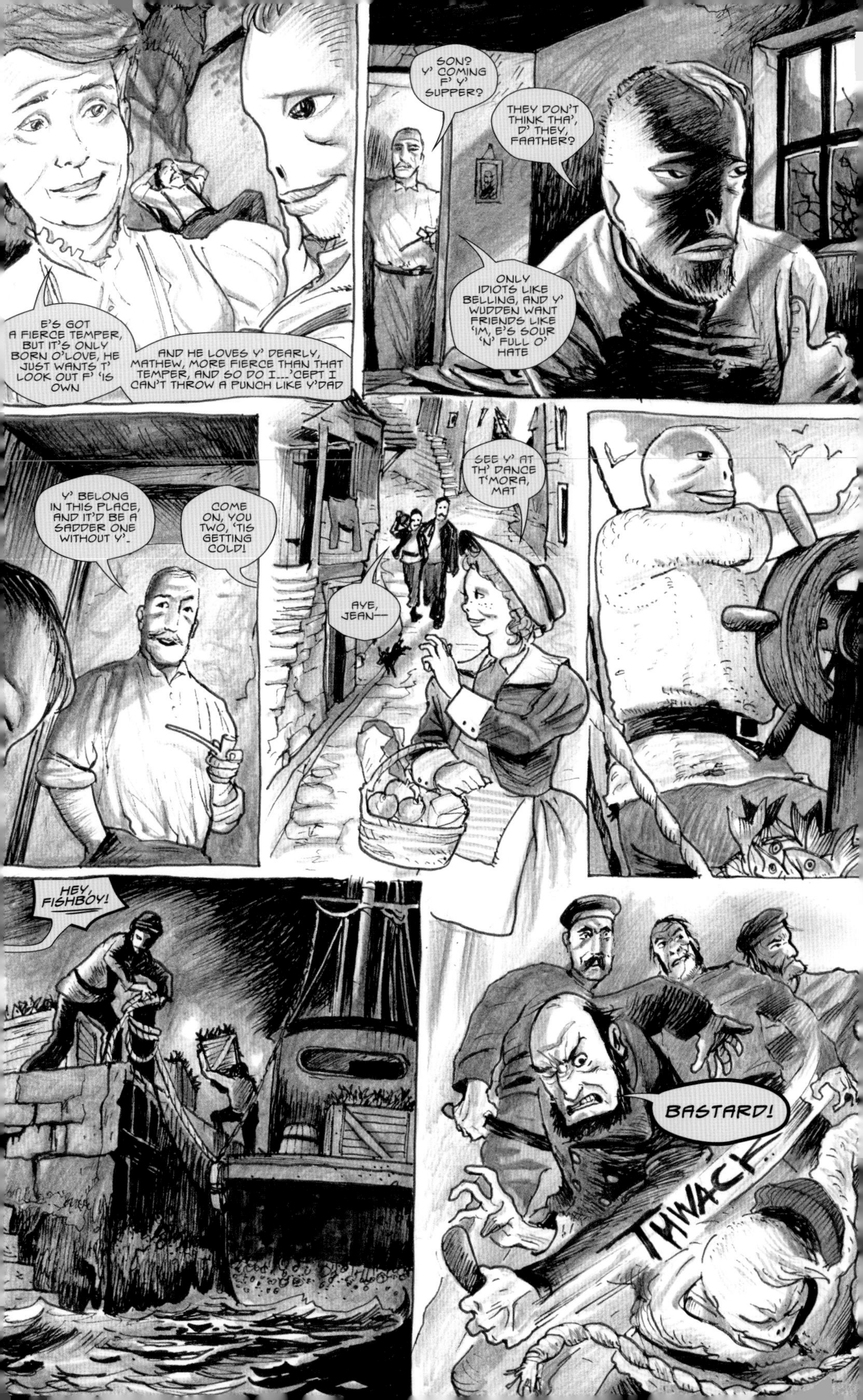
E'S GOT A FIERCE TEMPER, BUT IT'S ONLY BORN O'LOVE, HE JUST WANTS T' LOOK OUT F' 'IS OWN
AND HE LOVES Y' DEARLY, MATHEW, MORE FIERCE THAN THAT TEMPER, AND SO DO I...'CEPT I CAN'T THROW A PUNCH LIKE Y'DAD
SON? Y' COMING F' Y' SUPPER?
THEY DON'T THINK THA', D' THEY, FAATHER?
ONLY IDIOTS LIKE BELLING, AND Y' WUDDEN WANT FRIENDS LIKE 'IM, E'S SOUR 'N' FULL O' HATE
Y' BELONG IN THIS PLACE, AND IT'D BE A SADDER ONE WITHOUT Y'.
COME ON, YOU TWO, 'TIS GETTING COLD!
SEE Y' AT TH' DANCE T'MORA, MAT
AYE, JEAN--
HEY, FISHBOY!
BASTARD!
THWACK

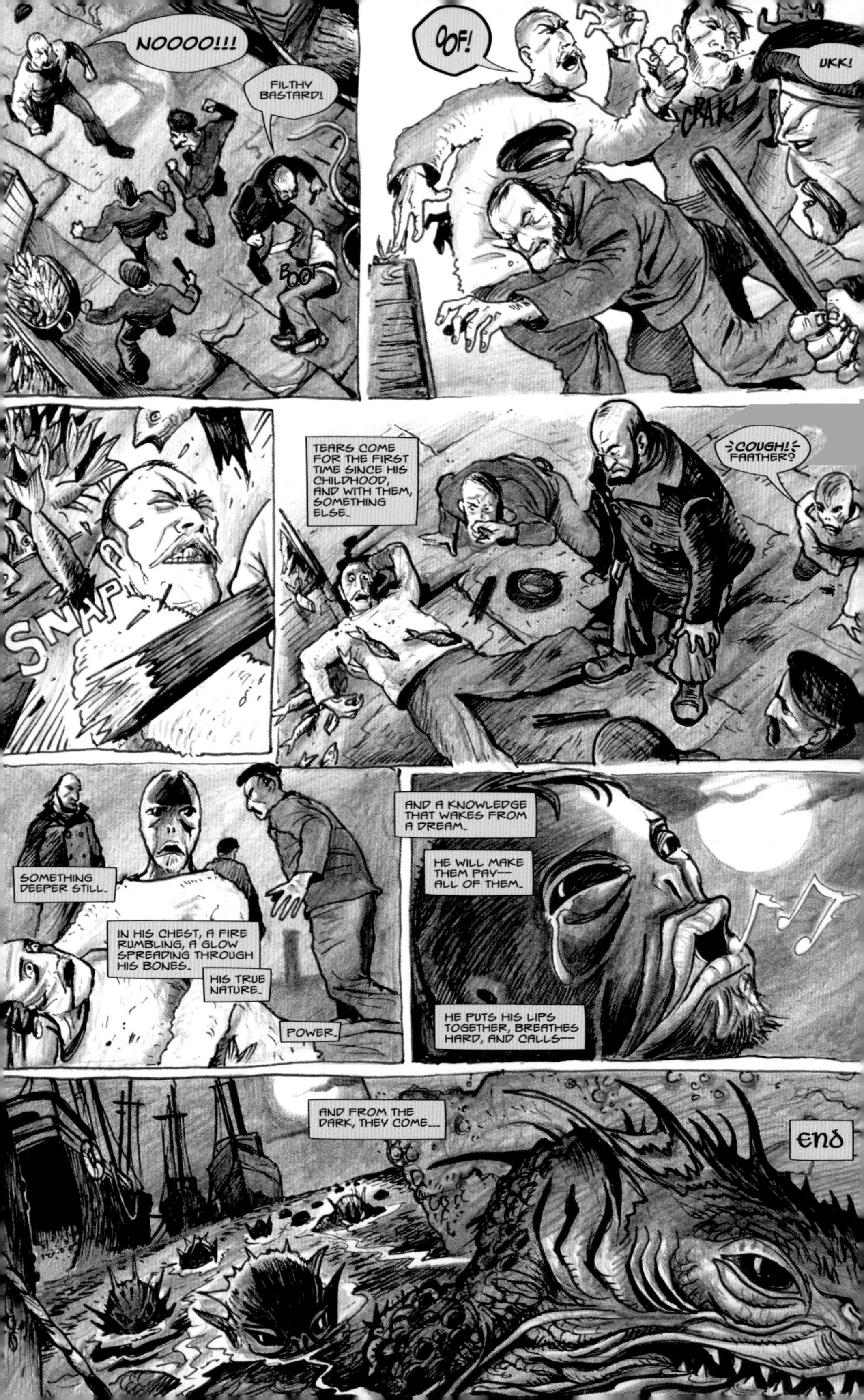
NOOOO!!!
FILTHY BASTARD!
BOOT
OOF!
UKK!
CRAK!
SNAP
TEARS COME FOR THE FIRST TIME SINCE HIS CHILDHOOD, AND WITH THEM, SOMETHING ELSE...
COUGH! FAATHER?
SOMETHING DEEPER STILL...
IN HIS CHEST, A FIRE RUMBLING, A GLOW SPREADING THROUGH HIS BONES...
HIS TRUE NATURE...
POWER...
AND A KNOWLEDGE THAT WAKES FROM A DREAM...
HE WILL MAKE THEM PAY— ALL OF THEM...
HE PUTS HIS LIPS TOGETHER, BREATHES HARD, AND CALLS—
AND FROM THE DARK, THEY COME...
END

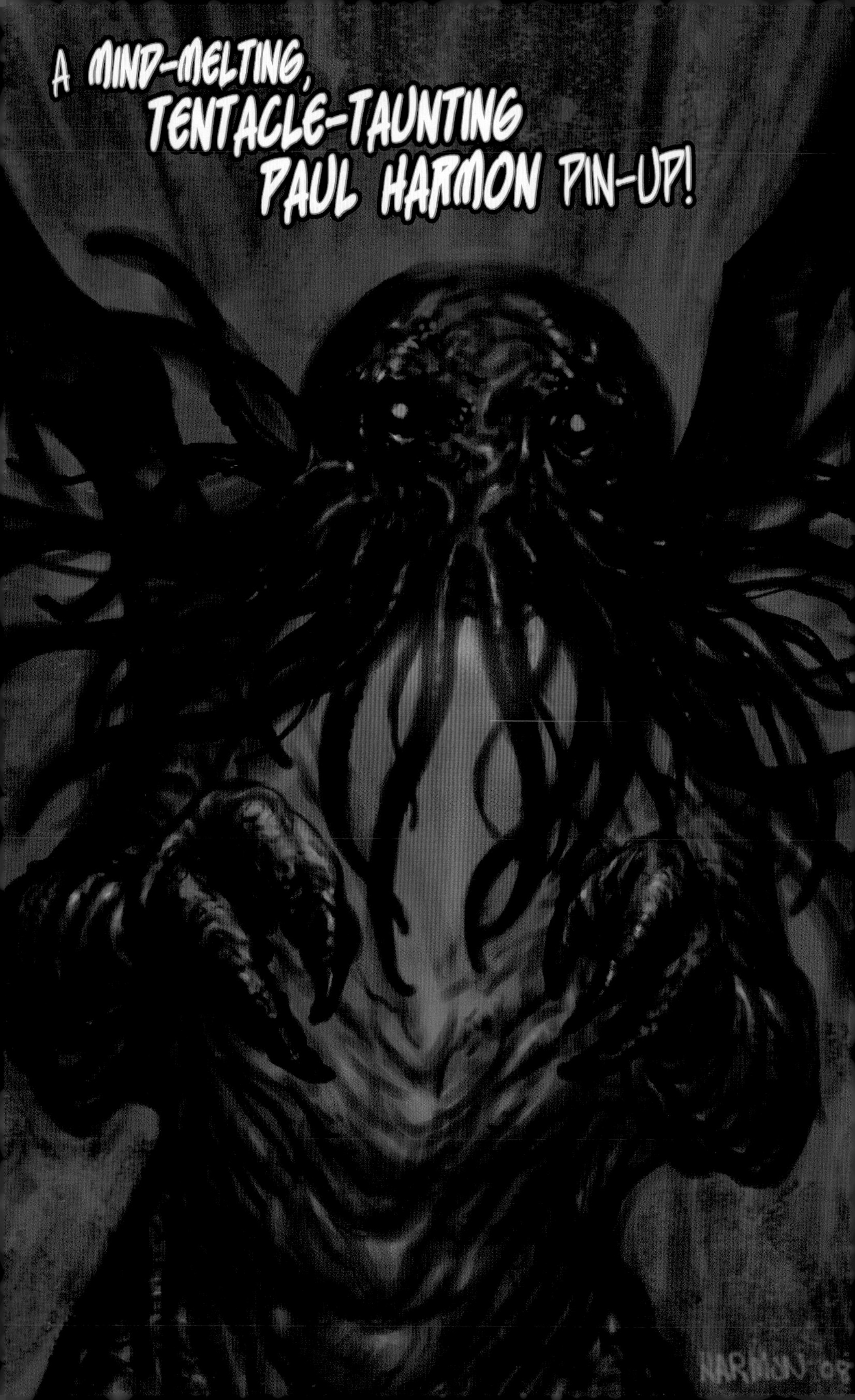
A MIND-MELTING, TENTACLE-TAUNTING PAUL HARMON PIN-UP!

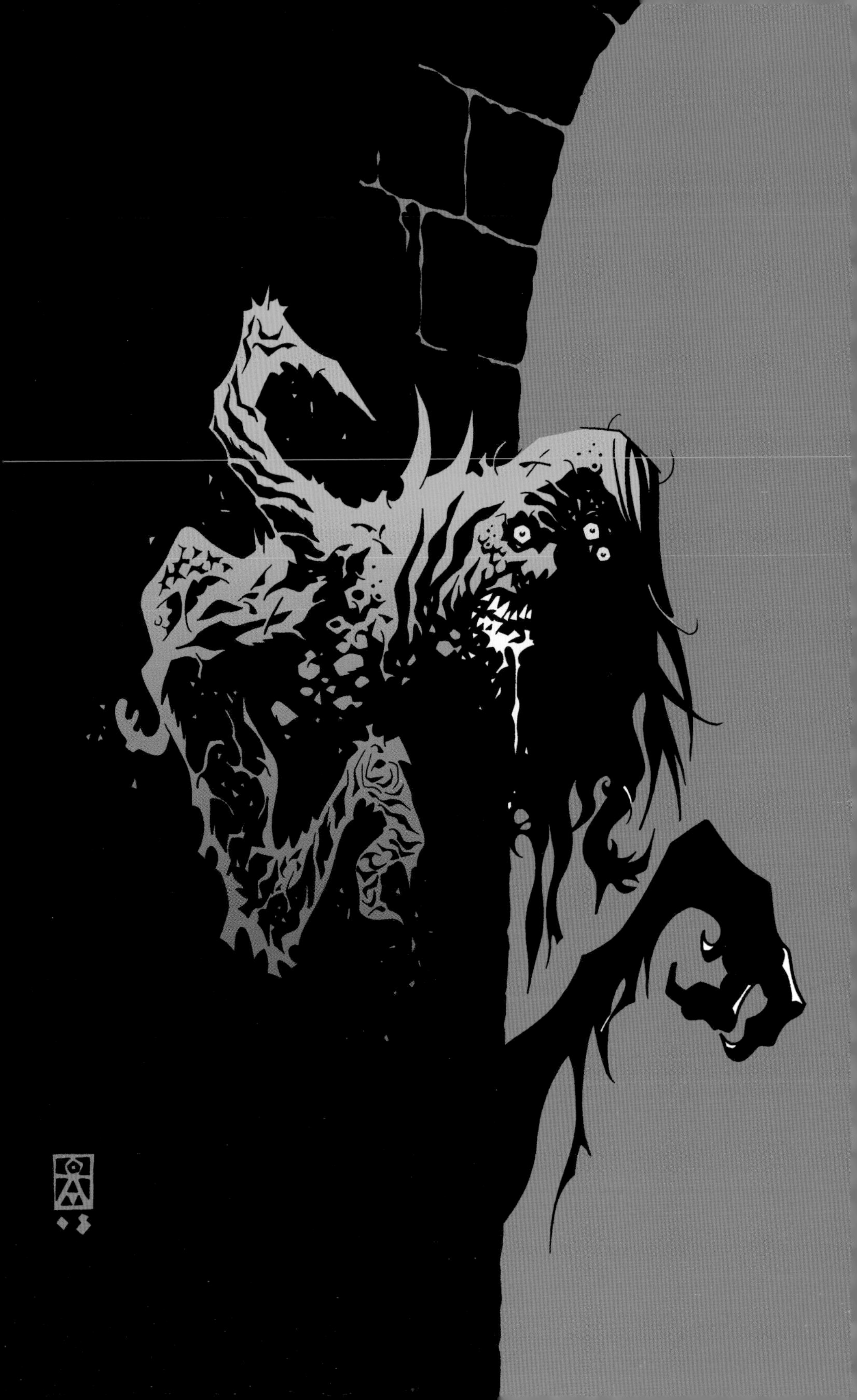

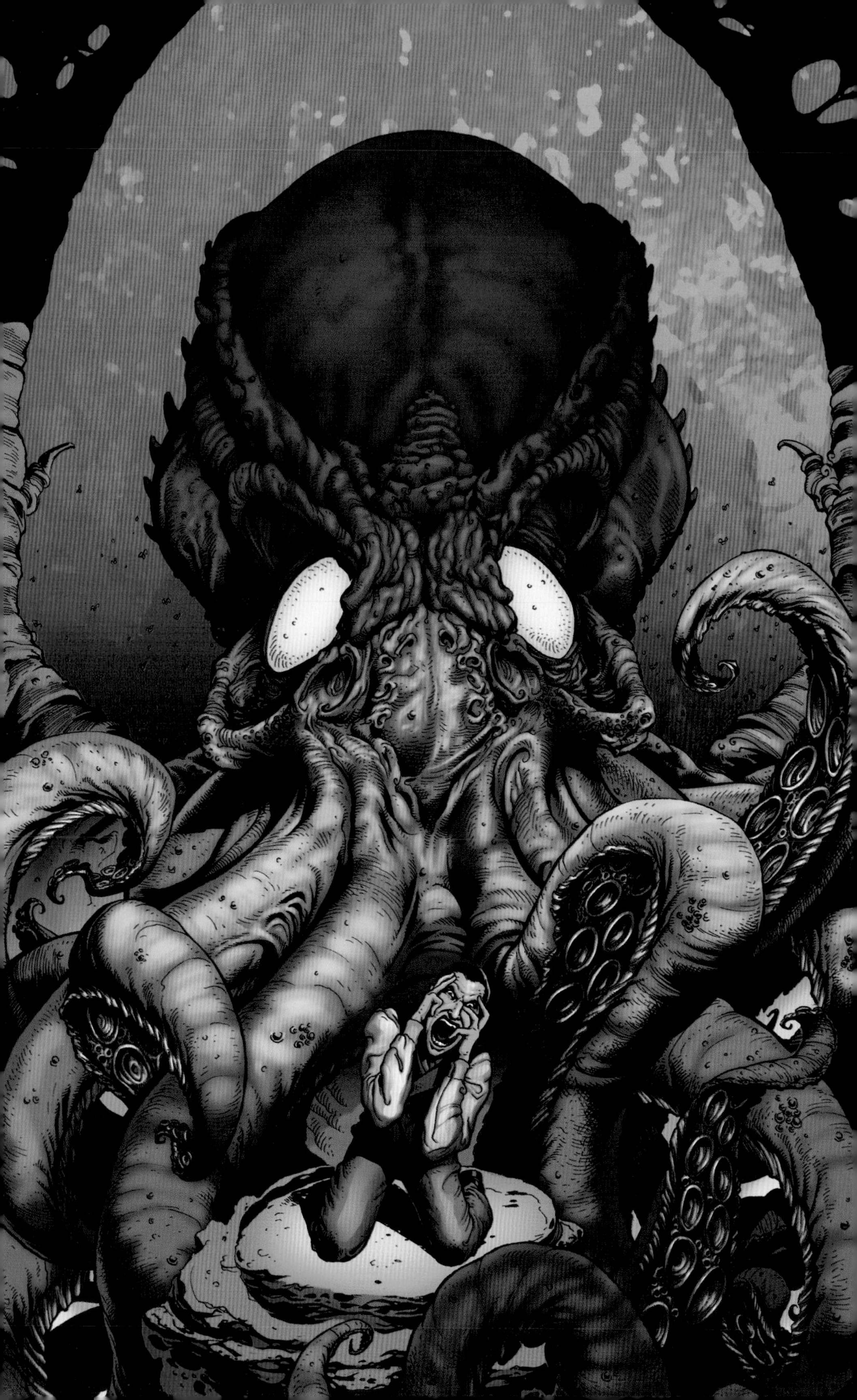

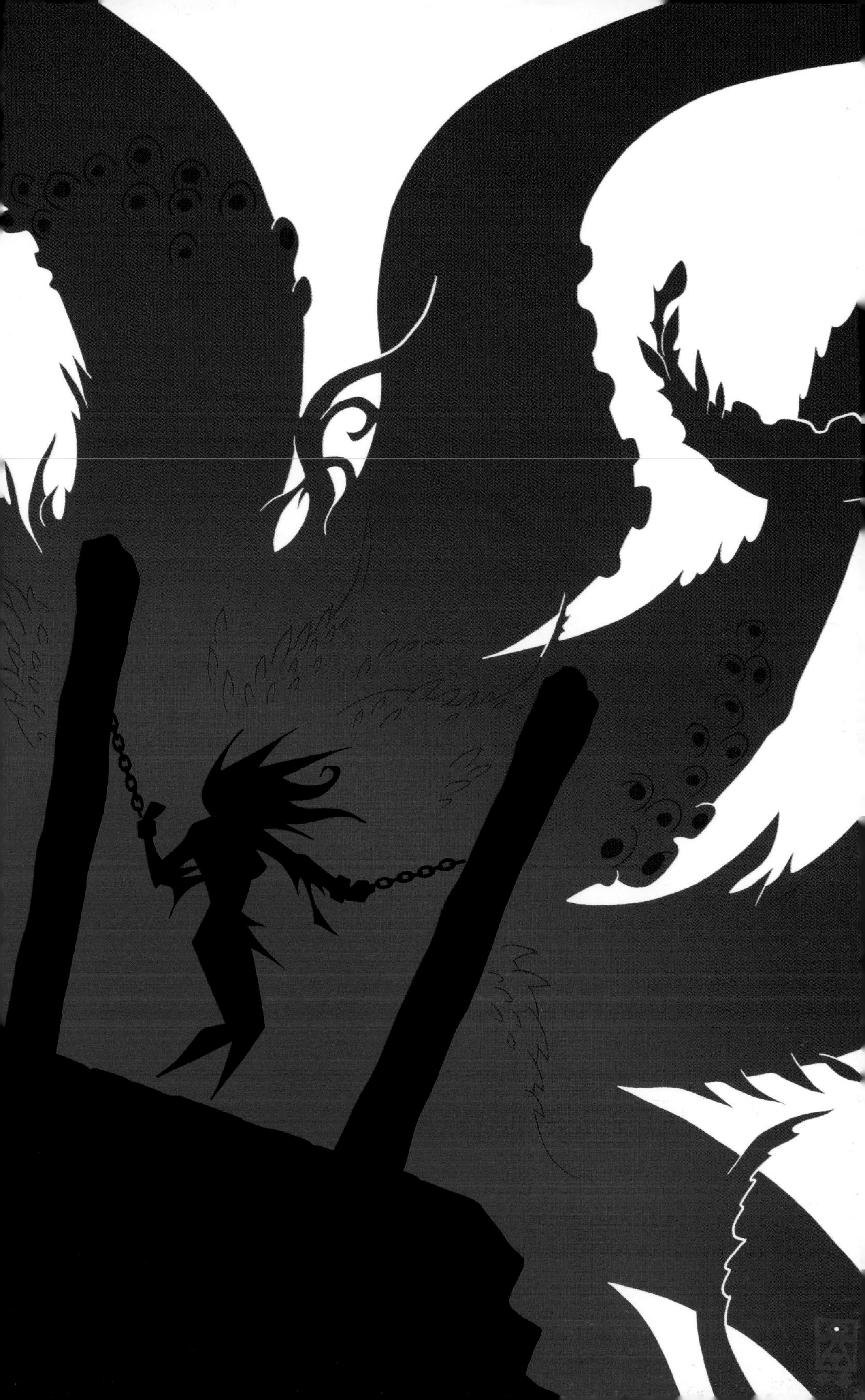

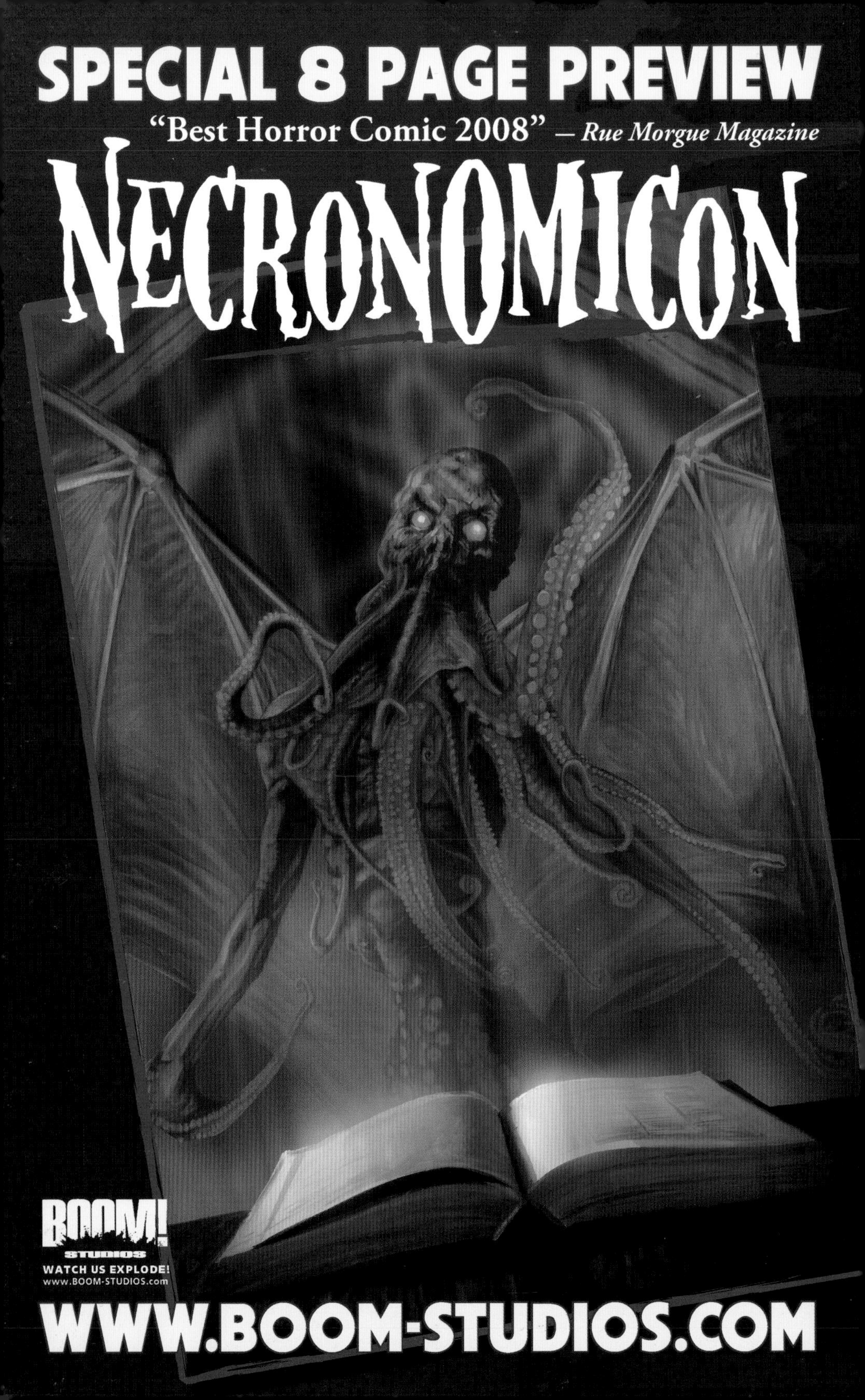

SPECIAL 8 PAGE PREVIEW
"Best Horror Comic 2008" – Rue Morgue Magazine
NECRONOMICON
BOOM! STUDIOS
WATCH US EXPLODE!
www.BOOM-STUDIOS.com
WWW.BOOM-STUDIOS.COM

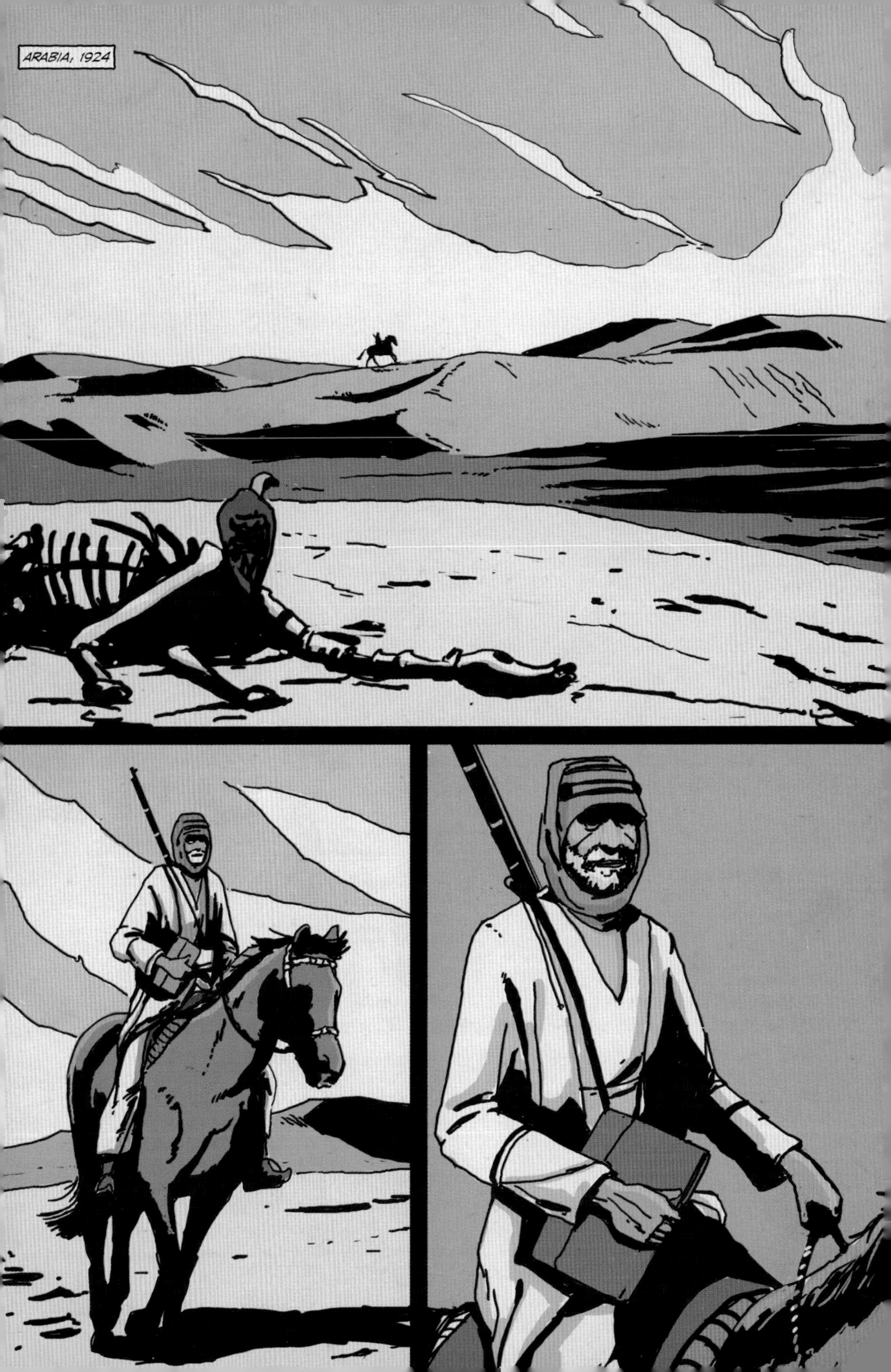
ARABIA, 1924

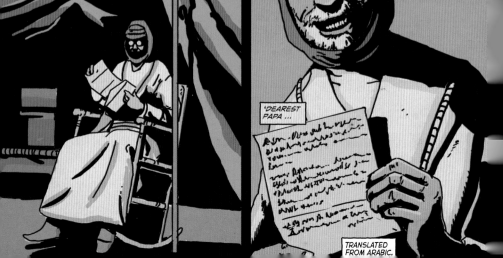

"DEAREST
PAPA ...

TRANSLATED
FROM ARABIC.

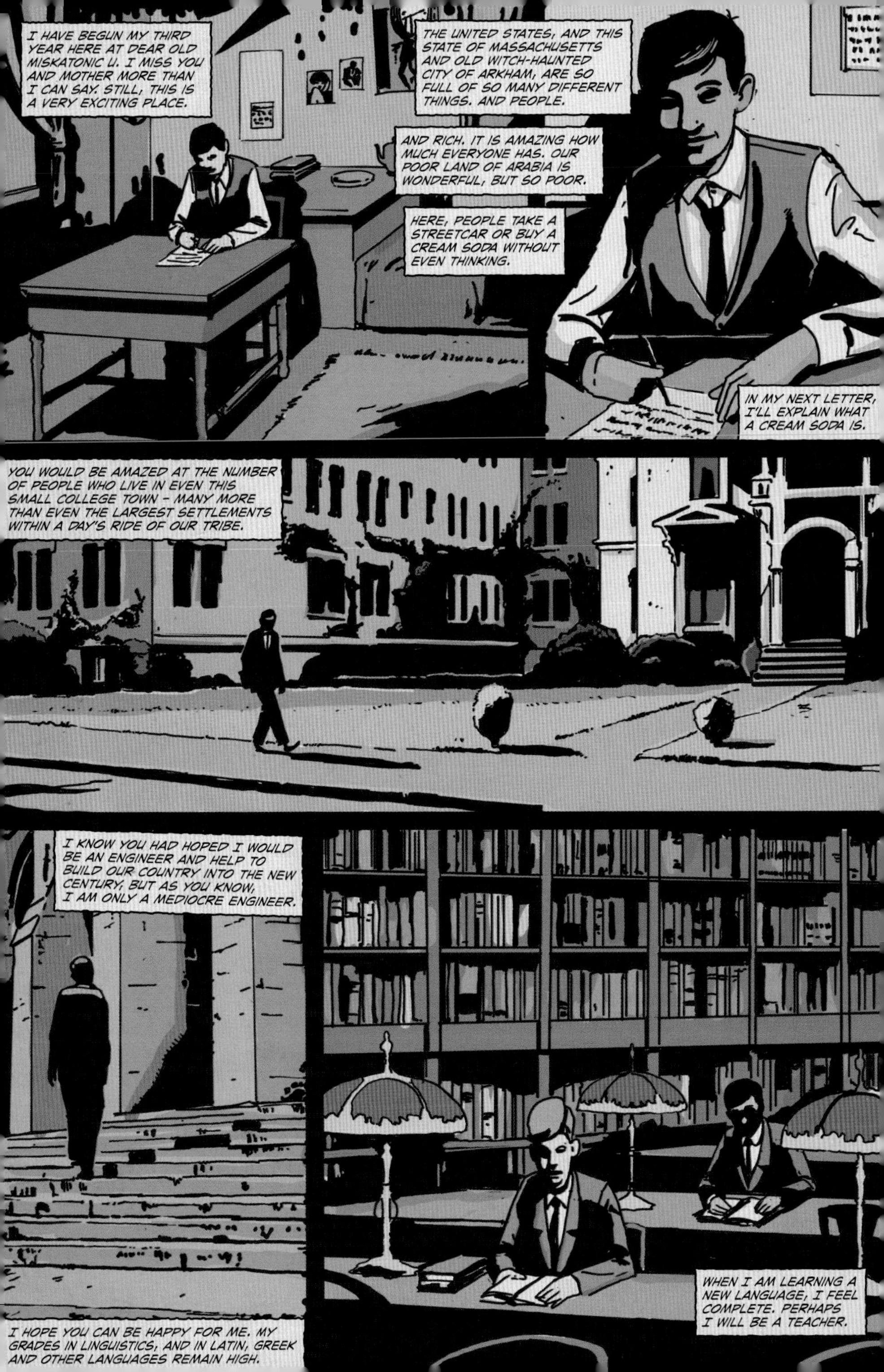
I HAVE BEGUN MY THIRD YEAR HERE AT DEAR OLD MISKATONIC U. I MISS YOU AND MOTHER MORE THAN I CAN SAY. STILL, THIS IS A VERY EXCITING PLACE.
THE UNITED STATES, AND THIS STATE OF MASSACHUSETTS AND OLD WITCH-HAUNTED CITY OF ARKHAM, ARE SO FULL OF SO MANY DIFFERENT THINGS. AND PEOPLE.
AND RICH. IT IS AMAZING HOW MUCH EVERYONE HAS. OUR POOR LAND OF ARABIA IS WONDERFUL, BUT SO POOR.
HERE, PEOPLE TAKE A STREETCAR OR BUY A CREAM SODA WITHOUT EVEN THINKING.
IN MY NEXT LETTER, I'LL EXPLAIN WHAT A CREAM SODA IS.
YOU WOULD BE AMAZED AT THE NUMBER OF PEOPLE WHO LIVE IN EVEN THIS SMALL COLLEGE TOWN - MANY MORE THAN EVEN THE LARGEST SETTLEMENTS WITHIN A DAY'S RIDE OF OUR TRIBE.
I KNOW YOU HAD HOPED I WOULD BE AN ENGINEER AND HELP TO BUILD OUR COUNTRY INTO THE NEW CENTURY, BUT AS YOU KNOW, I AM ONLY A MEDIOCRE ENGINEER.
I HOPE YOU CAN BE HAPPY FOR ME. MY GRADES IN LINGUISTICS, AND IN LATIN, GREEK AND OTHER LANGUAGES REMAIN HIGH.
WHEN I AM LEARNING A NEW LANGUAGE, I FEEL COMPLETE. PERHAPS I WILL BE A TEACHER.

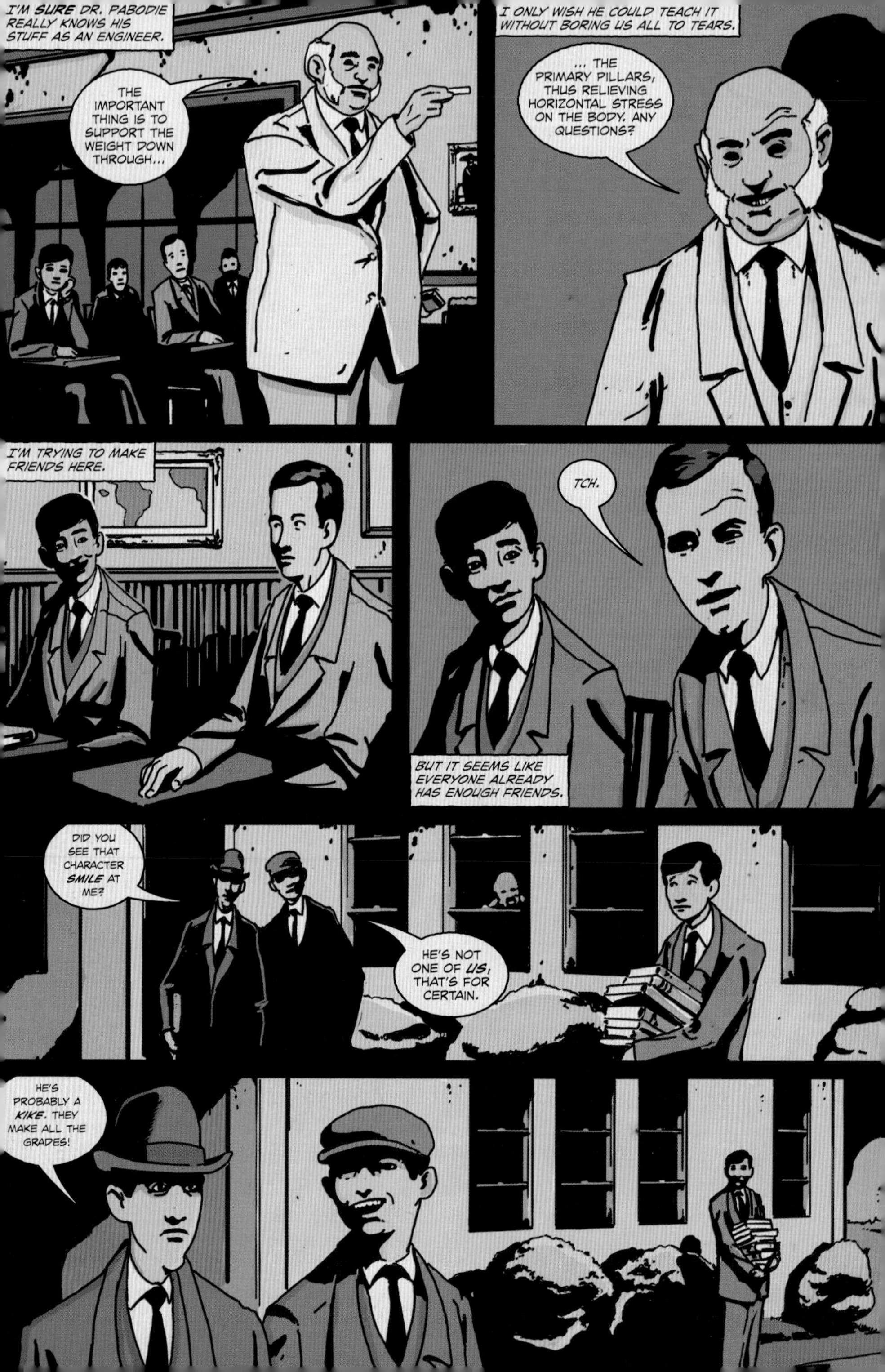
I'M SURE DR. PABODIE REALLY KNOWS HIS STUFF AS AN ENGINEER.
THE IMPORTANT THING IS TO SUPPORT THE WEIGHT DOWN THROUGH...
I ONLY WISH HE COULD TEACH IT WITHOUT BORING US ALL TO TEARS.
... THE PRIMARY PILLARS, THUS RELIEVING HORIZONTAL STRESS ON THE BODY. ANY QUESTIONS?
I'M TRYING TO MAKE FRIENDS HERE.
TCH.
BUT IT SEEMS LIKE EVERYONE ALREADY HAS ENOUGH FRIENDS.
DID YOU SEE THAT CHARACTER SMILE AT ME?
HE'S NOT ONE OF US, THAT'S FOR CERTAIN.
HE'S PROBABLY A KIKE. THEY MAKE ALL THE GRADES!

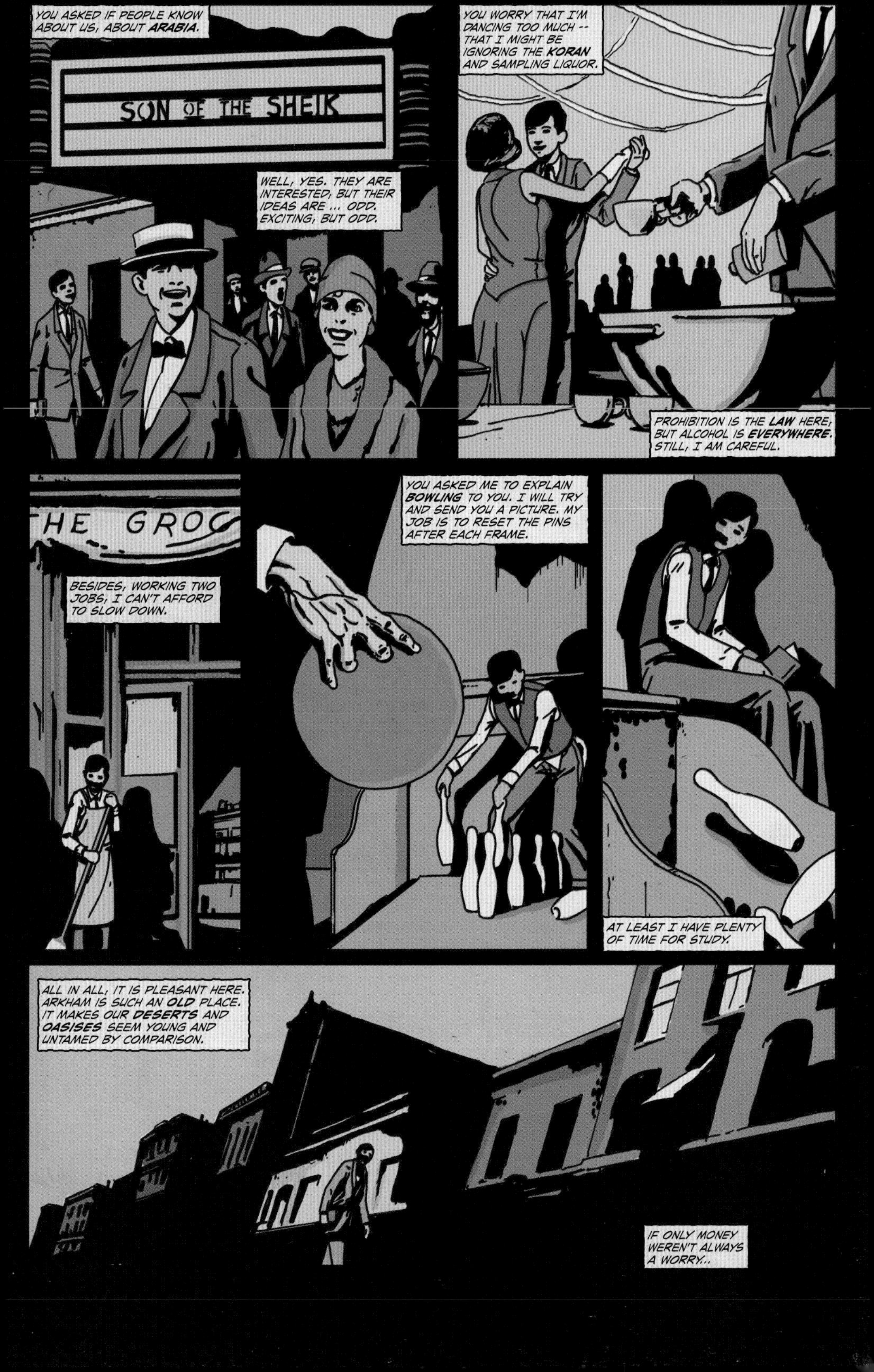
YOU ASKED IF PEOPLE KNOW ABOUT US, ABOUT ARABIA.
SON OF THE SHEIK
WELL, YES. THEY ARE INTERESTED, BUT THEIR IDEAS ARE ... ODD. EXCITING, BUT ODD.
YOU WORRY THAT I'M DANCING TOO MUCH -- THAT I MIGHT BE IGNORING THE KORAN AND SAMPLING LIQUOR.
PROHIBITION IS THE LAW HERE, BUT ALCOHOL IS EVERYWHERE. STILL, I AM CAREFUL.
THE GROC
BESIDES, WORKING TWO JOBS, I CAN'T AFFORD TO SLOW DOWN.
YOU ASKED ME TO EXPLAIN BOWLING TO YOU. I WILL TRY AND SEND YOU A PICTURE. MY JOB IS TO RESET THE PINS AFTER EACH FRAME.
AT LEAST I HAVE PLENTY OF TIME FOR STUDY.
ALL IN ALL, IT IS PLEASANT HERE. ARKHAM IS SUCH AN OLD PLACE. IT MAKES OUR DESERTS AND OASISES SEEM YOUNG AND UNTAMED BY COMPARISON.
IF ONLY MONEY WEREN'T ALWAYS A WORRY..

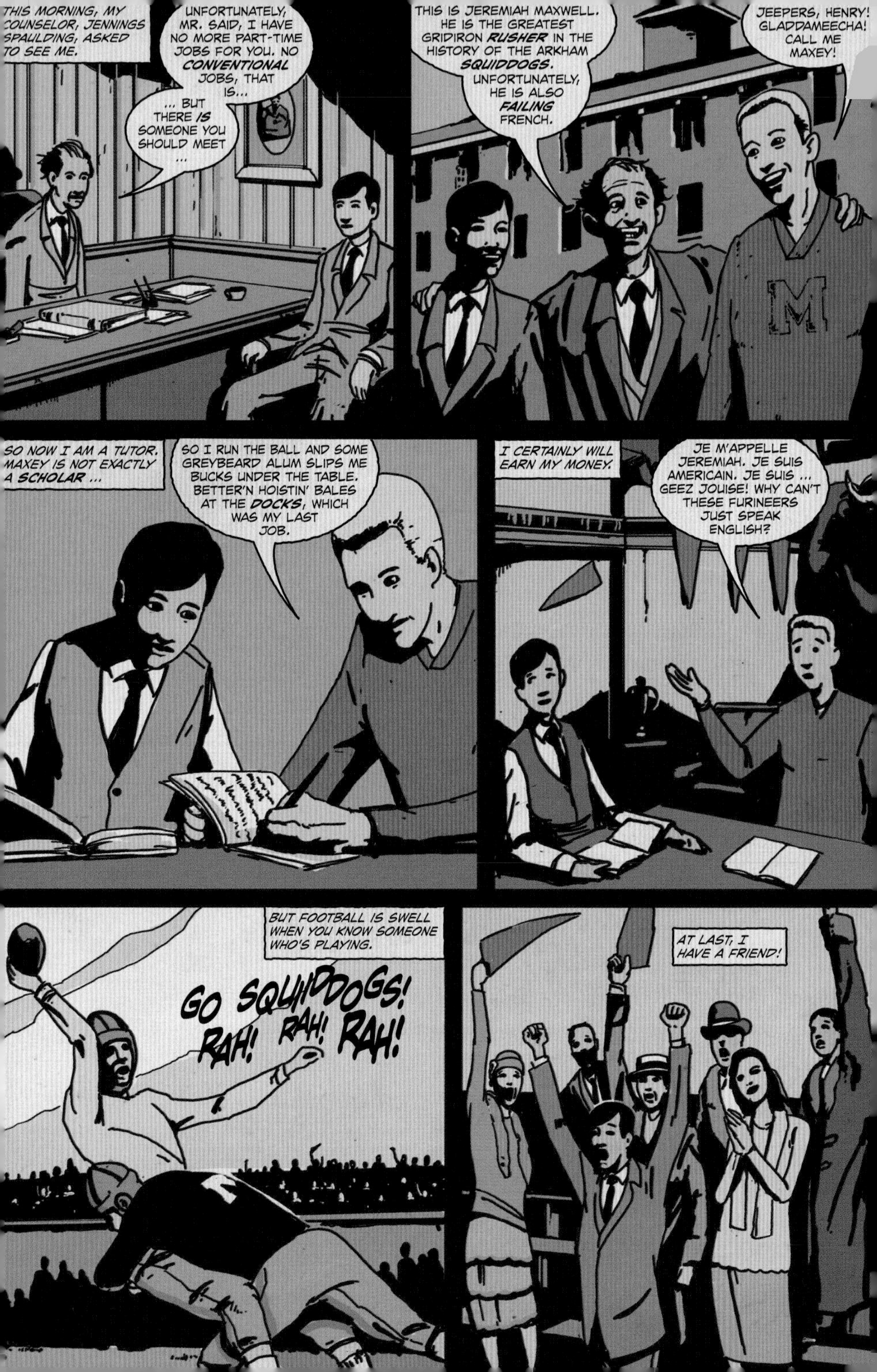
THIS MORNING, MY COUNSELOR, JENNINGS SPAULDING, ASKED TO SEE ME.
UNFORTUNATELY, MR. SAID, I HAVE NO MORE PART-TIME JOBS FOR YOU. NO CONVENTIONAL JOBS, THAT IS...
... BUT THERE IS SOMEONE YOU SHOULD MEET ...
THIS IS JEREMIAH MAXWELL. HE IS THE GREATEST GRIDIRON RUSHER IN THE HISTORY OF THE ARKHAM SQUIDDOGS. UNFORTUNATELY, HE IS ALSO FAILING FRENCH.
JEEPERS, HENRY! GLADDAMEECHA! CALL ME MAXEY!
M
SO NOW I AM A TUTOR. MAXEY IS NOT EXACTLY A SCHOLAR ...
SO I RUN THE BALL AND SOME GREYBEARD ALUM SLIPS ME BUCKS UNDER THE TABLE. BETTER'N HOISTIN' BALES AT THE DOCKS, WHICH WAS MY LAST JOB.
I CERTAINLY WILL EARN MY MONEY.
JE M'APPELLE JEREMIAH. JE SUIS AMERICAIN. JE SUIS ... GEEZ JOUISE! WHY CAN'T THESE FURINEERS JUST SPEAK ENGLISH?
BUT FOOTBALL IS SWELL WHEN YOU KNOW SOMEONE WHO'S PLAYING.
GO SQUIDDOGS! RAH! RAH! RAH!
AT LAST, I HAVE A FRIEND!

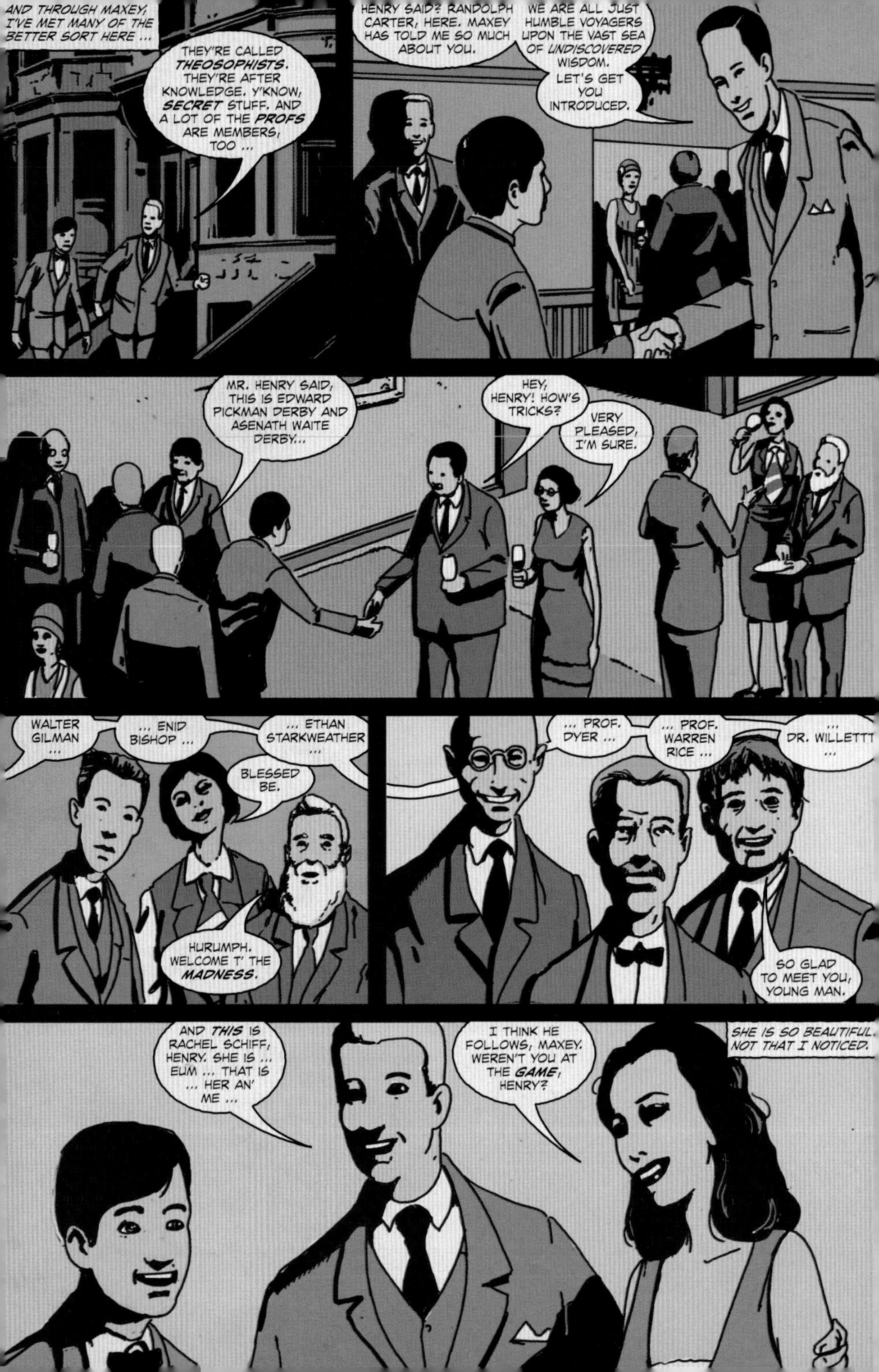
AND THROUGH MAXEY, I'VE MET MANY OF THE BETTER SORT HERE ...
THEY'RE CALLED THEOSOPHISTS. THEY'RE AFTER KNOWLEDGE. Y'KNOW, SECRET STUFF. AND A LOT OF THE PROFS ARE MEMBERS, TOO ...
HENRY SAID? RANDOLPH CARTER, HERE. MAXEY HAS TOLD ME SO MUCH ABOUT YOU.
WE ARE ALL JUST HUMBLE VOYAGERS UPON THE VAST SEA OF UNDISCOVERED WISDOM.
LET'S GET YOU INTRODUCED.
MR. HENRY SAID, THIS IS EDWARD PICKMAN DERBY AND ASENATH WAITE DERBY...
HEY, HENRY! HOW'S TRICKS?
VERY PLEASED, I'M SURE.
WALTER GILMAN ...
... ENID BISHOP ...
... ETHAN STARKWEATHER ...
BLESSED BE.
HURUMPH. WELCOME T' THE MADNESS.
... PROF. DYER ...
... PROF. WARREN RICE ...
... DR. WILLETT
SO GLAD TO MEET YOU, YOUNG MAN.
AND THIS IS RACHEL SCHIFF, HENRY. SHE IS ... EUM ... THAT IS ... HER AN' ME ...
I THINK HE FOLLOWS, MAXEY. WEREN'T YOU AT THE GAME, HENRY?
SHE IS SO BEAUTIFUL. NOT THAT I NOTICED.

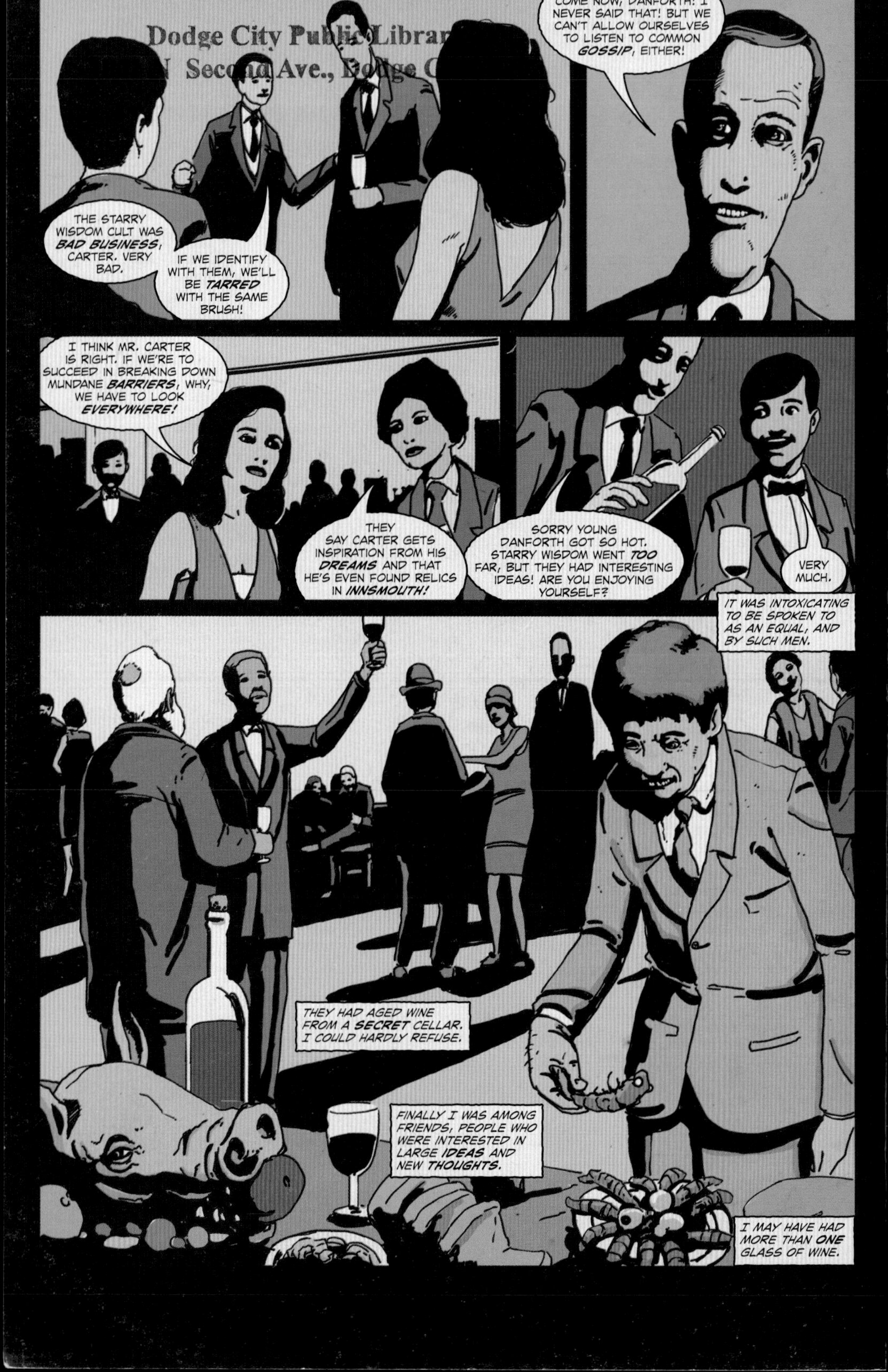
THE STARRY WISDOM CULT WAS BAD BUSINESS, CARTER. VERY BAD.
IF WE IDENTIFY WITH THEM, WE'LL BE TARRED WITH THE SAME BRUSH!
COME NOW, DANFORTH! I NEVER SAID THAT! BUT WE CAN'T ALLOW OURSELVES TO LISTEN TO COMMON GOSSIP, EITHER!
I THINK MR. CARTER IS RIGHT. IF WE'RE TO SUCCEED IN BREAKING DOWN MUNDANE BARRIERS, WHY, WE HAVE TO LOOK EVERYWHERE!
THEY SAY CARTER GETS INSPIRATION FROM HIS DREAMS AND THAT HE'S EVEN FOUND RELICS IN INNSMOUTH!
SORRY YOUNG DANFORTH GOT SO HOT. STARRY WISDOM WENT TOO FAR, BUT THEY HAD INTERESTING IDEAS! ARE YOU ENJOYING YOURSELF?
VERY MUCH.
IT WAS INTOXICATING TO BE SPOKEN TO AS AN EQUAL, AND BY SUCH MEN.
THEY HAD AGED WINE FROM A SECRET CELLAR. I COULD HARDLY REFUSE.
FINALLY I WAS AMONG FRIENDS, PEOPLE WHO WERE INTERESTED IN LARGE IDEAS AND NEW THOUGHTS.
I MAY HAVE HAD MORE THAN ONE GLASS OF WINE.